Practical Semantics

Trends in Linguistics
Studies and Monographs 3

Werner Winter

Editor

Mouton Publishers
The Hague · Paris · New York

Practical Semantics

A Study in the Rules of
Speech and Action

Hans Jürgen Heringer

Mouton Publishers
The Hague · Paris · New York

ISBN 90 279 7736 4
© Copyright 1978
Mouton Publishers, The Hague

Printed in Germany

PREFACE

This work is a modified version of my 'Praktische Semantik' published in 1974. Like the original it should be understood as a progress report. I think it will be criticized for two main reasons:

(i) People acquainted with the work done in Analytical Philosophy will say that a more developed discussion is needed to represent adequately the results of Ordinary Language Philosophy. I hope that they will understand that I wrote for linguists and that I tried to show the implications of these results for further empirical investigations.

(ii) Others will make the criticism that the formal apparatus is not worked out in a satisfactory way. This criticism ties up with certain standards for satisfaction. I understand the formal apparatus only as a kind of heuristic help for both linguist and agent, though I am sure it could be improved sufficiently to satisfy these critics.

As with any other work this is the product of many people and I am indebted to numerous friends of mine.

I am very grateful to Miss Th. Loff for the first translation of 'Praktische Semantik' and especially to Mr. K. Mulligan who improved our English and suggested various modifications.

I also wish to express my gratitude to Prof. W. Winter for his valuable comments and for accepting the manuscript to be published in this series.

Tübingen, August 1975   H. J. H.

CONTENTS

Preface

VIII

1 THEORIES OF MEANING

In the past linguists have not thought much about what meaning is. More often than not they just presupposed an answer to the question and made semantic descriptions accordingly. Such a procedure would have been legitimate if the consequences of the empirical semantic descriptions had been drawn and the answer to the meaning question modified, or if they had been aware of the restrictions resulting from the presupposed answer. I hope to show in what follows that when we consider existing semantic descriptions and the aim of such undertakings certain answers can be excluded and that therefore future semantic descriptions must take this into account. Our considerations of course must take place within an empirical theory which alone can answer the question about the meaning of a sign in language.

I start from the fact that we can distinguish between two aspects of the linguistic sign which, following Hjelmslev, we call expression[1] and content. The expression of a linguistic sign is a pattern for its phonic realization; the content is that which can be achieved by it in communication. It is also said that the expression stands for the content, the assumption being that the content exists in some way apart from the sign which is a mere proxy for such a content. I shall return later to this widespread view.

The character of the relation between expression and content has been widely discussed in linguistics. This is particularly true of the problems of the one-one relation and its "conventionality"; both are closely associated with the type of theory presupposed. If one assumes that one expression can express several contents (polysemy or homonymy) while still remaining only one sign, then the assumption seems to be that one can distinguish contents without using differences in signs or expressions. This seems to be possible only if these contents do not depend on language. But the assumption that contents do depend on language leads us to postulate a one-one relation between expression and content.

Another question concerns the age-old problem of whether the relation between expression and content is natural or arbitrary. If natural, one could not explain how different expressions from different languages may stand for the same content, and how the content of a sign could be changed. If arbitrary, this can be explained, but the arbitrariness must not be too arbitrary, otherwise every speaker might associate any given expression with any given content. He is prevented from doing so by the *langue*, a convention in the society which uses this *langue*. The convention is not due to an explicit contract, but to the fact that the *langue* is taught to each new member of the society. We will now outline and criticize aspects of three familiar theories of meaning: the referential theory, the conceptual theory, and the behavioral theory.[2]

1.1 REFERENTIAL THEORIES

Referential theories start from the fact that we talk about things with signs of natural languages, e.g., we use 'Paul' talking about Paul. Other nouns, which are not proper names are assimilated to this model which is sometimes represented as follows:

(1)   word ——————— thing

where the line designates the symbolic function *stat pro*. In naive referential theory, widespread in normal life and sometimes implicit in linguistic statements, it is said that in

(2)   I entered the house with her.

'house' stands for a thing, namely the house in question. The thing so referred to is called the referent of the sign. But the search for the referent becomes more difficult with other words. One is forced to assume that the referent of 'beautiful' is the property of beauty, that the referent of 'entered' in (2) is the action of entering, etc. Notice that the same signs reappear in these descriptions of the reference.

The theory outlined leads us into difficulties: the expressions 'on April 26, 1939' and 'on my birthday' would have the same referent and *ergo* the same meaning. If anyone else used the two expressions they might not have the same referent and would therefore have different meanings. Thus the meaning of expressions varies with their utterances. The reason for this is that meaning is not understood as part of the *langue,* probably because the distinction between *langue* and *parole* is not made. This is exemplified by 'house' in (2): in various possible utterances one can refer to different houses.

The consequence of such a view of meaning is that no speaker can know the meaning of an expression like 'I' for it would change with nearly every utterance of 'I'. If someone heard A uttering (2) for the first time, he could not know that 'I' means A. This shows that knowledge of the meaning of 'I' seems to be neither knowledge of A nor knowledge of the relation between 'I' and A, but something that allows the hearer to understand that 'I' means A in this case and probably B in a different case.

A second deficiency of the referential theory is that it obviously takes care only of the meaning of words, mostly of nouns, and not of those of other linguistic signs. What for example is the referent of (2)? The designated state of affairs? But what about an interrogative sentence? The weakness of answers to such questions is that a whole universe of entities has to be postulated: objects, properties, procedures, circumstances, questions, etc. And the postulation of this universe is justified only by the fact that it "explains" meaning and that it supports the theory of meaning in question. As long as one does not have any other empirical evidence about the elements of this universe, this "explanation" is a pure tautology. An indispensable condition would be some information about how to describe the elements of this universe, for semantic descriptions in this vein seem to lead only to repetitions, such as "the meaning of (2) is that I entered the house with her."

Other absurdities of referential theories become evident from the following examples:

(3)   He has no house.
(4)   Your apple is sweet.
(5)   Sigfried has died.

What is the referent of 'house' in (3) if it is true? Or, if the meaning of 'apple' in (4) is an apple, I could eat the meaning, and then 'apple' would have no meaning any more. Another difficulty resembling that with (3) arises with (5). If (5) were true, there would be no referent and accordingly no meaning to 'Siegfried'. Thus (5) could not have any meaning.[3]

Two modifications of the referential theory, which try to cope with some of these problems, remain to be dealt with. The first is that the referent is said to be a set of objects, etc. rather than an object. This also leads to difficulties. For, whatever the relation of my utterance of 'house' to the set of all houses, I am not necessarily speaking about the set of all houses. Otherwise, by uttering

(6)   The house is large.

I would say the same as by uttering

(7)   The set of all houses is large.

The second modification consists in supposing the meaning to be the relation between the expression and the referent rather than the referent alone. One consequence is that different relations would belong to different expressions: But specifying these relations involves specifying distinct referents, so that even here objections concerning the peculiarity of such referents as those of 'which', 'went', etc. prove insurmountable and − still worse − the dilemmas posed by 'unicorn', 'gnome', etc. remain.

In spite of all this, the referential theory was of fundamental importance for the construction of formal languages. It was extended by Frege, who introduced several categories of referents: in addition to objects as referents for proper names and descriptions, he has functions for predicates, and truth values (the True and the False) for sentences, which, however, he classes among objects. In this way he was the first to extend semantics to sentences and to explain how the reference of a sentence is composed of the references of its parts by interpreting functions as mappings from objects onto truth values.[4]

But what was said about the references of sentences remained confined to indicative sentences, for only their referents may be truth values. In the construction of logical languages this was no disadvantage; for the descriptions of natural languages it was. Frege showed as well that such a theory needs completing, for signs with the same referent can characterize this referent in different ways. If a, b, and c are straight lines which connect the corners of a triangle with the midpoints of the opposite sides, then the point of intersection of a and b is the same as that of b and c, but this point is given in different ways, as Frege says. These different ways of giving the point would be included in the sense of the signs 'the point of intersection of a and b' and 'the point of intersection of b and c'. That is why a semantic theory ought to have at least two components, in which reference and sense would be described.[5] Frege begins to describe senses, but he can neither show the relation between sense and reference, nor can he describe the composition of the sense of a sentence.

Frege's theory enables us to see why simple referential theories deal with only one of the important capacities of natural languages: that the speakers can refer with it to things in the world. But such theories cannot avoid a number of deficiencies:

(i) They cannot explain the nature of reference because they do not explain how it is possible to refer in different situations to different things with the same expression.

(ii) They generalize one aspect of language in an inadmissible way, lumping together all categories of expressions with proper names.

1.2 CONCEPTUAL THEORIES

The second type of theories of meaning to be dealt with copes with such difficulties as the one that the meaning of 'apple' cannot be eaten and that one has
to attach a meaning to 'gnome' and the like. These theories do not postulate
a direct relation between signs and objects of reality, but some intermediate
mental units, for example concepts. The geometrical picture for this is the
famous triangle

(8)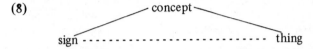

where expressions and things are only indirectly related via conceptual units.

But can one really explain the character of meaning by concepts? In my
opinion the term 'concept' is not clearer or more familiar than 'meaning', properties which might have enabled it to fulfill the task of explanation or regi-
mentation. There are many different uses of 'concept' both in philosophy and
in ordinary life. Sometimes 'concept' is used for what is common to synonymous predicate-expressions − which is nothing other than their meaning −
sometimes it is used for certain entities independent of language. If concepts
were the meanings of predicate-expressions such as 'goes', 'is green', 'is a
nervous woman', 'is a ϕ that ψ-s', then some meanings would be concepts but
others would not. But then what about the meanings of these other expressions? And if concepts were the meanings of synonymous predicate-expressions, they would be the meanings of predicate-expressions, hence meanings.

Concepts in the sense of predicate-expressions are well known in linguistics in so-called concept-systems. Such systems were conceived as universal
systems in which every expression finds its place. They were used as ordering
systems for expressions. But they are themselves systems of expressions ordered with the help of semantic relations; and having a place in such a system means being synonymous with the expression defining the place. Empirical work in lexicology and lexicography demonstrated that there is no universal system with a fixed place for every expression of every language. On the
contrary, there are many places for each expression, and there must be various
systems for different languages, and there is no place defined covering just
the meaning of one expression. So, empirical investigations show that neither
the assumption of a pre-established universe of concepts nor a Platonic realm
of ideas can help the linguist when he describes the meaning of a word. In the
end, all such systems are nothing but expression-systems themselves demand-
ing semantic description.

Another position on concepts would locate them not in a Platonic heaven
but in the heads of the speakers or perhaps in their hearts. Such theories take

the sign as a token for an idea which is independent of language. The linguistic communication works as follows: the speaker has an idea of a house which he evokes in the hearer when uttering the word 'house'. The relation between word and idea is most often interpreted as association.

If this theory of meaning is to be taken seriously, one ought to explain more precisely what an idea is. In communication nothing is evoked in me which I would call an idea.[6] If there really is someone who, when hearing (2), has the idea of a house, one would want to know what type of house: a house with a flat roof, one with a high roof, a farm-house of the Black Forest type, etc.? If it were always a distinct idea, we would have the *langue-parole* problem here as well. If it were a question of a general idea of houseness and thus of the same idea in every speech act, one could not explain how it is possible to speak of a particular house.

As with referential theories, it would be important to know which ideas are evoked by the words 'and', 'to', and 'it' in the following sentences:

(9)   People come and go.
(10)   Nobody dares to scold him.
(11)   It is raining.

or which idea might correspond to the expression 'round square'. Do you have an idea of a round square? The conceptual theory seems to adopt still other mental units besides ideas, e.g. a thought as the meaning of a sentence. The question which then arises is how thoughts are related to ideas, and how they are composed of them. According to the use of 'thought' familiar to me, it does not make sense to say the meaning of the sentence 'good morning' is a thought which is composed of the ideas of the good and the morning.

Another important objection to understanding meaning as an idea is that ideas can only be imagined as subjective ideas, so that every speaker might attach a different idea and hence a different meaning to an expression. In order to avoid these difficulties another entity has been postulated, common ideas, which are to be intersubjective. In order to obtain such common ideas one would have to explain how one could compare the subjective ideas of different speakers. Presumably any way of doing this which does not presuppose meanings is impossible, for everyone can know only his own ideas directly and those of his partner only via communication.

A specific argument against the belief that common ideas can be ascertained is color-blindness. Assume that a color-blind person, who on account of physiological defects clearly cannot distinguish between red and green, doesn't have different ideas of them. His ideas would then differ from those of other people who can distinguish between red and green. But frequently color-blindness is not noticed either by the color-blind person or by others, and the color-blind person uses 'red' and 'green' without deviation, by going on features such as order of the lamps of the traffic light, differences between the surfaces of objects, etc. As long as linguistic communication works well, ideas may be different. The discrepancy of ideas could only come to be noticed through the failure of linguistic communication. One could imagine a color-blindness so subtle that it cannot be discovered and would therefore be uninteresting.

The following main criticisms have to be made of conceptual theories of meaning:

(i) Concepts are at best the meanings of certain expressions. But then they are meanings.

(ii) Conceptual theories of meaning cannot deal with the *langue-parole* problem. The distinction between individual and common ideas is not clear and common ideas cannot be introduced without using meanings.

(iii) Information is needed, first about how to identify and describe ideas and second about the consequences of this theory of meaning for empirical descriptions. If the assumption that there are ideas is to explain anything, it must be possible to make statements about them which cannot otherwise be made about meanings, and there must be ideas which are not meanings. If not, the two terms are identical in use; and thus one of them is useless.

1.3 BEHAVIORAL THEORY

The difficulties of the conceptual theories of meaning are said to be avoided in the behavioral theory. It aims at being more elementary and tries to reduce all cases where the assumption of ideas is not irrelevant to simple, observable elements. The behavioral theory of meaning starts from a simple communication-situation: a speaker receives a stimulus S from the outer world that makes him utter a chain of sounds r as response, this works as a stimulus s on his communication-partner so that he acts in a certain way, response R. A schematic representation is

(12) $S \longrightarrow r \ldots \ldots s \longrightarrow R,$

where r, s and the dotted line belong to the set G of events which are regarded as verbal. Everything to the left of r belongs to a set F of so-called practical events preceding the act of speech, everything to the right of s to a set H of so-called practical events following elements of G. All speech-events consist of three parts: (i) production of sounds, (ii) transmission of sounds by soundwaves (in the air), (iii) reception of sounds. The meaning consists of the important events G is related to, namely F and H, more precisely the important events of F and H. The sets of events F and H and events of F and H are not linguistic and so neither is meaning in this theory. Meaning is exactly described by the description of everything in the speaker's world.[7] That is why scientific semantics is dependent on every other science and therefore impossible. Interestingly enough, other scientists do not seem to understand their activity in this way. A physicist would hardly admit to scrutinizing meanings. Nor could this theory explain the verbal behavior of the speakers, if such a semantic description is to complete the explanation. If meaning plays a part in communication this could not be meaning as described in the theory, for normally not every speaker is acquainted with all the different theories concerning his world, but some understanding of meaning must be involved in communication. In addition Bloomfield seems to assume that the scientists in question have another approach to the world than a verbal one. But even the results of their sciences consist of verbal descriptions of the world. This is part of the meaning of 'description'. In this sense 'NaCl', as the meaning of 'salt', is neither better nor worse than 'sel'; if anything it is worse, for it is less synonymous. It would not be a semantic description at all but a definition or a changing of the meaning.

According to Bloomfield's definition one is forced to assume that the meaning is a property of the speech act in question and thus belongs to the *parole*. If A asked B

(13) Are you going for a walk?

and B shook his head, the shaking of his head would belong to the meaning of (13). If B nodded, the nodding would belong to the meaning of (13). Thus the meaning of an expression may change considerably. If B accidently scratched his head because he has dandruff, this would belong to the meaning of (13). Only relevant parts of F and H are then said to belong to the meaning of an expression, an assumption clearly made by Bloomfield later.[8] But what are relevant parts? Presumably all parts which are the same in all or many uses of (13). This is to admit (i) that not the utterance of (13), but what is common to all utterances of (13) has a meaning, (ii) that the meaning may at best be the subset of events of F and H, which corresponds to what is common to all utterances of (13).

A speaker who is master of a language must know which elements from the sets of events F and H concern the meaning of (13) and so must be able to determine whether two situations or events are the same. Only in this way can A know that the nodding of B does not belong to the meaning of (13) but that it is an answer to (13). How does the behaviorist observer succeed in doing this? First of all he needs characteristics such that events from F are associated in different historical situations with a certain kind of stimulus. He must be able to classify events from the G-phase in the same way. He must know, for example, that the different physical events involved in uttering 'good morning' are somehow the same and that there are differences between speech-events and phonic events (belch, noise of jet-fighters, etc.). It is very doubtful whether he can come to know this without abandoning his principles. But if he succeeded, he would at least need a language which described such characteristics and thus he would already be interpreting. Such an interpretation of verbal behavior would, however, be insufficient. If the behaviorist wanted to describe verbal greeting behavior he would have to know both the common features of stimuli in the F-set and the common features of all instances of greeting in the G-set. But this seems to be possible only when he knows what greeting is. What, otherwise, are the common features of all instances of greeting? It seems to be somehow assumed that the behaviorist knows all this in advance and that his language for description contains the whole language of the observed speakers.[9]

If one had a language for description which made it possible to classify the events from F, G, and H to any extent, the problem of their association would arise. How are the relations which are represented by the outer arrows to be understood? The arrows represent sequences of events in the bodies of the partners of communication.[10] One could regard the relation between the events as causal, like the conditioned behavior of animals, for Bloomfield says the language of men differs from that of animals only by being more differentiated. A causal interpretation is not possible, however, for Bloomfield makes the correct empirical assumptions (i) that the speaker might utter an unexpected sentence in certain situations and (ii) that the hearer may react otherwise than expected (displaced speech).[11] But then the observer will no longer be able to find out the meaning, for he does not know whether it is displaced speech or not. In this way F and H become useless for the semantic description. An ignorant observer cannot determine meaning from them. There are two attempts to cope with these difficulties. Morris wants to avoid the difficulty that the hearer can react otherwise than is to be expected from (12) and the meanings of the respective expressions by supposing that the hearer must only have the disposition to react in such and such a way. In order to ascertain this disposition one could establish the conditions under which the hearer will act in such and such a way.

But the singular case does not establish the disposition. It gives no evidence for the general hypothetical statement that if the condition were fulfilled he would react in this way. For even if he does not act in such and such a way, he might still have the disposition. This is exactly the difficulty. A disposition is not empirical in this crude way.

Skinner tries to specify the stimuli from F so that they get only one response from G at any given time. But even then one cannot predict the responses from the stimuli, for obviously only some of the events from F function as stimuli. Which ones function as stimuli of this sort can only be determined by means of the responses, thus *ex post facto*. If one does not regard the arrow-relation as causal and assumes that habits learnt by ostension are involved (12) still remains scientifically useless, for one element $x_i \in F$ may cause different responses $r_i \in G$, so that x_i is not necessary, much less sufficient for r_i. Hence it is neither possible to forecast $r_i \in G$ nor to explain the succession of x_i and r_i.

A behavioral theory could at best be developed for independent utterances. Should one understand the meaning of parts of utterances as parts of events? If in an utterance the word 'apple' appears, an apple need not be part of an event from F or H. The sentence might be

(14) There is no apple here.

This is a characteristic use of words. How should one describe in this theory the meaning of 'and' and 'at' in

(15) Men and women wonder greatly at such theories.

Up until now no attempts to determine stimuli for such words have been made known.[12] And as concerns the composition of the meaning of a sentence from its parts, none of the many speculations in this theory deal with the problem.

In contrast to the other theories, the behavioral theory of meaning does not start from the view that it is the sign that designates something or expresses something, thereby ascribing acts of the speakers to the signs. It has the advantage of including human behavior. But the differences between behavior and action have been ignored and thus could not be explained. Speech acts, such as lying, and the like, or misunderstandings have not been considered at all.

Furthermore it has to be criticized because (i) it cannot cope with the problem of eliciting relevant parts from F and H, (ii) it cannot solve the *langue-parole* problem, (iii) it seems to be characteristic of the behavioral theory of meaning that semantic descriptions can be made by an uninvolved observer, as in an experiment with rats. This is the residue of an empiricist theory of science which holds that only direct observation can be relied upon. But as observations come into the description only by way of sentences, they can only enter interpreted into the theory. And when a behavioral theory of meaning interprets the behavior of the communication partners in a way differing from their own understanding, who is to have the last word?

The rejection of the behavioral theory of meaning does not mean that the behavior of the speakers has nothing to do with the meaning, just as little as the rejection of the referential theory means that the world of objects has nothing to do with the meaning. What we need is a theory which takes every important component into consideration in a consistent and coherent manner, one which must make as few unproved assumptions as possible.

1.4 USE THEORY

A theory capable of getting rid of the weak points in the theories dealt with above and of taking care of their good points in a coherent description is the so-called use theory which was established above all by Wittgenstein. The meaning of a sign is here considered to be the rule for its use. Thus: (i) language is related to the whole of human action, for the use of language is a part of human action; (ii) language is not regarded as a system of signs which exists independently of speakers and social groups; (iii) through the assumption of rules, the relation between *langue* and *parole* and the possibilities of forming, changing and learning signs are taken into consideration.

How linguistic action is woven into the whole of action may be illustrated by an example: if a command is given to someone by uttering a chain of expressions, it consists not only of uttering this chain of expressions. To understand which command has been given one has to know what one has to do to obey it or what one has refrained from when not obeying it. This does not mean that linguistic action is to be reduced to other sorts of action, as with the behaviorists, but only that the meaning of the sentence uttered in an act of commanding determines the alternative acts open to the partner, if he does not act deviantly. The same holds for speech acts in general.

From the point of view of this theory, other semantic theories have overgeneralized particular speech acts; in the case of referential theories, the generalization is of the use of signs to refer to objects, which is only one kind of speech act, one usually involving certain signs such as some pronouns and some noun-phrases.

Another generalization of this type was the restriction to assertion originating in the development of logical languages where certain logical languages containing only truth-functional sentences have been taken as a standard. Only such a restriction made it possible to consider assertion, so to speak, as a constant operator and to take into account not the speech acts but only the signs used. In this way some linguists came to understand language as a system of signs and to forget the speakers in their description.

The use theory gives up the idea that words, like labels, are attached to objects given in the world. There is no need here to assume such a pre-established world. The description of speech acts can demonstrate, rather, that different social groups make different assumptions about the world by referring to different objects or by referring differently. Thus the ideal of discovering or constructing the only language that truly describes the world has been given up. Instead there is the idea of relating our language to our world, for we do not have the world in itself or without language. The alternative assuption would be empty and unprovable. Indeed the very proving of such an assumption would be a speech act.

On the other hand, a theory where the meaning of a linguistic sign is considered as the rule for its use would be able to explain on the basis of which existing or adopted modes of action social groups or individuals make this or that assumption about the world. Only this theory could give something like an explanation of how different social groups have different worlds. In this way it ought to be able to explain how people came to assume that there is only one world which has been realized or copied more or less adequately and approximately in different languages.

Of course, the instruction "describe the use" as a method of description of a language is still insufficient. Wittgenstein himself gave good examples of how to profit from it, but he did not describe the procedure. In order to be able to describe the different functions of our languages in general Wittgenstein uses the concept of language game. Language games show that language is not only an instrument of telling.[13] The act of uttering sentences, understanding the partner, and the acts of both partners belong to the language game.

Wittgenstein's language games are less complicated than our colloquial speech. Therefore they are particularly appropriate for making colloquial speech understandable. Even language games which are not very complicated have properties never dreamt of by logicians. Though language games need not be played in this form, they are not to be understood as ideals or as regulatives but as paradigms which can explain the games we in fact play. The point is to clarify our colloquial speech, not to substitute ideal language games for colloquial games.

We learn from the concept of language game that different language games can be played in very different contexts. When playing a certain language game one can only act in a certain way. And of course the language game will be established according to the necessities of action. That is why to imagine a language is to imagine a form of life. [14] The language determines the form of life and is a product of it.

A language game does not only exist when it is played. It is defined by the rules according to which it may be played. We wish to call these rules patterns and, as 'rule' is used in different ways, we want to draw from these a use which captures what is essential to human action.

Imagine yourself teaching a child the difference between red and green. In order to achieve this you are playing a little game with him. You have got two kinds of chips, red ones and green ones, and you move them one after the other forming two heaps, one heap of red chips and one of green chips, giving a paradigm to the child of what he has to do. Then you encourage the child to form two heaps himself. But the child does not — he cannot — understand what you want. So you take his hand and help him form the heaps and then when the child understands what he has to do he takes your hand and forms heaps by pressing your fingers around the chips and laying them down. He did not understand that taking the hands of the partner did not belong to the required act.

But how could the child come to know that this did not belong to the act? He would have had to know that taking one's hand is often done to make someone do something and that he had to subtract this from the whole act because it was not relevant here. This shows that to know what is relevant is part of what has to be learned. Guiding the hand is not part of our game. The rules of the game do not mention it. We say that what is relevant is indicated by the rule.

Assuming that the child has now understood that he has to sort out the chips himself, let us continue the game. In order to achieve the correct sorting he must put all chips of one color in one heap. But this is just what he should learn. What does 'the same' here mean to him? It means that he has to grasp or to understand the rule of your action. Because it is a part of knowing the rule to know what counts as doing the same here.

There is another property of rules which we can learn from our example. If the child happens to sort the chips out right on his first attempt, you could not be sure that he had mastered the rule. You would let him repeat the action and if he repeated it several times in the right way you would say that he knows the difference now although you could not be sure that he would not make a mistake next time. This shows that the criterion for having mastered the rule is repetition and at the same time that there is no ultimate certainty for someone having mastered a rule.

Up until now we have established three main attributes of rules:

(i)   The rule regulates what is relevant for an act to be of this or that kind. So it says what an act counts as.
(ii) The rule regulates which acts count as the same.
(iii) A rule is not established by one single act according to the rule. The cri-

terion for its rule character is repetition.

Sameness and repetition are features not only of rules but also of the regularities observed by the physicist or behaviorist. The difference lies in the fact that regularities of events are only ascertained by men. Stars in their movement do not follow rules. If the behavior of a star does not correspond to the forecast made on the basis of the relevant regularity we would not say the star had made a mistake or deviated. We would revise our formulation of the regularity because it was wrong. But in the case of the formulation of a rule, there would also be the possibility that the agent had made a mistake, that he had deviated. Since men follow rules, they can also deviate from them in congenial circumstances. A rule would not be a rule unless one could deviate from it and unless one's partners could see this and react accordingly. To deviate from a rule does not necessarily mean to act somehow irregularly, as if one were making some sort of mistake. Often the deviating person wants to act according to another rule, a competing rule which may not belong to this game.

Such a deviation may be creative because it may be regarded as the proposal of a new rule. Deviation is a condition for every change of a game. If the partners understand and accept the new rule, that is, act according to it under certain circumstances, they have changed the game and so have perhaps formed a new group. The decisive phase here is that a second person accepts the rule. Only then is it no longer private. The acceptance of a new rule does not happen in a vacuum, but through common action and therefore on the basis of common rules already recognized. Even when accepting new rules an individual is dependent on the rules he has already mastered and thus dependent on a social group. Understanding historical development in this way, we do not start from some absolute origin of rules but always presuppose rules. From these new rules develop; more precisely, they are developed. We call this the historical openness of the rule.

The possibility of changing rules is a result of what we call their conventionality. 'Conventionality' here means, negatively, that not every social group must have and follow the same rules. There is no fixed set of rules for all human beings but different rules grow up in different societies in the flux of their history. Note that a host of rules and the use of signs is not systematic in a naive sense. Nor is there a logical *must* forcing us to use an expression in some particular way. 'Conventionality' also means that the interacting persons must know the rules and that they expect the partner to follow the rules. But this is not due to a kind of *contrat social* at the beginning, with people agreeing explicitly on the use of the signs or on the rules.

The conventionality of rules implies that they are not innate but learned. We can consider the ability to learn rules guaranteed by the assumption of an innate capacity to grasp the regularities behind acts. In this way a child learns rules by making hypotheses about the regularity of the acts of its partners. These hypotheses are changed in the face of new acts, by his own and by reactions of his partners to them. The rule is acquired by common practice. Thus it is not a condition that the rules be explained (in the normal strong sense of the word). For then we could not imagine a beginning in the learning process. In order for someone to grasp hypotheses concerning the rules it is sufficient to give him examples, to act paradigmatically: you show him how to do something which he then imitates.[15] There is then no last or circular explanation.

Because of conventionality there is no genuine but only a historical justification for a rule. Why do people call this animal 'dog'? Because it has four legs, can bark, etc. That would be no justification, but an explication of the rule. A justification arises when I point out that I call it a dog because my compatriots understand me and because this is what I have learned. Justifications are always related to whole language games and by this to whole forms of life. There is no absolute criterion here.

Now we can incorporate two more properties in our catalogue:

(iv) Rules are social and conventional.
(v)   Rules are part of the history of a social group. They are elaborated and changed in the sequence of acts which is the history of the group. And they are learned by the individuals of the group

Rules guiding human action are not mnemonic phrases which may sometimes be called 'rules' as well. A rule is no sentence at all. One can obey a rule unconsciously and without being able to make it explicit.[16] Obeying a rule consciously seems to be something of an exception, e.g., when a beginner who wants to learn a rule, tries to guess it first. Usually there is a dangerous certainty and naturalness involved in following a rule. It is dangerous because this naturalness induces us to consider our rules to be the only right ones and to be objectively given; we therefore find it difficult to accord the competing rules of other social groups similar status as rules and as justified to the same extent.

On the other hand, the certainty involved in obeying a rule seems to be necessary, for reflection and calling into question interferes with obeying the rule. It deprives us of our certainty. Besides, the permanent qualification 'the rule might be different' is redundant. Perhaps one can draw the conclusion that one is allowed to forget the relativity of one's own rules as long as, and only as long as, there is no conflict. In case of conflict, rules must be judged according to their being more or less sensible and that demands reflection. But reflecting on a rule is not obeying the rule.

Since rules are not sentences, we must clearly distinguish between rules and their linguistic expressions or formulations. A standard form of a rule-formulation would be:

(16) One can V.,

where 'V' stands for parts of the predicate like 'laugh', 'answer questions', etc. An act according to the rule, e.g.

(17) A follows the rule of V-ing.

implies (16) and that A knows that (16) but not that A knows a formulation or can formulate the rule. However, in the course of learning a formulation of the rule is often given to us. One could therefore strengthen the relation between rule and rule-formulation by assuming that A can follow a rule only if a formulation of it exists at all.[17] But then it would be necessary to give the criteria for rule-formulations, e.g., it should not be demanded that one must be able to analyze the action of laughing in order to be able to obey the rule of laughing. Just 'laugh' as an expression of the rule could do the job.

Rule-formulations of the form (16) consist mainly of three parts: the subject part, a modal part, and the remainder of the predicate representing the rule. Within the abstract form of a rule-formulation A, the general 'one' occurs as the subject part. This may be substituted for in special formulations by other subject expressions such as 'whoever is married', 'the beginner', etc., all having one thing in common: that they are used to refer to all agents of a certain type. On the one hand, 'one' resembles 'we' because we do not refer to all and every one with it but only to the people belonging to the group. In asserting that one says 'I was there' we do not mean that every human being says this but only English-speaking people. Whereas 'we' refers to members of a group from the inside and presupposes that the speaker is a group member, 'one' is more neutral since it refers to people in general while not necessarily including the speaker. And it is therefore very useful for the formulation of rules.

On the other hand, 'one' is akin to 'every' since it is also used with distributive generality; this means that we refer distributively to each member of the group.[18] But there is a difference: With 'one' one does not refer to each and every member of the group without exception. 'One' has a normative element in it indicating that every one should act in this way. But if anyone who is a member of the group does not act (under the appropriate circumstances) in this way, the assertion in the *one*-form will not be falsified. It is merely the case that this person has deviated. However, if you deviate too often or follow other rules you are not accepted as a member of the group.

Within the second part of the rule-formulation 'can' is the fundamental expression since it is presupposed by all the other modal expressions occurring here ('must', 'may', etc.). The modal part displays rule-formulations as an instance of normative discourse. This need not always be obvious since the modal part may be suppressed.

(18)   In English one does not say 'We was there'.

At first glance this may look like a fact-stating sentence and some linguists, observing the behavior of English speaking people, might mean by it that, as a matter of fact, nobody ever uttered 'We was there'. But then it is clearly not a formulation of a rule since firstly it could be false that nobody ever uttered 'We was there' and all the same the rule could hold and, secondly, the rule-formulation applies not only to past but also to future acts. The question is whether it makes sense to utter sentences such as (18) to state a fact in a linguistic description. When it is used to formulate a rule it is of the form (16). Note that (16) can be used not only to formulate a rule but for other purposes as well, e.g. in order to introduce a new rule or to propose it.

The third part of the rule-formulation is an expression of the rule. This part in fact comprises the whole of the rest of the sentence. We express by it what one can, must, etc. do. In order to do this it is only necessary that the rule exists, i.e. that this part is meaningful, whereas the rule-formulation, contrary to introduction or proposals of new rules, also implies that the rule holds, i.e. can, must, etc. be followed.

To know a formulation of the rule is not necessarily to have masterd it. Think of having learned some formulation of a rule of a foreign language. You possibly need practice or a more detailed description of the rule to apply it. When I have formulated a rule for someone, he may not know what V-ing is. I can then go on and describe the rule for V-ing. I can announce my description:

(19)   V-ing takes place in the following way: . ..

Here the rule-expression is shifted to the subject position in order to refer to the rule in question and the dots stand for a text used for the description. As with descriptions in general, I describe the rule to someone (i) by telling him further particulars, giving the relevant parts of the structure of the rule and (ii) by uttering a text where I refer to the rule at least once; (iii) I therefore have to use an expression for the rule with which I can refer to the rule. Referring to the rule is a precondition for describing it; (iv) by describing different aspects of the rule. The main aspects are characterized by the questions: Who? What? How? Why? Under what conditions?

To conclude the exposition of the concept of a rule, let us have a brief look at some close relatives. Rule-formulations of the form (16) state what, according to a certain rule, one can do or must do in a certain game. A more detailed formulation for this would be

(20) When you want to play the game X, you must do Y given condition C (in order to do Z).

So, only one who wants to play the game, one who wants to follow the rule, can break the rule. That is the difference between rules and laws (also called moral rules), where there is no such alternative.[19] They concern also those who do not want to play the game and may have the form

(21) When condition C is satisfied you should always do Y.

Of course, the necessity of playing a game can be given by a law. But that does not disturb the value of the distinction between rule and law, just as it does not call into question that for the most part it is not clear that one can play another game. For the limits of the game are already given by the rules which do not take other games into account at all.

A rule has something in common with a command. For a rule, too, is something which is to be obeyed. A typical expression of a command is:

(22) Do V!

In a command as well as in a rule someone is expected to do something. But often a command is addressed to one single person and always to specified persons. A rule has a claim on each person of a group, in general. Within the standard version of a command the pattern V occurs as in the standard rule-formulation. It seems that (22) presupposes (16) and because of this it also indirectly presupposes existence of the rule. Other differences between rules and commands are that a command is an act or the product of an act of a single person, which a rule is not.

The rule is the product of a social group. Commands require a single act, rules concern all acts of a certain type. Commands require only future acts, rules concern past, present, and future acts. Often laws serve as justification for commands. It is true that one can judge acts to be right or wrong according to a rule, that is whether or not they are in harmony with the rule. But, because of their similarity to commands, one cannot judge formulations of rules to be true or false, for they are not assertions which alone can be judged to be true or false. This can be demonstrated with a declarative sentence like

(23) I played bridge.

used to make an assertion, which may be true or false according to the situations in which it is made, whereas a rule-formulation does not change its truth value in this way; it seems to be more general.

Though a rule-formulation has something in common with a command, it could be judged in some sense to be true or false, that is, with respect to adequacy and validity. E.g. (18) could be an inadequate formulation of the corresponding rule for English, since it does not take into account the conditions or the binding force of the rule. This might have the consequences that a rule other than that intended is what gets formulated. Or the formulation may be said to be false because the rule does not hold. Both possibilities show that giving true rule-formulations in this sense is of the greatest importance for social science since they are part of the description of societies. Notice, however, that an assertion of (18) is not falsified by someone saying 'We was there' if this act is not correct.

In the discussion up to now one sort of rule has predominated. We call these constitutive rules and separate them from strategic rules.[20] As an expression for strategic rules we take:

(24) If you want to play the game X and reach the goal R it is better to do Y than Z given the conditions C.

Constitutive rules do not allow any alternatives unless one foregoes playing the particular language game to which the rules belong. They are like definitions; they define the game. Strategic rules are based on alternatives in the game, as is shown by the expression (24), they are only possible within the frame of constitutive rules, because (24) implies both the rule-formulation (25) and (26)

(25) You can do Y.
(26) You can do Z.

This shows that for strategic rules both the existence and the holding of the corresponding constitutive rule is a precondition. In this they are related to commands and to laws, although these do not allow for alternatives.

A foul in soccer is given by the constitutive rules. Committing a foul belongs to the rules of soccer. If someone touches the ball once with his hand, the game does not become handball. The strategic rules evaluate conduct within the game. If someone repudiates these evaluations, sanctions are definitely established in the game. They are part of the game. I can play soccer both defensively and offensively. But under certain circumstances it may be better to play defensively. If one infringes upon this strategy, the sanction may be to lose the game. Of course, the distinction between constitutive and strategic rules is not sharp. For if I permanently infringe upon the strategic rules, it may be that I am really playing another game. If a soccer team plays the ball with the hands only, a soccer game can no longer take place. Though the rules provide for this, the whole point of the game is lost.

With this explanation of the language game and the use of 'rule' we have already hinted at some consequences for possible descriptions of the use of sentences. But we do not have a method for the description. The starting point put forward by Alston[21], who introduces as an important part of the description the conditions in which an expression can be used, is also not sufficient. What we need are descriptive techniques which allow a systematic description of the make-up of our linguistic action and of how the acts we perform in speaking are embedded in the rest of action. Thus what we need is a theory of action.

NOTES

1. I do not use the usual term 'form' instead of 'expression' because its vagueness and ambiguity give rise to various misunderstandings.
2. Cf. Alston (1964: chapter 2).
3. Cf. Wittgenstein (1953: § 40).
4. Frege (1891, 1892; both reprinted in 1954). The original German 'Bedeutung' (translated as 'reference') is normally used for 'meaning'.
5. Cf. Carnap's distinction between extension and intension, especially Carnap (1964: 118-33).
6. Cf. Wittgenstein (1953: § 6).
7. Bloomfield (1933: 139).
8. Bloomfield (1933: 141).
9. Cf. Black (1949: 182).
10. Bloomfield (1933: 26).
11. Bloomfield (1933: 141).
12. Cf. also Black (1949: 174) concerning 'black'.
13. Wittgenstein (1953: § 363).
14. Cf. Wittgenstein (1953: § 19).
15. Cf. Lorenz (1970: 149-241).
16. Cf. Wittgenstein (1953: § 219): "I obey the rule blindly".
17. Ganz (1971: 26-37) proposes to do so.
18. Cf. Vendler (1967: 74-9). Notice that 'one' is singular, whereas 'we' is plural and used sometimes collectively.
19. However, for laws there has to be an alternative act in the game; cf. below for laws as special cases of strategic rules.
20. A similar distinction is that of Searle's between constitutive and regulative rules; cf. Searle (1969: 37-8).
21. Alston (1964: 41-4).

2 THEORY OF ACTION

2.1 WHAT IS AN ACT?

A policeman shot a Greek dead. He took the electric torch in the Greek's right hand for a pistol. What did the policeman do? Possible answers to this question are:

(27) He killed the Greek.
(28) He defended himself.
(29) He shot the Greek by mistake.

The same act can be conceived and be described as belonging to different types of acts.

In general we want to call answers to questions like (30), (31), and (32) descriptions of acts.

(30) What is A doing?
(31) What did A do?
(32) What will A do?

The answers have the form (33) and (34) or similar forms:

(33) A is doing y.
(34) A is Y-ing.

'A' represents the agent; 'what', 'y' and 'Y' represent actions, 'do' is something like a copula.

For our purpose, however, such a limitation of acts is still too broad. We have to place some further restrictions on it. First, we have to restrict the domain of A to human beings or groups of human beings, i.e. we do not include stones, energy, or animals as agents. Perhaps that should be revised for animals, for now and then we attribute acts to them in everyday life. But if it is assumed that our understanding of acts depends upon language, they are to be excluded. Then the adequate question-form would not be (30) but

(35) What are you doing?

Such a restriction is related to the fact that often one cannot understand acts as an observer whereas the agent himself is quite certain of his act.

Other important restrictions on the sentence-form (30) would be to recognize the answers to (30) as descriptions of acts only if it makes sense to ask questions like (36) and (37):

(36) Why does A do y?
(37) For what reasons does A do y?

In this way answers like

(38) A coughed.

are excluded as descriptions of acts, provided that A coughed because he has a cough, since it does not make sense to ask (37) and at the same time to assume that A's coughing was caused by a cough. However, if A coughed as a sort of ironical gesture, (38) would indeed describe an act of A.

Another restriction would be that one must be able to transform sentences which describe acts into meaningful commands:

(39) Cough!

can make sense as a request during an X-ray examination, when A co-operates with the doctor, but not as a request to produce a normal cough caused by illness.

In some theories, especially theories of a behaviorist turn, attempts to avoid descriptions of acts like (27), (28), (29) have been made in order to make so-called objective descriptions.[1] In these descriptions, acts are usually described as events where there are no longer any agents. Such a description presents an extreme case among possible worlds, namely a world in which everything *happens*; the other extreme would be that mythical world in which everything is *done* (by a deity). The difference between these two worlds suggests that far-reaching decisions must be made whenever we define or identify acts and events. Theories in which acts are described as events are based on two principles: (i) acts are regarded as events which are objective and causally connected; (ii) the descriptions of acts are made by an uninvolved observer.

Principle (ii) is probably related to the principle of objectivity. In order to realize both principles, descriptions like the following are given: The pistol in the policeman's hand pointed at the Greek. Thereafter his finger curled itself around the trigger and thereby released a shot. The bullet hit the Greek right between the eyes, after which he dropped dead. It is regarded as worthwhile to make more minute descriptions, perhaps using a complicated apparatus, chemical experiments, etc.

Nevertheless descriptions of acts cannot be reduced to such a description of events. There are many questions which do not apply to events but to acts, for instance questions like (36), (37), or

(40) What did A want to do?

Events cannot be judged according to the agents' intentions, for there are no agents. Similarly, this is true for the question whether someone did something on purpose, by mistake, willingly, voluntarily, and whether he may be held responsible for something. It makes no sense to ask such questions concerning events.

Both the principle of objectivity and impartial observation are out of place as concerns acts, for the agent's acts are connected with intentions which must be understood. And the understanding of these intentions, like that of acts, is based upon (i) the interaction of partners, (ii) a common rule according to which they act. Thus, we interpret the action of a man as a product of obeying certain rules which he has learned. That is the reason why the distinction between acts and patterns according to which acts are performed must be made, on the analogy of the distinction in 1.4 between following a rule and the rule. Hence the considerations put forward there are valid for act-patterns and acts as well, e.g., the distinction between regularity and rule which also defines the difference between events and acts; events do not follow rules although we can see that they occur with regularity. Events cannot make mistakes. But, when acting, we follow rules, and with acts in particular the possibility of deviation, which exists only for rules, must be taken into consideration.

This understanding of acts does not mean that a detailed description would be useless. On the contrary, the understanding of acts may depend upon a description in detail. But only relevant properties are taken into consideration and thereby reference is made to the rule. Something may only be said to be relevant when it is judged in connection with criteria or rules.[2]

Nor does this understanding of acts mean that a scientific theory of action would be impossible, which people who laid stress upon *Verstehen* supposed or, perhaps, were supposed by their opponents to suppose. As soon as we give up the restricted view of science based on the idea of an ultimate accuracy, measurability, observability, etc., and also the standpoint of natural sciences, namely that objects of science may be controlled, in the case of human action we should say: manipulated, we have no reason to consider the description of acts based on understanding as unscientific. A scientific theory of this type would also open up for us a new perspective on itself: for its assertions are not objective in the sense of an ultimate objectivity independent of men. They are based on interaction, and they can only be justified by way of communication; that is, they are based on interaction.

One consequence of this is that a semanticist, like a psycho-analyst, cannot simply diagnose a defect and then remedy it. The persons concerned must remedy the defect themselves. The scientists offer them their solutions and opinions. In a certain sense they even persuade them to act according to these proposals. The point is not to establish a technical use of 'act' but to achieve a better understanding of how we are using the word 'act'. Only in this way could such a theory give us a better understanding of what we are doing, or help us find a way to realize how our acts are interrelated.

As matters stand at present, fixing a new use of 'act' would not in any case be useful. Here, only the question of what plays a part in action is to be settled, in order to be able to construct a language of description which takes this into account. The evaluation of competing uses of 'act' can only be made within an empirical theory which, however, presupposes a language of description. Therefore we settle the question of what shall be regarded as an act by means of the particular interests with which we are concerned. These interests must be given and explained here; whether they are worth-while is another question. But the difference between this understanding of action and the more technical one lies above all in these interests.

2.2 FORMAL THEORY OF ACTION

The formal language of description for action proposed below is meant to make it possible to get a clear view of the relations between acts and to provide for the possibility of placing a formal linguistic theory within a theory of action.

2.2.1 The α-relation

We start from the distinction between act and act-pattern[3] which hitherto we have occasionally disregarded. We identify act-patterns with rules, and acts with performances, i.e. instances or products of following these rules. We use 'x' and indexed 'x's' ('x_1', 'x_2' etc.) as variables for acts. Signs for act-patterns are chains of capitals ('ASS', 'KIL' etc.), variables for act-patterns are 'HA', 'HB', 'HC', etc. If an act x_1 is done according to the pattern HA we use the following representation:

(41) $x_1 \alpha$ HA.

This is to be read: x_1 is of (pattern) HA. The negation of (41) is (42) or (43):

(42) not $(x_1 \alpha$ HA).
(43) $x_1 \notin$ HA.

Read: x_1 is not of (pattern) HA. Thus, the domain of the asymmetrical α - relation consists of acts and its range of act-patterns.

Acts are not independent of space and time. But they cannot be identified by giving their space-time coordinates; this emerges when we consider the formulation just given, where by 'their' we refer to acts, which must be identified in some other way. Acts are identified by attaching them to patterns. Therefore definite descriptions of the form 'the act the policeman did at 8:51 P. M.' cannot be used to individuate acts but presuppose such individuation. For instance, as acts are not usually instantaneous, one would have to specify the act's beginning and end, say 8:51 P. M to 8:52 P. M. Doing this involves taking for granted that we know that this act was completed at 8:52 P. M. and this depends on our knowing it to be of a certain pattern. Only in this way can we be certain that it was not only a part of the act. Thus, the beginning and the end of an act change according to the pattern to which the act belongs. If the policeman's act was murder, other parts belong to the act which may even be discontinuous in time. However, there are descriptions which make reference to a pattern in a weaker form: the correct use of 'what you have just done' presupposes only that the person addressed performed an act at all. The special pattern according to which the act was performed need not be known or, at least, need not necessarily be describable. For these reasons the variables x_1, x_2, etc. in our language of description are used only in the way variables in other formal languages are used, namely to indicate by their uniformity the identity of possible instances. This is necessary, for one act may belong to several patterns. [Shoot] and [defend oneself] are two different act-patterns. But if, as in 2.1, someone shoots and thus defends himself, he obviously has performed only one act, for here shooting and defending oneself cannot be separated.

It has been supposed that we have here two different descriptions of the same act.[4] But this should not be understood in the sense of alternative descriptions having equal rights. They should be understood, rather, as complementary descriptions each of which gives only one aspect of the act, no one description characterizing it sufficiently. The case seems to be analogous to the case where I buy a house and I buy something red where I need not have bought two things and I need not have performed two acts; it is possible that I bought a red house. The same with acts; that I shot someone and I killed him does not imply that I performed two acts. It is possible that I killed him by shooting him. It does not seem very sensible to take the question of whether there are two acts or only one for a question of description in the ordinary sense of 'description', because in describing something we have to refer to it and this presupposes that we can individuate it and that we know what it is. So, description presupposes individuation. Our description of something as an act of shooting does not make it an act of shooting any more than our description of something as a house makes it a house.[5] How many acts have been done and what act has been done is a question of interpretation which, in the case of acts, is carried out by assigning an act to a pattern. However, if we replace the description of acts by assigning them to patterns, we have to say that one act x is done according to a more complex pattern involving the two patterns HA and HB and a special relation between the two patterns, namely that HA can be followed by following HB. A description of such an act as an act of HB-ing lays stress upon only one aspect of the act and neglects the other, of being according to HA. A detailed description of this relation between patterns could allow us to convey the burden of individuation to certain prominent acts, the so-called basic acts.

The problem of individuation of acts gives rise to another problem. For example, one can understand "yes" as an answer to the question

(44) Did he cook?

according to the form $x_1 \alpha$ HA. But "no" as an answer can be understood not only as not $(x_1 \alpha$ HA$)$ but also as

(45) He did not do anything.

In all cases where (45) is given as an answer to (31) such an x_1 need not really exist. For the x_1 in question exists only as produced by the agent.[6] Therefore only in the case that there is at least one HX, such that$_1 \alpha$ HX, does x_1 exists; and only then do all predications of the form '$x_1 \alpha$ HY' or 'not ($x_1 \alpha$ HY)' make sense. Only then is (46) valid:

(46) $x_1 \alpha$ HY or not ($x_1 \alpha$ HY)   for every x_1.

The reference to time distinguishes the α-relation from the ϵ-relation of set theory. It is mirrored in sentences describing acts. Whereas an act-pattern is described by an infinitive expression, say 'murder Mikis', where one cannot speak of truth or falsity, acts are described by uttering sentences like

(47) Joseph murdered Mikis on Monday.

'Joseph', 'Mikis' and 'Monday' must refer to certain objects, (47) to a certain act of Joseph. If (47) is false, the last reference fails.

The verbal morpheme and the α-relation are similar in meaning. This similarity makes for a fundamental distinction between logic and theory of action. Whereas sentences of logic are formulated in the ahistorical present tense and the statements within the calculus are conceived as invariant and timeless, the sentences of action theory show different relations to time. One of them is that the acts themselves are done at a specific time. Furthermore, the theory of action cannot fail to take into account the fact that varying interpretations are possible and usual and that the practice of agents as well as of theorists may change the assignments of acts to patterns and the patterns themselves. Action theory has to emphasize that the world does not exist independent of time, that the world is made by the action of man, is thus interpreted by men, and may be interpreted differently at different times.

A pattern does not have, like a set, the property of extensionality, so that one does not have to know which x's are according to the pattern in order to know the pattern. Only owing to this fact can we judge future, not-yet-existing acts according to this pattern, which does not necessarily change if new x's are performed according to it.[7] These properties of patterns play a part in their acquisition and historical transformation. For, in order to master a pattern, one need not remember either every x of HA which one has come to know up to now, or even every act which has ever been done according to HA. But as the acts according to a pattern do play a part in its acquisition and in its transformation — inasmuch as I can only discover the pattern mastered by another person by supposing that he differentiates: $x_1 \alpha$ HA, $x_2 \not\alpha$ HA, but $x_2 \alpha$ HB etc. — it follows that the patterns according to which different people act are never identical and that they are permanently in motion. Indeed, how many x_i must my partner show me in order for me to be able to recognize his pattern? Here there is no limit.[8]

There is not one single empty pattern as is the case with sets. We may construct or invent new patterns according to which no one ever acted and we would have to say that these patterns exist though they are empty. But we could not say that they are identical. It would make a great difference whether we acted according to the one or to the other.

Of course such an empty pattern could not be said to hold. This would not even be correct of a pattern according to which only one act has been performed.[9] For rules are defined by the similarity of acts so that at least two similar acts are necessary in order to say that the rule holds. The formation of act-patterns depends upon the intention of an individual to act according to a pattern. But only by repetition and not privately is the pattern introduced.

2.2.2 *The arrow-relation*

If the policeman killed the Greek by shooting him it does not make sense to ask what he did first, the killing or the shooting. Therefore the one cannot be the cause of the other as far as the *by*-relation is concerned, for that presupposes a chronological order. Nor is it the case for the *by*-relation that one act is a temporal phase of the other. Phases of shooting might be [draw the pistol], [fire]. But one can neither fire by drawing the pistol, nor draw the pistol by firing.

As the *by*-relation does not apply to all cases which we describe with the conjunction 'after' – x_2 of HB is done after x_1 of HA has been done or vice versa – it also excludes the conjunction 'while', say [shoot the greek while singing a song]. Although we have simultaneity here it would be odd to say that he shot him by singing a song, the reason being that for simultaneity there must be two acts whereas a condition for the *by*-relation is that only one act is done, but according to two patterns:

(48) $x \, \alpha \, HA$ and $x \, \alpha \, HB$.

In contrast, for the 'after' case and for the 'while' case the following holds:

(49) $x_1 \, \alpha \, HA$ and $x_2 \, \alpha \, HB$ and $x_1 \neq x_2$.

The close connection of the patterns through the *by*-relation is seen from the fact that if, in a special case, one had not acted according to HA one also could not have acted according to HB and vice versa. Further, as far as the *by*-relation is concerned it is impossible for different agents to act according to the different patterns. This is due to the subject identity condition for gerund constructions. Significantly, not only gerund constructions occur with 'while' and 'after' but also clauses with different subjects which is impossible for 'by'.

Here the pattern in the *by*-gerund is rather a kind of modification of the other one.

We shall now introduce a special way of representing the case of doing an act x according to HA by doing x according to HB:

(50) $x \alpha (HA \rightarrow HB)$.

We have thus formed a complex pattern with the help of $\rightarrow$ and the brackets. But we also use '$\rightarrow$' to describe the relation between the patterns in:

(51) $HA \rightarrow HB$.

We read: HA generates HB and call (51) a generation.[10] We have already seen in 2.2.1 that the two expressions HA and HB in (50) were not synonymous: Not all cases of [defend oneself] are cases of [shoot someone] nor vice versa. For one can defend oneself by hitting someone's arm, and one can shoot and thus murder someone. For this reason there is a surplus on both sides.[11] However, as (50) holds for HA and HB, it appears (i) that it must be possible that acts according to both have the same result, and (ii) that (50) holds only if, under the same conditions, the agent would not have acted according to HA, if he had not acted according to HB.

The arrow of generation '$\rightarrow$' has the following properties:

(52) If $(HA \rightarrow HB$ and $HB \rightarrow HA)$ then $HA = HB$ antisymmetrical
(53) If $(HA \rightarrow HB$ and $HB \rightarrow HC)$ then $HA \rightarrow HC$ transitive
(54) $HA \rightarrow HA$ reflexive.

The transitivity of '$\rightarrow$' does not make reference to the agent's intention. Our policeman may really have defended himself and may have intended to do so, but he need not have intended to shoot the Greek, even if he defended himself by shooting the Greek. This is due to the intensional context 'intended'. Assuming '$\rightarrow$' to be reflexive is rather unusual, for usually we do not say: one turns on the light by turning on the light. But that may be admitted as a redundancy which does no harm. Later we shall see that this assumption is significant.[12] It is already implied in (52).

From our examples and from (53) we already know that the generated pattern itself generates other patterns. So, the policeman defended himself by shooting the Greek, by pulling the trigger, by curling his finger round the trigger. An analysis of this would have the following form:

(55) $HA \rightarrow HB$.

HB → HC.

HC → HD.

In accordance with (53) we might as well write:

(56) HA → HB → HC → HD.

Acts, the patterns of which cannot generate further patterns, that is, which do not occur on the left of the arrow, are called basic acts.[13]

A basic act is e.g. the curling of one's finger, for we can find no description such as 'A curls his finger by V-ing'. Attempts have indeed been made at such a description, e.g. a neurophysiological description. However, it is not the conventional arrow-relation which is described here, it is only said that certain nerves and muscles are activated when curling one's finger and how this might be the cause for the movement of the finger. But, the agent's act is not usually [move this or that muscle] but [curl the finger], or perhaps even [move the muscles by curling one's finger]. Once more it is evident that these modes of description do not compete.[14]

Our definition does not mean that basic acts could not be complex in another way, e.g. both [curl the finger in the evening] and [curl the finger at 8:51 P.M.] are basic patterns, though they are related to one another and can be analysed together. Moreover, a basic act may consist of different phases in time; e.g. an act according to [curl the finger one millimetre] is most often a phase of an act according to [curl the finger] which may also be a basic act. But usually the former is not generated by [curl the finger].[15] Here the agent's intention could be of importance. If he wants to curl the finger at one stroke, his doing so is a basic act.

It must be possible to make every basic act intentionally and willfully (under normal conditions of course). That is the reason why coughing because one has a cough, mentioned above, is not a basic act and no act at all; ironical coughing is, however. The corresponding pattern is generated by [give a sign]. But that does not mean that every basic act must be made intentionally and willfully. It is possible to do something under compulsion, automatically, lost in thought, etc.

In order to be able to perform basic acts, certain requirements must be fulfilled just as for other acts. Besides, the action competence of men differs in the internalisation of basic patterns: A person whose right hand is paralyzed cannot perform an act according to [curl the right forefinger]. Others are masters of more patterns than people usually are, e.g. [wiggle one's ears]. We can imagine people who are masters of quite unusual basic patterns such as [see infra-red], [see double]. Notice that there is not a special class of basic act-patterns. Act-patterns basic in one string may be generating patterns in another string.

A theory of action should not only deal with the explanation of acts already performed, but above all with the possibilities of these acts. In order to do so, it would be necessary to explain that one can defend oneself by shooting someone or by arresting someone or. . .

In addition to the mere possibility of acting in a certain way, which is described by the relations between the patterns as in (51), the fact that there are alternative possibilities is of great importance:

(57) $x_1 \, \alpha \, (HA \rightarrow HB)$ or
$\quad x_2 \, \alpha \, (HA \rightarrow HC)$ or
$\quad x_3 \, \alpha \, (HA \rightarrow HD)$.

In summing up we may write for (57):

(58) $x_i \, \alpha \, (HA \rightarrow \begin{Bmatrix} HB \\ HC \\ HD \end{Bmatrix})$.

The three generations are strict alternatives, for we do not want to allow the possibility of performing one act x_i according to $HA \rightarrow HB$ and according to $HA \rightarrow HC$.

In order to describe the possible acts it is sufficient to describe the relation between the patterns as presented in (58) as follows:

(59) $HA \rightarrow \begin{Bmatrix} HB \\ HC \\ HD \end{Bmatrix}$.

We call (59) a partition of HA. The expression on the right side of the arrow is called a family; HB, HC, HD are called members of the family. In general, partitions remain open, for there are many patterns which may be generated by one pattern, and new patterns continually enter its partition. For example, I can greet someone not only by doffing my hat, by giving him a smile, or by shaking hands with him, but also, under certain circumstances, by giving him my foot, and he will understand that as a greeting. This example makes it quite clear that a partition of a pattern is always conventional.

In spite of its openness, a partition is not trivial. For some generations are excluded, others very unlikely. It is impossible to give someone one's foot by greeting him. For, in order to give someone a foot, one must usually give him a foot. There are hardly any other possibilities. Of course one could introduce the convention that some sort of greeting is accepted for giving the foot; but then one obviously would have changed act-patterns.

Partitions cannot normally be used to define act-patterns, e.g. by strengthening the arrow to '=' and by enumerating all possibilities. This fails because (i) the partitions remain open; (ii) there is the surplus mentioned above for every generated pattern, so that even in the degenerate case where a partition is identical with a generation HA $\rightarrow$ HB, there would still be acts according to HB which are not according to HA. However, we shall come to certain special cases later where such a definition seems to be possible. In those cases which have been allowed for by the reflexivity of $\rightarrow$ the definition is not realized by the arrow.

We secure the strict alternativity of the generations within a partition by postulating that the members of a family must differ from one another. Let HB, HC and HD be members of a family then:

(60) If $x_1 \; \alpha \;$ HB then $x_1 \; \not\alpha \;$ HC and $x_1 \; \not\alpha \;$ HD   for every x_1.

Empirically we fulfill these requirements by treating overlapping HX and HY as a whole, namely HZ. This may be allowed because of the possible surplus. Moreover we can assume that we always take into account the difference within partitions in our current treatment of acts, so that examples according to (59) like

(61) GREET $\rightarrow \left\{ \begin{array}{l} \text{SHAKE HANDS} \\ \text{SAY GOOD MORNING} \end{array} \right\}$.

which at first glance seem to allow the possibility of doing HA by doing HB and HC, are to be understood rather differently. Here we have a sort of redundant greeting (not a twice repeated greeting), which occurs when doing two acts: $x_2 \; \alpha \;$ HB and $x_3 \; \alpha \;$ HC where both pass for HA, e.g. in this way: $x_1 \; \alpha \;$ HA and $x_1 = \; < x_2, x_3 >$. We shall come to talk about this possibility of forming pairs of acts in 2.2.5.

Up to now we have not paid any attention to the fact that one cannot act according to a certain pattern in any given situation: one can only reconcile two people if they have quarrelled and are still quarrelling. And one cannot greet someone by shaking hands with him if one is speaking to him by telephone. Thus, there are requirements for patterns which must necessarily be fulfilled so that someone may act according to this pattern. We introduce these conditions into our language of description in the following way:

(62) HA if C1.

The condition for doing HA is given by a truth-functional sentence C1. Its truth is a necessary condition for the possibility of acting according to HA. To ask for the conditions means to ask for certain typical features of a situation in which an act according to HA can be performed. The situations are not to be understood as static in a strict sense. C1 may even require an act or the result of an act.

One might think of distinguishing between different categories of conditions. The condition for someone's chopping wood, namely that there is wood, might be regarded as a sort of physical sentence. By way of contrast, the condition for someone's giving an order to somebody else, namely that he has a certain position in the corresponding hierarchy, is a social one. This division, however, diverts us from the fact that all of these conditions are conventional, because they are part of the rule, that is, part of the corresponding act-pattern. If it were possible to chop wood without having wood, a different pattern would be involved. Therefore the conditions must not be regarded as somehow independent from the act-patterns. It is our action which defines the condition in question. Thus, we create the social hierarchies only by the possibilities of action; for the position of an individual within such a hierarchy consists in his possibilities of acting. While learning the possibilities of acting we also learn to associate situations with such types of situations.

Therefore a description of a rule must contain a description of the conditions under which the rule may be obeyed.[16] Here, the description of the social situation, needs, etc., come into play. The naive objectivist assumption that this situation is somehow already given does not hold nor is it more concrete than the abstract rule.

Conditions need not refer to individual act-patterns; they may also hold for generations. For example it is possible both to turn on the light and to turn the corresponding switch, and still fail to turn on the light by turning the corresponding switch, if the circuit is broken. Likewise it is possible to maintain that Cicero died and to utter 'Marcus is dead', but it is not possible to maintain the former by uttering the latter, if I do not know that one can refer with 'Marcus' and 'Cicero' to the same person. That is why we must make clear the scope of these conditions to whole generations by means of brackets:

(63) (HA → HB) if C1.

We can proceed in the same way with partitions: The conditions for the members of the family are written inside the braces as in (64), those for generations after the braces, so that every condition refers to the line of the partition on which it stands:

$$(64) \quad HA \rightarrow \left\{ \begin{array}{ll} HB & \text{if C1} \\ HC & \text{if C2} \\ \cdot & \cdot \\ \cdot & \cdot \\ \cdot & \cdot \end{array} \right\}$$

$$(65) \quad HA \rightarrow \left\{ \begin{array}{ll} HB & \text{if C1} \\ HC & \text{if C2} \\ \cdot & \cdot \\ \cdot & \cdot \\ \cdot & \cdot \end{array} \right\}$$

Since the members in (65) themselves generate other patterns it is possible that the description of an act comprises several stages. E.g. Goldman's example of killing someone (KILL) by giving him a heart attack (HEART) by check-mating him (CHECKM) by moving one's queen to king's-knight-seven (MOVE), may be described by the following partitions:

$$(66) \quad KILL \rightarrow \left\{ \begin{array}{ll} HEART & \text{if C1} \\ SHOOT & \text{if C2} \\ \cdot & \cdot \\ \cdot & \cdot \\ \cdot & \cdot \end{array} \right\}$$

$$HEART \rightarrow \left\{ \begin{array}{ll} CHECKM & \text{if C3} \\ FRIGHT & \text{if C4} \\ \cdot & \cdot \\ \cdot & \cdot \\ \cdot & \cdot \end{array} \right\}$$

$$CHECKM \rightarrow \left\{ \begin{array}{ll} MOVE & \text{if C5} \\ \cdot & \cdot \\ \cdot & \cdot \\ \cdot & \cdot \end{array} \right\}$$

The linear representation may cause difficulties for the association of the conditions in chains of generation. E.g., one cannot arrive at a clear association by bracketing for the chain KILL → HEART if C1 → CHECKM if C3 →

MOVE if C5, which is possible according to (66). But when applying (56) it is sufficient to accept the conditions of a chain of generation all together. So, according to (66) an act according to KILL → HEART → CHECKM → MOVE if C1, C3, C5 would be possible, where the condition is the conjunction of all conditions of the single patterns and generations.

2.2.3 *The operators* ⊓ *and* ⊔.

For the description of an act we want to admit that the act may simultaneously be performed according to several patterns without the arrow-relation existing between them. A description of [play drums] (HA) may contain among other things [move the hands] (HB) and [move the feet] (HC). In the partition of HA we assume a pattern HX as a member which is composed of HB and HC:

$$(67) \quad HA \rightarrow \left\{ \begin{matrix} HX \\ . \\ . \\ . \end{matrix} \right\}$$

HX may be defined by

$$(68) \quad HX = HB \sqcap HC,$$

where '⊓' stands for an operation which forms out of two act-patterns a new one. We read 'HB ⊓ HC': HB bench HC or HB and HC. We define (68) by

(69) $HX = HB \sqcap HC$ if and only if x consists of x_1 and x_2 and x_1 is
simultaneous with x_2
for every x α HX and some x_1 α HB, x_2 α HC.

Because there is possibly no expression for HX we use the composed pattern HB ⊓ HC for it. In generations we introduce square brackets instead of '⊓' which allows for the abandonment of the linear representation. Accordingly a possible generation of our example would be

$$(70) \quad HA \rightarrow \begin{bmatrix} HB \\ HC \end{bmatrix}$$

As HB and HC themselves generate other patterns, (71) would be possible, too:

$$(71) \quad HA \rightarrow \begin{bmatrix} HB \rightarrow \ldots \\ \\ HC \rightarrow \ldots \end{bmatrix}$$

Of course the patterns formed by do not occur only as generated patterns but also as generating ones. For example one can make oneself sleepy (HA) and enjoy oneself (HB) by drinking beer (HC), without enjoying oneself by making oneself sleepy or vice versa. An act according to this generation might have the following description:

$$(72) \quad \begin{bmatrix} HA \\ \\ HB \end{bmatrix} \rightarrow HC$$

This must be distinguished both from (73) and (74):

(73) HA → HB → HC.
(74) HB → HA → HC.

The properties of ⌐ result from the properties of the defining 'and':

(75) HA ⌐ HB = HB ⌐ HA   commutative
(76) HA ⌐ (HA ⌐ HC) = (HA ⌐ HB) ⌐ HC   associative
(77) HA ⌐ HA = HA   idempotent

Because of (76) we can spare ourselves an inner bracketing for the ordering in iterated applications of ⌐.

In addition to ⌐ we introduce the operation ⌣ which also forms new act-patterns from pairs of act-patterns. It is defined by

(78) HX = HB ⌣ HC if and only if x α HX ⇐⇒ x α HB or x α HC

and has analogous properties to ⌐:

(79) HA ⌣ HB = HB ⌣ HA   commutative
(80) HA ⌣ (HB ⌣ HC) = (HA ⌣ HB) ⌣ HC   associative
(81) HA ⌣ HA = HA   idempotent

'HA ⌣ HC' is to be read: HA trough HC.

The families of partition are special cases of ⌣-related patterns in which the related patterns are distinct. If we take this as an additional condition, we can introduce a linear way of representation of partitions for certain purposes. Accordingly (59) would be written as

(82) HA → HB⊔HC⊔HD⊔...

As usual the points indicate the openness of the partition. If ⊔operations also occur in generating patterns, we shall use braces as we use square brackets for ⊓, as long as no misunderstandings could arise. Thus, a possible generation of [drink beer](HC) might also be:

$$(83) \begin{Bmatrix} HA \\ HB \end{Bmatrix} → HC,$$

of which (72) would be a special case, if HA = [make oneself sleepy], HB = [enjoy oneself].

2.2.4 *Subpatterns and specifications*

It may happen that two patterns are more closely related than is represented by a partition. Indeed, for HA = [kill someone] and HB = [kill someone today] (84) is valid:

(84) HA → HB,

even if it may sometimes sound rather strange. Still (84) does not represent completely the relationship of the two patterns. HA seems to be somehow contained in HB. In order to show this one could imagine two different analyses of HB where HA appears as a part of it:

(85) [kill someone and do something today].
(86) [kill someone by doing something today].

According to condition (48) both of the analyses are to be understood in the sense that there is always one act in question, not that one kills someone and simultaneously does something else today. However, we succeed with neither of the analyses because the second parts of the patterns contain the referring expression 'something', which is used to refer anaphorically exactly to the pattern HA. Just that is the condition for there being only one single act at any time. But then both analyses are nothing but (84), (85) however in a weaker form and thus less adequate. Therefore we introduce a new way of representation which shows the relation between HA and HB by utilizing the fact that HB is, as it were, a special case of HA. This is based on the fact that 'x α HB' implies 'x α HA', thus that the surplus mentioned exists in (84) only on one side. For 'x α HA' does not imply 'x α HB'. For this new representation we define a new relation between act-patterns which we mark with ' ⊏ ':

(87)   HB ⊏ HA if and only if x α HB ⇒ x α HA.

We say: HB is a subpattern of HA.

Subpatterns have the following properties:

(88)   If HA ⊏ HB and HB ⊏ HC then HA ⊏ HC   transitive
(89)   If HA ⊏ HB and HB ⊏ HA then HA = HB   antisymmetrical

In our example the relation between the two patterns is already evident in their linguistic expressions. Since our abbreviated representation of 'HA' and 'HB' does not make that clear, we introduce into our language of description new means by which we can define HB by HA as follows:

(90)   HB = HA (M1)

where HA(M1) is called a specification of HA. M1 is an operator which causes the change in HA, so that the implication mentioned above holds. Operators of this kind are called specificators or simply specifications, too. Now (84) should be represented as (91) which formally shows the relation between the two patterns:

(91)   HA → HA (M1)

We also assume specifications in other cases which, at first glance, seem to be less obvious. Let HC = [kill someone with a knife], then HC, like HB, cannot be analysed as follows:

(92)   [kill someone and use a knife].

For here it is not certain that only one act is concerned. One might as well use a knife for another purpose, say in order to cut a slice of salami,[17] so that: x_1 α HA and x_2 α HD (= [use a knife]) and $x_1 \neq x_2$. (92) would not justify a generation like

(93) HA → HD.

For this purpose we ought to add to HD at least another 'for this purpose' and thereby refer to HA and then the pattern would again be identical with HC. Here, too, it is better to describe HC as a specification of HA, e.g. HA (M2). These two examples demonstrate that there are different specifications for a pattern which do not exclude one another. The specifications, however, are not limited to the different adverbials in the expressions of the patterns (say A1, A2,. . .), they also concern complements. Thus HE = [kill Mikis] is related to HA as a specification. This specification is based upon the implication of the descriptions of acts, which correspond to the expressions of patterns; that is, (95) implies (94):

(94) A kills someone.
(95) A kills Mikis.

For these reasons we replace HA by the specification HA (X1) in which X1 is to be understood as a variable for the direct object from (94); the specification is to be understood as existentially quantified. The pattern that includes (95) would then be HA (B), if 'B' were a name for Mikis.[18]

Special cases of both kinds of specification are those cases where the specificator itself is an act-pattern, like [help], [learn] (HF), etc. Here again the difference between generation and specification becomes evident. For, if [learn to kill someone] is represented as HF (HA), (96) is valid:

(96) HF (X) → HF (HA),

but not

(97) HF (HA) → HA.

Here we recognize important possibilities of applying the theory of action to a didactic theory, for it would enable us to formalize the methods of learning. So, (97) shows us that within a method following (97) at least one restriction, which is often not justified, would have to be made.

When there are several specifications we separate the specificators by commas. As a property of double specification we assume

(98) HX (M1, M2) = HX (M2, M1),

so that we do not need bracketing for the succession of the specifications.

This presupposes that the kind of specification is given by indexing and not by succession. The necessity of differentiating between several kinds according to the syntactic positions within the description of the pattern becomes fairly evident when one pattern contains different complements. For example, (99) is not valid:

(99)   [give Emma a child] = [give Emma to a child].

Now we can render our definition of the basic act more precisely: HX is a basic pattern if and only if (i) HX is not further decomposable under →, (ii) there are only specifications of HX on the right of the arrow and they cannot be decomposed. If HA is a basic pattern, all specifications of HA must be basic patterns. This is another difference between generation and specification.

For every given specification (100) and (101) are now valid:

(100)   HX (M1, M2) ⊏ HX (M2).
(101)   HX (M1, M2) ⊏ HX (M1).

Furthermore it holds that:

(102)   HX (M1) ⊏ HX.
(103)   not (HX ⊏ HX (M1)).
(104)   HX (B) ⊏ HX (X).   existential instantiation

where B is an individual constant. As special cases of (102) and (103) we have:

(105)   HX (HY) ⊏ HX.
(106)   not (HY ⊏ HX (HY)).

As mentioned above, the assumption of the contrary of (106) may lead to considerable restrictions.[19]

By means of specification, the semantic relation of identity can be represented, as has already been done in (90). Thus it seems to be possible to define [murder someone] by a threefold specification of [kill something]:

(107)   MURD (X) = KILL (X, M1, M2),

where the scope of X must be restricted to man, M1 = with intent and premeditation, M2 = for base motives.[20] Semantic relations like these often cause peculiarities in generations and partitions (like the distinctness of the members mentioned above) and also in the rules of inference which we will now talk about. We shall choose some valid rules of inference and discuss why some others are not valid. Replacement to the right of the arrow is defined by (108) and (109):

(108)   HA → ...HB...
         HX ⊏ HB
         _____

         HA → ...HX...

We obtain a special case of (108) if we substitute a specified pattern for HX.

(109)   HA → ...HB...
         HB (M) ⊏ HB
         _____

         HA → ...HB (M)...

In contrast to (108), introducing a rule like (110) may lead to strange consequences:

(110)*   HA → ...HB...
         HB ⊏ HX
         _____

         HA → ...HX...

To be sure, it often seems possible to make inferences in accordance with (110), because a shift of the surplus from HB to HX will not be harmful in the generation. But if the relation between HA and HB is closer than usual, e.g. if HB ⊏ HA holds, then this relation may be destroyed. For example one can kill Paul by poisoning Paul. As [poison Paul] ⊏ [poison someone] holds, we might conclude with (110) that one could kill Paul by poisoning someone. This generation is valid. However the surplus of HX is very great, since HX is only generated by HA if this someone is Paul. If all generations which are special cases of this kind were not listed themselves but derived from superior generations by means of subpatterns, one could admit (110) as a valid rule of inference without any disturbing effects. Because of the asymmetry which is described by (102) and (103), there cannot be a corresponding special case for (109).

But we do not want to admit (110) here because still other, not very meaningful sentences might be derived by it:[21]

(111)   HA → . . .HA. . .
        HA ⊏ H*
       _____

        HA → H*

Since here only theorems are used, HA → H* would be a theorem. If we accept this we could use (108) in the following way:

(112)   HA → H*
        HZ ⊏ H*
       _____

        HA → HZ

In this case the arrow would become trivial because it holds between all pairs of patterns.

In addition to the replacement to the right, there is one to the left:

(113)   HA → . . .HB. . .
        HA ⊏ HX
       _____

        HX → . . .HB. . .

It causes an increase of the surplus of HA and seems to be generally acceptable. However, the following replacement is not a valid rule of inference:

(114)* HA → . . .HB. . .
        HX ⊏ HA
       _____

        HX → . . .HB. . .

At least this rule of inference is not valid for distinct members of a partition, for then:

(115)   KILL → . . .POIS. . .
        SHOOT ⊏ KILL
       _____

        SHOOT → . . .POIS. . .

That can be avoided by introducing poisoning (POIS) and shooting (SHOOT) as specifications of KILL: POIS = KILL (M), SHOOT = KILL (N). For such a case an exception would have to be introduced in order to prevent the contradictory specificators M and N from occurring in patterns which generate one another.

The rules of inference must still be examined more precisely as to the conditions for the member chosen out of a partition. It looks as if at least the conditions for the member of the major premise must be transferred to the conclusion. Often further restrictions of the conditions must be made. One ought to be able to infer this restriction from the minor premise. We have further special cases of the rules of inference with certain specifications. The replacement to the right according to (108) looks like

(116)　HA → . . .HB (X). . .
　　　　HB (A) ⊏ HB (X)
　　　　―――――――――――
　　　　HA → . . .HB (A). . .

As we have seen, one must be careful with a conclusion according to (110), if there are variables with an identical reference in a sentence:

(117)　HA → . . .HB (A). . .
　　　　HB (A) ⊏ HB (X)　　　　according to (104)
　　　　―――――――――――
　　　　HA → . . .HB (X). . .

Usually, when substituting, all identical variables would have to be substituted in the same way. Therefore the replacement to the right is not admitted as existential instantiation.

(118)　MURD (A) → . . .POIS (A). . .
　　　　POIS (A) ⊏ POIS (X)
　　　　―――――――――――――
　　　　MURD (A) → POIS (X)

Obviously it is impossible to murder Paul by poisoning someone if this someone is not Paul himself. Certain ways of speaking, e.g. that one kills a woman by killing her child Claudia, are therefore either intended as a metaphor or the killing of the woman is only a consequence. But in no case may one conclude according to (118).

The replacement to the left, however, is possible as an existential instantiation without preserving the variables:

(119) MURD (A) → . . .POIS (A). . .
       MURD (A) ⌐MURD (X)
       _____

       MURD (X) → . . .POIS (A). . .

Cases where there are no identical variables are of course not subject to these
rules. E.g. [turn out the light by turning the switch] would have the form:
HA (X) → HB (Y). Of course here also a relation between the variables holds,
for one cannot turn any given switch in order to turn out a certain light. Perhaps this relation can be represented in a fuller analysis.

2.2.5 The cross-operation

Let $<x_1, x_2>$ be an ordered pair of acts, then

(120) $<x_1, x_2> \neq <x_2, x_1>$,

if one does not make further restrictions. We shall call the pattern that includes
all pairs such that $x_1 \alpha$ HA and $x_2 \alpha$ HB the product of HA and HB and write
HA † HB. That is to be read: HA cross HB. Accordingly (121) and (122) are
valid:

(121) $<x_1, x_2> \alpha$ HA † HB.
(122) HA † HB $\neq$ HB † HA.

Here is one difference between cross-operation and the ⌐-operator, which
does not have a definite order because of its commutativity. In most cases,
product-patterns are not institutionalized act-patterns; sometimes they are,
especially if x_1 is before x_2 so that $x_1 < x_2$. An example of this would be
[make a square knot] = HA, which consists of the following components:
HB = [make a loop], HC = [make a round turn], HD = [pull the free end
through the loop] (see diagram). Thus HA is a subpattern of HB † HC † HD
which is defined by $<$ and some other conditions, e.g., to continue with the
right end of the rope and not to let it go in the meantime, etc.

   If we write 'HFOR' for the subpattern defined by $<$ we can generally
assume:

(123)   HFOR ⌈ HB † HC † ... † HN if and only if x α HFOR ⇒

$$x_1 < x_2 < \ldots < x_n$$

with x = $<x_1, x_2, \ldots, x_n>$ and x_1 α HB, ..., x_n α HN

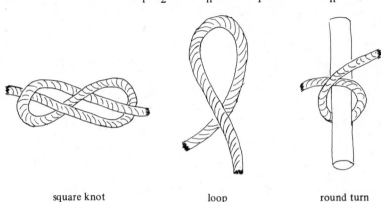

square knot   loop   round turn

We call all instances of HFOR sequence-patterns and acts according to sequence-patterns sequences. If we have instead of $<$ the stronger relation $<\cdot$ (directly before), we talk of direct sequences.

It is not of prime importance for an empirical theory of action to describe, as it were constructively, the possibilities of forming new patterns, but to describe existing patterns. Therefore those cases are interesting where a sub-pattern of a product is itself a pattern which is institutionalized, and on which one acts all in one go; that is, one does not perform first an act x_1 of HB and then one x_2 of HC, but only x_i of HA. One need only intend to do x_i of HA. The decomposition into phases is, so to speak, automatic. For these cases we write 'HAUT'. Examples are: [pronounce a word] in opposition to [pronounce a word phoneme by phoneme], something, then, like spelling. Obviously we can pronounce many sentences all in one go without being conscious of the pronunciation of every word. In contrast, pronouncing word by word, say when pronouncing a sentence to a foreigner, is acting according to the pro-duct-pattern. The intention to do x_i of HA and the carrying out of this inten-tion do not require that $x_1 <\cdot x_2 <\cdot x_3$.[22] Someone may have done HB when the bell rings. He may now interrupt his doing HA, open the door, and then continue with HA. Because of the interruption $x_1 <\cdot x_2$ does not hold, but the intention was, all the same, to do HA. Of course it may be that A no long-er knows how to continue, so that he must begin once again, because he does HA automatically; that is, he knows nothing about the phases and their succes-sion. All the same, the description of several phases is not inappropriate. For he himself may recognize the composition of HA; he may even profit by knowing its make-up, if he wants to explain or to teach HA to somebody.

The decomposition of HAUT into phases is important for learning because it is often an advantage to practice different phases of movements separately, even where basic acts are concerned. We have:

(124)   HAUT ⊏ HA ⊹ HB.

For the special case of identity of components of the product-patterns, we use the abbreviated representation:[23]

(125) $HA^2 = HA \dagger HA.$
(126) $HA^n = HA \dagger \ldots \dagger HA$
$$\underbrace{}_{\text{n times}}$$

This way of representation is useful for all repetitions or acts with phases that are repeated. It cannot be used directly for the definition of REPEAT (HA). REPEAT (HA) → HA is indeed valid, but existence of the x of HA already done is a condition for this generation. That is the reason why 'having repeated HA' includes 'having done HA^2'.

Product-patterns have the following properties:

(127)   If HA ⊏ HB then HA † HC ⊏ HB † HC
(128)   If HB ⊏ HC then HA † HB ⊏ HA † HC
(129)   If HA † HB → HB † HA and HB † HA → HA † HB then HA = HB

Of course the rules of inference from 2.2.4 are also valid for product-patterns. So the following conclusion according to (108) is justified:

(130)   HA → ...HB † HC...
HD ⊏ HB † HC
────────────────
HA → ...HD...

However, here as well, conclusions according to (111) seem to be possible only if we allow for changes in conditions of the major premise. Then (131) and (132) would be valid as special cases:

(131)   HA → ...HFOR...
HFOR ⊏ HA † HB
────────────────
HA → ...HA † HB...

(132)　　HA → ...HAUT...
　　　　　HAUT ⌈HA † HB
　　　　　―――――――――――――
　　　　　HA → ...HA † HB...

Now I want to give examples for act-patterns, which are described with the apparatus developed so far. Let HA = [play a major scale on the piano], HB = [play any given tone x], HC = [play the next highest tone which is defined by the scale of x], and so on to HI, HJ = [move the right hand], HK = [move the left hand]. Then (133) would be a description of [play a major scale, by playing eight tones one after the other, by moving the right hand], (134) a description of [play a major scale by playing eight tones one after another, by playing the first four tones by moving the right hand and the last four tones by moving the left hand]:

(133)

$$HA \rightarrow HFOR \rightarrow \left\{ \begin{array}{c} HB \\ HC \\ \cdot \\ \cdot \\ HI \end{array} \right\} \rightarrow HJ$$

(134)

$$HA \rightarrow HFOR \rightarrow \left\{ \begin{array}{c} \left\{ \begin{array}{c} HB \\ \cdot \\ \cdot \\ HE \end{array} \right\} \rightarrow HJ \\ \\ \left\{ \begin{array}{c} HF \\ \cdot \\ HI \end{array} \right\} \rightarrow HK \end{array} \right\}$$

Here the cross-operation is represented by the angled brackets. Goldman's[24] example of [drive a nail into the wall] = HA might be described with HB = [drive the nail a little way into the wall], HC = [swing the hammer], HD = [swing his hand]:

(135)

$$HA \rightarrow HFOR \rightarrow \left\{ \begin{array}{c} HB \rightarrow HC \rightarrow HD \\ HB \rightarrow HC \rightarrow HD \\ \\ HB \rightarrow HC \rightarrow HD \\ HB \rightarrow HC \rightarrow HD \end{array} \right\}$$

As an abbreviation for (135) one could use (136):

(136) $HA \rightarrow HFOR \rightarrow (HB \rightarrow HC \rightarrow HD)^4$.

In both cases the nail would be hammered into the wall with four strokes. An act according to (137), one with no sequence, would of course be more economical, if this hand-swinging took no more time than that in (135):

(137) $HA \rightarrow HB \rightarrow HC \rightarrow HD$.

(138)   must also be distinguished from (136):

(138)

$$HA \rightarrow HFOR \rightarrow \begin{pmatrix} HB \rightarrow HC \\ HB \rightarrow HC \\ HB \rightarrow HC \\ HB \rightarrow HC \end{pmatrix} \rightarrow HD.$$

I cannot imagine how people manage such a thing, excluding cases where different agents are involved, or where a machine is used which has a stuttering gear, so that its hammer strikes four times through a single pulling of the lever.

According to (122) the cross-operation is asymmetrical. Therefore we introduce a special way of representation for the inversion of the components of a product. If $HA = HB \dagger HC$, the following holds:

(139) $HA^{-1} = HC \dagger HB$.

HA^{-1} is called the inverse pattern of HA, and the acts according to HA^{-1} are called inverse acts of those according to HA. If the sequence pattern contains more than two components, the components are shifted pairwise, around the central component (which may be null). Here we deal only with the inverse pattern of HFOR. Note that the inverse of [tie a square knot] = HA is not [undo a square knot] = HD. For all components must be inverted, say

(140) $HD = HC^{-1} \dagger HB^{-1} \dagger HA^{-1}$.

But that would also be insufficient because when undoing a knot, one proceeds in a different manner than when tying a knot. E.g. one can undo a loop by letting one end drop. We imagine HA^{-1} to be something like a film that is played backwards. We also see the persons acting, that is, we have interpretations for their x of HA^{-1}; however, this world may seem to us in part very strange, because e.g., of the frequency of acts according to HA^{-1} (going backwards frequently and so on) or the particular succession of acts, for instance when someone is fishing. Backwards, we see that he pulls the line out of the water very quickly and at one stroke. Of course we presume that he has thrown it in before. Then he throws it out again, somewhat slowly. Now he has a rather large bait on the line, which he has taken out of the basket. Of course he will bring it out only later, but the film no longer shows that. Here we make the correct connections to contexts. But as far as isolated basic acts are concerned, one often cannot decide whether one is seeing the film backwards or forwards. For example, one cannot decide whether there is an act according to HA = [raise the arm] or backwards according to HA^{-1} = [lower the arm]. Even in context this often cannot be decided, if we have plausible interpretations for all HX^{-1}.

It seems to be questionable whether one can assume inverse acts for basic acts at all given our definition (139). But every act and every pattern can be decomposed as finely as desired. It might happen that we do not know institutionalized patterns for the components. But then we help ourselves with specifications, e.g. [raise the arm one millimetre]. Thus we can obtain any degree of fineness by specifying in space and time as finely as we want. The inversion of acts entails, as we have seen in our film, changes within the results. There is a time when the fisher finally has a fish in his basket, but not so when inverting the acts. Such differences may well be shown in the description of acts of writing. Let WN = [write an N], HMN = [move the hand in N-manner] [25], V and H be specifications for the movements 'vertically' and 'horizontally', '$\succ$' stand for the relation between the act and its result. Noew we can make the following description:

$$(141) \quad WN \rightarrow \begin{bmatrix} HMN\,(V) \\ HMN\,(H) \end{bmatrix} \succ N$$

$$(142) \quad WN \rightarrow \begin{bmatrix} HMN\,(V)^{-1} \\ HMN\,(H) \end{bmatrix} \succ N$$

$$(143) \quad WN \rightarrow \begin{bmatrix} HMN\,(V)_{\cdot} \\ HMN\,(H) \end{bmatrix} \succ N$$

$$(144) \quad WN^{-1} \rightarrow \begin{bmatrix} HMN\,(V)^{-1} \\ HMN\,(H)^{-1} \end{bmatrix} \succ N$$

Of course, the two generations in the middle are not correct because they are not generations for WN and the result is not N. (144) however, might well appear within a partition of WN by adding $WN \to WN^{-1}$ in front of it. Of course the results are related to the type of symmetry of the letters. For WW = [write a W] we would have a different distribution:

$$(145) \quad WW \to \quad \begin{bmatrix} HMN(V)^{-1} \\ HMN(H) \end{bmatrix} \quad \succ \quad \text{M}$$

$$(146) \quad WW \to \quad \begin{bmatrix} HMN(V) \\ HMN(H)^{-1} \end{bmatrix} \quad \succ \quad W$$

$$(147) \quad WW \to \quad \begin{bmatrix} HMN(V)^{-1} \\ HMN(H)^{-1} \end{bmatrix} \quad \succ \quad \text{M}$$

In both cases a decomposition into phases is possible, so that one could also obtain these results by inverting the phases or the specified phases. But it seems to me as if both analyses may have a very direct practical application, if one considers that our movements of writing might be much more economical: e.g. many people write an N by doing $HMN(V)^2$ instead of $HMN(V)$, more exactly $HMN(V) \dagger HMN(V)^{-1}$ (me, too, by the way). This seems to be related to a tendency to begin block letters on their top left.

2.2.6 Omissions and deviations

In addition to using the minus sign in negative exponents in inversions, we want to use it for negative acts according to HA which would be acts according to -HA. A negative act does not simply mean not-doing HA. That would force us to assume that every agent performs at any time an infinity of acts, because the number of acts not performed would be infinite. Even if an act serves to prevent a certain change[26] so that the act with the result not-R would be the negative of that with R, we do not want to assume negative acts. That would be a special case of [prevent].

On the contrary, negative acts are to stand for omissions in a strict sense. Omissions are made in those cases where certain conditions C are fulfilled and a general law is accepted: whenever C holds, you must perform an act of HA. If one does not do HA in this situation one has performed an act according to -HA. For example, if one does not make compliments to the hostess at dinner or if one is told to perform an act according to HB and one does not do so, then one has performed an act according to -HB. It is evident that the law in question does not describe causal relations but conventional ones.

Therefore one can infringe upon it. Because of their importance in social interactions, omissions are important for a theory of action and their description
is justified. Now we want to point out some properties of negative acts:

(148) It is not the case for every x that x α HA or x α -HA.
(149) -HX $\sqsubset$ H*   for every HX.
(150) HA $\neq$ - HA.
(151) If x α HA then x $\not\alpha$ -HA   for every x.

Generations must admit descriptions like $\left[\begin{smallmatrix} HA \\ -HB \end{smallmatrix}\right]$, both before and after the arrow.
If we write HA - HB for this, then

(152) If x α HA - HB then x α HA and x $\not\alpha$ HB   for every x.

A special case of (152) is (153):

(153) If x α H* - HB then x α H* and x $\not\alpha$ HB   for every x.
(154) It is not the case for every x that if x $\not\alpha$ HA then x α -HA.
(155) HA - HB $\sqsubset$ HA.

When introducing the concept of rule, we encountered the possibility of
deviating as a fundamental property of the rule. As laws are not rules, omissions are not deviations from any rule, and therefore they are differently
named here, though often in ordinary language no differentiation is made.
Now I shall give some hints as to how to use the categories of our language
of description for the explanation of deviating acts. We distinguish between
two large groups of deviations, mistakes, and omissions: in the first group
there are acts which cannot be attached to certain patterns, in the second
group we have three cases:

(i) We are all familiar with this experience: you want to perform a certain
basic act, according to HA perhaps, and you do not succeed. E.g., when
playing ping-pong you want to move your arm so that you succeed in returning the ball with a smash, but you smash it into the net. Often we do not
know what our mistake has been. Maybe it is a temporary weakness, maybe a
systematic mistake. In general it is a question of training where an expert may
of course be of help. In other cases there are in addition external circumstances
which prevent the performance of x according to HA; for example when my
paddle is damaged. Here, it may be that I have judged the circumstances
wrongly, that I did not know some of them, or that a disturbance occurs at the
last moment. In most cases we recognize such cases when we do not attain the

desired result, but we often perceive already during the action that the act will go wrong.

(ii) Somewhere in the chain of generation a defect occurs. Of course the reason may be the quite special one that the basic act fails. But there are many more possibilities. They are all probably related to the conditions of the generation. Let us suppose that the defect occurs between the triplets of dots in . . .→ HX → HY → . . . It might be that the conditions for HX or HY had not been fulfilled. The agent's social role is part of these conditions, e.g. if I were to marry two lovers by uttering the corresponding formula, I would not perform an act according to 'marry someone' because this act-pattern is reserved for certain agents. But I may have performed an act according to HY. It would be different if the conventional arrow-relation were not valid under these circumstances. E.g., when I want to turn on the light by turning the switch but it is the wrong switch, perhaps one which is dead. The case is similar when an act according to HY admits several HXs and it is hard to decide according to which HX the act is performed: e.g., if someone, by uttering S, asserts that S and perhaps even lies, this would be hard to decide. So, it may be uncertain what the leftmost pattern was in the string of generation.

(iii) This leads us to the third kind of failure which is not only the agent's affair, but due to the fact that the partners do not assign the act correctly or that the partners and the agent do not agree when assigning acts to patterns. These difficulties in deciding whether x was performed according to HX become clear in trials which are supposed to ascertain after the event whether x α HX or x α HZ, the latter being proposed by the opposing side. It often amounts to a question of power. So long as this decision is made by experts after long discussions and so long as the laws are so complicated – in the extreme case, when the laws are written in a strange language – then they cannot help the agent better to understand his action. Hence a subsequent justification with the help of money and a good lawyer, just as much as a subsequent reversal of the verdict, is a perversion of a reasonable idea of law.

(iv) The second group is defined by laws stating that one must act according to HA or -HB in such-and-such situations. One makes a mistake if one acts according to -HA or HB. All conditions which might be infringed upon in the first group are fulfilled here. One can do -HA or even HB, but one should not.

As infringements upon such laws cause sanctions, they demand an authority which judges acts, in most cases with particular reference to their assignment to patterns as in (iii). This authority may be the social group to which one belongs or oneself, e.g. if one infringes upon laws imposed upon oneself in order to give up smoking.

(v) A second case within this group occurs when certain conditions which the agent believes to be fulfilled are not believed to be fulfilled by the partner. This often happens with mental illness, which is partly defined by the fact that someone has beliefs which are not conventional for a given society.

All these cases of deviation presuppose social conventions and bring us back to the important feature we mentioned when introducing rules and patterns, but have neglected up to now: namely that acts are not private but social activities. In the next section we shall turn to this aspect and consider especially the possibilities of justifying the theory of action in this light.

2.3 INTERACTION

It is now high time to turn away from our lonely agent and turn towards the common action of several agents. For, according to our discussion of rules, human action can only be possible as social action, and thus only a theory of action that is based on interaction is capable of explaining human action.

We want to understand interaction as a product-pattern $HA \dagger HB \dagger \ldots \dagger HN$ with at least two components, such that

(i)   at least two partners P1 and P2 are involved.[27]
(ii)   each of the partners acts according to at least one component.
(iii) the act(s) of the partner who does not begin shall be understood as a reaction to an act of the partner who begins.

In order to specify which partner acts according to which pattern we introduce indexes into the patterns. We write HA_i, if Pi acts according to HA. An interaction I_{12} of the partners P1, P2 is defined by

$$(156) \quad I_{12} = HA_1 \dagger \ldots \dagger HB_2 \dagger \ldots \dagger HN_i \quad \text{with i = 1 or 2}$$

The agent indexes are referential indexes, such that

    (157)   The policeman shot the Greek.
    (158)   Miller shot the Greek.

are related to the same pattern, provided that one refers with 'Miller' and 'the policeman' to the same person, which is not necessarily always clear.

A consequence of condition (ii) that every partner must act according to at least one component in the interaction is that every interaction has at least two components. Of course, each of the components may consist of a product-pattern as long as it is not interrupted by some act of the other partner. If we call such product-patterns moves, we can say more precisely that every interaction must consist of at least two moves. We call the number of moves of an interaction its dimension. There is a strictly alternating interaction if the first partner acts according to the odd-numbered moves and the second according to the even-numbered:

$$(159) \quad IA_{12} = HA_1 \dagger HB_2 \dagger HC_1 \dagger \ldots \dagger HN_i$$

In this case every component is exactly one move. According to condition (iii) not all those product-patterns which fulfill (i) and (ii) are interactions Interactions are certain subpatterns of such product-patterns,[28] which are made possible by the existence of the corresponding rules. The relation between the successive HX_1s and HY_2s is neither natural nor causal, but learned and dependent on society. For reactions are not just consequences but independent acts of a partner. It is of fundamental importance for an interaction that both partners know of and expect this relation between HX_1 and HY_2. This is also a question of understanding, because the standards of interaction are not so rigid that failure threatens if the partner does not act exactly according to the pattern expected. A partner who knows that rules are flexible and that two partners rarely ever act according to identical rules will rather leave a margin and search for an interpretation of his partner's act within the limits of the interaction, unless the latter's acts directly contradict the rule he is following. Hence one should not underestimate the elasticity of rules and should not restrict the creativity which the rules allow to the partners by premature codification. For even the most rigid codification does not prevent deviation and in the end cannot hide the fact that different social groups and different agents follow different rules.

For these reasons we do not assume that an interaction fails if, e.g., P1 acts according to HX and P2 interprets P1's acts as being according to HY and HX $\neq$ HY. This assumption would necessarily involve the failure of every interaction. Nor are interactions defined in such a way that they do not leave alternatives to the partners. E.g. an interaction where P1 orders P2 to do something and P2 refuses to obey does not thereby fail.[29] For refusing is just as much a move in interaction as obeying an order. According to our definition, omission can be understood only by the position of a pattern in an interaction.

An interaction is called cooperation or cooperative interaction if both partners want to obtain the same result by it and are able to do so. An interaction is called competition or competitive interaction, if both partners want to obtain by it contradictory results so that only one of them can reach his objective. E.g., a football game is a competition, because each team plays in order to win, and if one wins (reaches its goal) the other loses (does not reach its goal). However, singing in chorus will be a cooperative enterprise because all agents involved want as a result as excellent a performance as possible. Cooperation is what singing in chorus means. Our definition of competition shows that competition is not a fight without rules by everybody against everybody.

For even a competition is an interaction, one where rules must be obeyed for the interaction to succeed. For these reasons competition in a certain sense will presuppose a kind of cooperation, if is regarded as the aim of the partners to carry out this interaction. But this does not affect the value of the distinction between cooperation and competition.

Within an interaction the role of each of the partners is determined by way of indexing. The role R_i of the partner Pi in I is the ordered set of conditioned patterns according to which Pi can act in I; not at will, however, but in the way determined by I; e.g. one's partner's acts are a condition for one's own acts. The role R_i in I is a projection from I onto the components according to which Pi acts.

There are very often conditions for the adoption of a role by an agent where certain properties are required of the agent. In the degenerate case these properties may refer to the fact that he can play exactly this role; in other cases they may refer to other possibilities of acting, or to knowledge, power, status, etc. Thus, neither these conditions nor the general conditions for acting according to a pattern are to be regarded as independent of the act-pattern.

Because such conditions overlap or are dependent on one another, an agent can certainly play different roles. He may act as a doctor, or as a father, etc. But the possibilities of adopting a role also depend upon the agent's action competence, because one's action competence will not enable one to play any role. Perhaps the agent has not internalized certain basic act-patterns or generations which are, of course, neither innate nor unalterable, for the act-patterns of every agent are permanently changing.

Additional restrictions on the roles of an interaction are possible because some moves generate conditioned alternatives. These conditions are related to properties of the agent who plays this role. All this cannot be discussed in detail here.

We still have to introduce another important differentiation of interactions concerning roles, by distinguishing between symmetrical and complementary interactions using different concepts of symmetry. An interaction is to be called symmetrical if

(i) $R_1 = R_2$ or
(ii)   P1 and P2 can play either of the two roles.

An interaction shall be called complementary if there is no HX such that

(160) $HX \in R_1$ and $HX \in R_2$.

A weaker definition would be

(161) $HY \in R_1$ and $HY \notin R_2$ for some HY.

It would be premature to judge these definitions. They should demonstrate only that our language of description offers different possibilities for precise definitions among which we can make our choice on the basis of empirical criteria. As a further interpretation of symmetry, understood as a social ideal,[30] one could assume a symmetry between the action competence of both partners.

Since the components of an interaction can be partitioned, it may happen that an interaction symmetrical according to (i) is not symmetrical in this sense, for both partners know different partitions of the components. Symmetry understood in this way would require

(iii) $H^*_1 = H^*_2$

or at least the same competences as concerns the act-patterns which are components of the interaction.

Presumably symmetry as an ideal can only refer to (ii): in the case of (i) this ideal would lead to a drastic decimation of interactions, in the case of (iii) to some sort of supercompetence which, surely, nobody could acquire, otherwise it would turn out to be (ii), because the internalisation of the role must be regarded as a condition for its acceptance. To be sure, for the ideal of symmetry, the 'can' in (ii) should be understood to mean not only that the agent is master of this role but that he can perform it without being impeded by laws and interdictions.

Roles as parts of interactions can be changed. They do not only fix the agent's possibilities of action within an independent system, but can also be creative.

We can give detailed representations of interactions in the form of trees. If the agent changes we go one step further down, so that every line describes one move of a partner. We interpret the vertices as components and the edges as the cross-operation of interaction. Since we deal exclusively with

sequence patterns here we restrict the product-patterns to HFOR, so that the
order of the tree from top to bottom corresponds to the order in time. Thus
(159) might be represented as

(162) HA
       │
       HB
       │
       HC
       ·
       ·
       ·
       HN

Indexes would here be redundant and can be dispensed with. Since in an interaction a partner is often in a position to choose between several alternatives for a move, e.g. in our example P2 might do HB by doing HX or HY,
we assume a branching in the tree for the case where these alternatives are
generated directly by the pattern in question. Thus HB need not appear in
the tree (and often not in the interaction either):

(163)   HA
           ╱   ╲
        HX   HY
        │   │
        HC   HC
        ·   ·
        ·   ·
        ·   ·
        HN   HN

Certainly the choice of an alternative will often influence the further development of the interaction, in such a way that P1 could not act according to HC.
The generation the partner chooses for his acts has a similar effect. This can
also be introduced into the tree, so that one obtains a detailed strategy tree:

(164)   HA   ⎧ HR if C1 → HT
           ╱   ╲   ⎪
        HX   HY → HP → HQ → ⎨
        │   │   ⎪ HS if C2 → ⎡HU⎤
        HC   HC   ⎩   ⎣HV⎦
        ·   ·
        ·   ·
        ·   ·
        HN   HN

P1 can influence the alternatives of P2. E.g. he can choose for HA a generation the result of which is just the contrary of C1 or implies it. In this way
P2 would be forced to do HS by the preceding phase of the interaction. Similarly P1 can prevent the performance of HR by preventing that of HT.

In order to preserve clearness of interaction trees, one can enumerate the
generations of the single moves in a special list, so that every vertex is labelled with only one act-pattern. This will be of advantage above all for complicated partitions and for repetitions of moves.

2.4 ACTION COMPETENCE

The action competence C^*_i of an agent Pi is given by the ordered set of act-
patterns according to which Pi can act. Since these act-patterns are socially
determined, the agent is always master of a subset of the act-patterns existing in the social group or groups he belongs to. The extent of this subset is
determined by Pi's life, socialisation, and predisposition.

One might suppose that the existence of C^*_i is taken into account in the
existing psychological models of personality. But it is there regarded not as
an integral part of the person, rather as a construct of a certain theory which
competes with other theories of personality. I do not want to discuss psychological theories of personality here, above all because they seem to be based
on questionable or even untenable theoretical principles. Nevertheless a proposal will be made concerning the uppermost components of the structure
of personality, in order to be able to consider the relation between these
components and the position of C^*_i and not in order to give a description,
empirically based, of the structure of a person.

I start from the assumption of four components of personality which seem
to be defined in a more or less conventional way. These components can be
defined by the following expressions:

(i)   What A can do (in the sense of 'act').
(ii) What A knows.
(iii) What A can say or understand.
(iv) What A feels.

Before entering into the particulars of C^*_i, which is to be defined by (i), the
problems of this division and the fact that there are multiple overlappings
and connections must be discussed.

As a definiens of the second component, 'knows' alone will not be enough.
One would have to add predicates like 'believes', 'takes for granted', etc.

Since there can only be propositions as complements of these predicates in the use intended here it is already becoming obvious that A's knowledge is related to his linguistic competence, which is to be defined by (iii). The assumption that (165) implies (166) strenghtens the relation between the expression defined:

(165)   A knows X.
(166)   A can say X.

The definition of the third component is still unsatisfactory because it seems to separate the linguistic competence from action competence. We shall see later on that the linguistic competence can be regarded as a part of the action competence, as is suggested by the fact that [say] is an act-pattern as well.

Yet the assumption that the linguistic competence is a genuine part of C^*_i also leads to difficulties; on the one hand, it is not certain whether the passive linguistic competence can be regarded as a part of the action competence; on the other hand, we have already noticed the fundamental relation between speech and action when discussing the concept of rule. It could then be assumed that the understanding of an act depends upon the internalisation of certain linguistic expressions and that the linguistic competence somehow determines C^*_i. We shall try to clarify parts of this dialectical relation between speech and action within the following chapter.

Another vague relation between the components (i) and (ii) must be pointed out here. On the one hand, the second component is the result of actions and interactions and thus influenced by C^*_i. On the other hand, it influences C^*_i because Pi's knowledge occurs in the conditions for act-patterns and generations of C^*_i. We show our knowledge in our actions.

The fourth component is rather traditional. But it is not only to include certain properties, predispositions of Pi, but to draw attention to the fact that everything that A feels can happen in space and time. We do not want to go further into the character of this division, which is obviously still provisional and unfounded.

For the description of C^*_i we start from our expression (i) which provides for an indefinite reference to act-patterns according to which A can act. The 'can' within this expression is a kind of operator which is distributed over all act-patterns and generations which can be inserted, so that we can confine ourselves in the main to the relations between the act-patterns. Still this 'can' must be discussed. It operates on act-patterns, certainly, but it makes a lot of difference whether I say (167) or (168):

(167)   A can HX.

(168)   A is HX-ing.

For (167) can be true, even if A is just now not HX-ing. A need have only the possibility of HX-ing, and it must be a live possibility for A. It is not merely a possibility in principle, say to be able to learn HX: A must already have learned to HX. All the same (167) certainly is related to (168). If (168) had never been true, that is, if A never had HX-ed, there would be no evidence to assume that he can HX. Though we do not always need evidence, other people can verify (167) only by means of (168). But this does not mean that there would be a certain point of time or a certain period of time when A would have to HX in order to prove the truth of (167). A might have learnt to HX many years ago without HX-ing ever again. All the same he might still be capable of HX-ing.

We have to separate this use from another use of 'can', which we do not want here. This last use can be got at by adding 'if I let him' or the like. It is possible that someone can play basket-ball and that he can truly state (167) when the corresponding substitutions are made. But of course, he cannot play if he has no ball, if he is fettered, or if he has no fellow-players. The two uses can be contrasted in (169) and (170), neither of which is contradictory because of the difference in the two 'can's', although it is not said that A cannot now HX in the first use:

(169)   A can HX, but now he cannot HX.
(170)   A can HX, but at the moment t he cannot HX.

The second use of 'can' is related to general conditions for acts according to HX. If a situation does not fulfill these conditions someone within this situation cannot act according to HX though he has internalized HX.

Finally, another use of 'can' must be pointed out and should be excluded from (167). 'Can' is used in this way in

(171)   Only men can speak.

In addition to the first use, what seems to be meant here is that only men can learn to speak. In this sense one speaks of innate abilities, where the different uses of 'can' are reflected by the use of 'ability'. Because of this vagueness we shall rarely use 'ability' in connection with C^*_i, but talk of act-patterns which are internalized.

In order to describe C^*_i we must now concentrate on the structure of the set of act-patterns the agent Pi has internalized. We start from the pattern H^*_i according to which he also acts whenever he acts. The structure of C^*_i is the structure of the partition of H^*_i. For H^*_i must generate every other pattern. The partition of H^*_i will also include the relations between the act-patterns which hold generally within the social group in which the corresponding act-patterns exist. So if we try to discover the parts of C^*_i which might be the same with different agents we shall find just such relations. The upper branchings, particularly, of such a C^*_i are based upon a classification of act-patterns.

Now we want to present some general structures of C^*_i, using a tree representation of the partition of H^*_i. On the first level we begin with the distinction frequently made between outer action (HOUT) and inner action (HINN), which is sometimes called open and covered action or, still less appropriate, physical and mental action. The paradigm for HINN is thinking, which, perhaps, remains the only case of HINN. We represent this part of C^*_i in a tree arranged from the left to the right, in order to distinguish it from interaction trees:

(172)

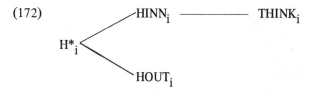

The edges of the tree represent the arrow-relation, and sometimes the subpattern-relation ⌐ as a special case of the arrow-relation. An example might be our partition on the first level, because this binary partition will be exhaustive and because neither HINN nor HOUT have surpluses which are not according to H^*_i. If one wants to introduce conditions for generations into the tree, these conditions can be introduced by indexing the edges with the corresponding sentences.

For the introduction of THINK into C^*_i, the difference between THINK and the component defined by (ii), where the verb 'think' also plays a part, must be pointed out: there we deal with 'think that' where propositions are required as complements, whereas the 'think' occurring here has other complements or, rather, is a one-place verb (or 'think of') related to REFLECT, CONCLUDE, PLAN, CALCULATE, etc. Therefore we may regard these patterns as patterns generated by THINK. Of course, these patterns themselves generate patterns as well. E.g. CALCULATE would generate ADD, MULTIPLY, etc. One would have to inquire which are the basic patterns of this branch.

In our partition, thinking acquires an importance which a lot of people would not attach to it; because usually thinking is opposed to action. I do not want to discuss the reasons for this distinction in detail. But there do not seem to be good reasons for not introducing thinking as action into the theory of action. The differences between HOUT and HINN will become evident if they are described by means of the theory of action. Provisional tests support the idea of understanding thinking as action: 'Try to think!' 'Le 'Learn to think!' All these commands indicate that we somehow regard thinking as action. Still I want to discuss, within our general considerations, one of the reasons why thinking has not been regarded as action, because this reason may be related to a behavioristic concept of action which regards as action only what is overt and visible. Certainly thinking is not visible, because it is private in a certain sense, namely that another person cannot perceive whether and what I am thinking. Nevertheless, thinking is not completely private, for (i) there are social consequences, so that the results of thinking may not remain hidden, (ii) it seems to be socially determined, since we obey learnt rules when thinking (maybe linguistic rules). Because of (ii) one can understand that there will often be patterns occurring within partitions of THINK which also occur within the linguistic branch, say ASK, CONCLUDE, INFER, etc.

The opposition of thinking and action depends certainly upon certain forms of life. The current idea of intelligent action, which is said to be preceded by thinking, is a manifestation of this form of life. Assuming this and, at the same time, assuming that thinking is action, intelligent action naturally leads us into a regress similar to that we have discussed in connection with wishing. But we can avoid this regress if we do not make the first assumption. 'Intelligent' is rather a specification of the action in question and does not necessarily refer to a preceding action.[31]

As concerns the lower branch of C^*_i, we can profit from some distinctions already made. We distinguished between interaction (INTERACT) and the action of one agent alone (HALONE). Since there must be at least one partner for INTERACT, one would have to introduce a specification in order to indicate with whom P_i is interacting. This specification will be kept up through the patterns generated by INTERACT, which are the patterns COOP for cooperation and COMPETE for competition, already introduced above. Thus we would obtain the following structure

(173)

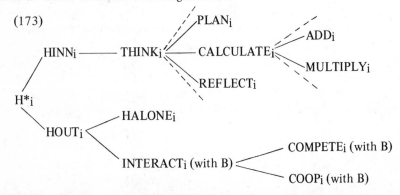

This tree shows that we assume that in HINN the distinction between inter-action and solitary action need not be made. The inner action is monologous per definition. Cases where we say that P1 and P2 are thinking together about Y are interactions, normally sequences where some components belong to THINK, and exactly these components remain monologous here as well.

We have already dealt with specifications when discussing the act-patterns of the second level, for which we do not have independent expressions. Other possible specifications might occur there already or even with H^*_i. Say, 'to act quickly', 'to act confidently', 'to act cleverly', etc.

Psychological theories have nearly always leaned on such specifications which have been regarded as properties of individuals. In this way one came to a static concept of intelligence which was described in terms of disposition. For the description of this or that property of a person what counted as im-portant was not only which specified patterns were internalized but how fre-quently they were followed. But it should now be clear that such a theory would presuppose the description of C^*_i, because (i) the properties in quest-ion are derived from the specifications of act-patterns and (ii) the generations, where such a specified pattern occurs, may be different for different agents.

Up to now we have not introduced this kind of specification into C^*_i, because they are already described as subpatterns. We do not need to give the specifications as long as they can be distributed beyond the edges. And, in-deed, such a distribution often seems to be possible. The specification in question need not absolutely occur as a specification, but it must be some-how included in the generated pattern. E.g. a ninety-year-old A acts clumsily by dribbling, where the clumsy action is already implied in DRIBBLE. Thus we formulate the strings of C^*_i in such a way that we need not introduce parallel strings for subpatterns generated analogously. The economy of this may well be shown with the specifications themselves. If we have, e.g., a part of a string [identify a man] → [point to a man] → [point one's finger at a man], we would not have to list these strings specially because it would be a special case of [identify something] → [point to something] → [point one's finger at something]. Described in a mixture of formal and colloquial lan-guage, however, this relation is not yet represented quite adequately, be-cause in most cases the generations are only meaningful if with 'something' and 'a man' the same objects are referred to. A description by specifications makes this clearer. Then the general form of both cases would be

(174) IDENTIFY (X) → POINT (to X) → POINT ONE'S FINGER (at X).

Of course, this string would include the still more special case [identify Paul] → [point to Paul] → [point one's finger at Paul], so that it would not have to be itemized either.

In the general form the relation between the specifications is indicated by the uniformity of variables. But as a general description, our description (174) would still be too restricted, for one can identify X by pointing to Y; say, if there are only two objects and one excludes Y by pointing to it.

In the process of developing the INTERACT-branch we come to another problem already touched upon. A kind of interaction that is especially important for linguistic theories is communication, COMMUNICATE. We cannot introduce it directly behind INTERACT, because the distinction between COMPETE and COOP is more general and applies to all interactions. Nor can we restrict COMMUNICATE to COMPETE or COOP. Here, a very important property of C^*_i becomes obvious, from which we have already profited in connection with THINK, namely that the same patterns may occur in different branches. Thus, C^*_i does not contain act-patterns but occurrences of act-patterns and differs from a mere classification of act-patterns under $\rightarrow$ and $\sqsubset$. There is another problem which though less general is very important here. I see strong arguments against labelling [communicate] only as a subpattern of [interact] , although I think communication is founded in interaction and impossible without interaction. One difference is the following: 'A interacts with B' implies that A acts and that B acts and the same holds for 'A and B interact'. This is also provided for by our definition. 'A communicates with B' does not seem to imply that B acts. For us to talk of communication being successful it is sufficient that B understand what A said. But understanding is not action. Another related difference is that 'interacts with' is symmetrical where 'communicates with' is not. The similarity of [communicate] and [interact] lies in the fact that both require (i) a partner for A and (ii) that the partner understands what A does.

All this does not mean that communication cannot be a case of interaction. Clearly, when A communicates with B, B can communicate with A and this will usually be the case. But we must admit [communicate] also in the HALONE-branch, although this does not mean that A can communicate when he his alone — this is excluded by the conditions (i) and (ii) —, but only that he can act alone.

The general part of the action competence of an agent, with which we shall content ourselves here, now has the following form (fig. (175), p. 65). Of course we have already left this general part with the branch CALCULATE. One would probably have to leave it when generating other branches. The individual strings always end up with basic patterns. The differences in the action competences of different agents will not only consist of the internalization of different basic patterns, but above all in different generations. Within these generations whole roles may occur,[32] which one individual, unlike others, has internalized.

(175)

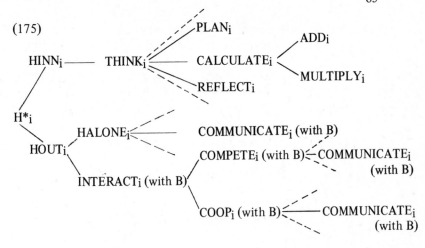

Our description of C^*_i makes it evident that the action competence of an individual can only be seen in connection with the rules of a social group. For the patterns in C^*_i are not private, and some of them can only be understood as components of interactions.

On the other hand, the action competence of an individual does not fully depend upon a social group; first, because an individual never lives in a completely homogeneous group, so that he can internalize patterns and generations which, in his social group, are not usual; second, because sociality does not usually require complete dependence. If only because of the openness of the rules the rules of individuals are never identical or equal to the intersection of the rules of particular individuals. Thus, the changing of rules can only originate in the individual.

Even if this dialectic of individual and group is not completely clear, one still recognizes that it need not be a question of reciprocal domination.

2.5 FORMAL SKETCH

Within this section a proposal for a stricter formalization of the language of action and for an axiomatization of an empirical theory of action will be given. This may be premature for the following reasons: first, a strict formalization may only be possible after further work with this language of description has been done. Second, formalization of the language of action is not of paramount importance. The semi-formal presentation given up to now is to be thought of as a heuristic help for the agents and therefore at least one requirement has to be fulfilled, namely that it can be understood by the agents. Third, there are two problems about which I have no clear ideas. One is the problem of quantifying into acts, the other is the problem of intention. This is why I may, in some of the following passages, oversimplify some things discussed above, or I may leave out some elements of the language of description, and ignore points already made, such that the differences between the theory of action and set theory are blurred. If this is the case, I shall be providing a fine example of what occurs when one needlessly formalizes.

First of all, we introduce three sets X, AP and AP*:

$$(176) \qquad X = \left\{ x \mid x \text{ is an act} \right\},$$

where $|X|$ is infinite. As was pointed out in 2.21 this set is not already given or fixed and, perhaps, cannot be represented as a set at all. The same holds for AP defined by

$$(177) \qquad AP = \left\{ HX \mid HX \text{ is a simple act-pattern} \right\},$$

where $|AP| < |X|$. Simple act-patterns are not basic patterns, which will be derived by classifying the set of act-patterns by means of $\rightarrow$, but those patterns which are not built up by means of $\sqcap$, $\sqcup$, or $\dagger$. Within an empirical theory, AP is determined by the patterns which exist in the social group being described.

The set of all act-patterns AP* is given by the recursive definition:

(178)   a   Let $\mu \in AP$, then $\mu \in AP^*$.
        b   Let $\mu_1, \mu_2 \in AP^*$, then $\mu_1 \sqcap \mu_2 \in AP^*$.
        c   Let $\mu_1, \mu_2 \in AP^*$, then $\mu_1 \sqcup \mu_2 \in AP^*$.
        d   Let $\mu_1, \mu_2 \in AP^*$, then $\mu_1 \dagger \mu_2 \in AP^*$.

Unlike AP, AP* will always include far too much in empirical studies. Nevertheless we do not introduce restrictions for the elements of AP*, for example by stopping the recursion, so that only act-patterns composed of at most two simple patterns occur. Even then AP* would still include too much, but surely too little as well. Therefore we understand AP* as constructive, so that the main task of an empirical description would consist in restricting AP*, based on AP to the point where it includes exactly the existing patterns of a social group. It is to be assumed that there are no simple functions for this.

Properties of $\sqcap$ and $\sqcup$ are:

(179) $HA \sqcap HB = HB \sqcap HA$ commutative
(180) $HA \sqcap HA = HA$ idempotent

(181)	$(HA \sqcap HB) \sqcap HC = HA \sqcap (HB \sqcap HC)$	associative
(182)	$HA \sqcup HB = HB \sqcup HA$	commutative
(183)	$HA \sqcup HA = HA$	idempotent
(184)	$(HA \sqcup HB) \sqcup HC = HA \sqcup (HB \sqcup HC)$	associative

Let

(185) $X \times AP^* = \left\{ <x, HX> \mid x \in X \text{ and } HX \in AP^* \right\}$,

then α is a two-place relation with

(186) $\alpha \subset X \times AP^*$.

α is exactly that subset of $X \times AP^*$, for the elements of which 'x is of HX' holds.

In $AP^* \times AP^*$ a relation $\rightarrow$ is induced by α for which (187) is valid:

(187)   If $x \, \alpha \, (HX \rightarrow HY)$, then $x \, \alpha \, HX$ and $x \, \alpha \, HY$, for every $x \in X$.

By contraposition we obtain from (187):

(188)   If $x \, \alpha \, HX$ and $x \, \cancel{\alpha} \, HY$, then $x \, \cancel{\alpha} \, (HX \rightarrow HY)$, for every $x \in X$.
(189)   If $x \, \alpha \, HY$ and $x \, \cancel{\alpha} \, HX$, then $x \, \cancel{\alpha} \, (HX \rightarrow HY)$, for every $x \in X$.

The relation $\rightarrow$ cannot be introduced here through a definition by means of α, for only within a description of the relations between the actions of a social group or of an agent can it be ascertained whether the relation $\rightarrow$ holds between two act-patterns. The relation $\rightarrow$ has the following properties:

(190)	$HA \rightarrow HA$	reflexive
(191)	$HA \rightarrow HB \wedge HB \rightarrow HA \Rightarrow HA = HB$	antisymmetrical
(192)	$HA \rightarrow HB \wedge HB \rightarrow HC \Rightarrow HA \rightarrow HC$	transitive

Accordingly, it is an order relation which could define a partial order on AP^*. However, it would be empirically more adequate to have the arrow-relation operate on occurrences of elements of AP^*, for every $HX \in AP^*$ can occur in different generations. We can easily form such occurrences by forming pairs $< HX, j >$ with $j \in N$, the set of natural numbers. But we do not want to inflate AP^* here in order to get a set of such occurrences of elements of AP^*.

68

We want to use it only to the extent that we shall need it later for the partitions of certain H^*_i. Yet the axiom of order

(193)   For all HX, HY: not (HX → HY and HY → HX) if HX ≠ HY

holds only if it is formulated for occurrences of elements of AP*. In this case the arrow-relation would be irreflexive and asymmetrical.

For a description of the action competence C^*_i of an agent Pi, we start from a subset of AP*, from which we obtain the set AP^*_i as a set of pairs < HX, j > by indexing the occurrences of HX ∈ AP*. The asymmetrical and irreflexive arrow-relation now provides a set-theoretical partition of AP^*_i into subsets K, such that:

(i)   Every given HX_i ∈ K can be compared with every HY_i ∈ K relative to →.

(ii)   Every K contains at most one occurrence of a type HX ∈ AP*.

We call the subsets K strings. For every string the following holds:

(194)   There is an HX_i, such that HX_i is a maximal element relative to →.

(195)   There is an HY_i, such that HY_i is a minimal element relative to →.

(196)   Let HX_i, HY_i ∈ K, then either HX_i → HY_i or HY_i → HX_i.

The minimal element of a string is a basic pattern. The set of basic patterns of an agent is identical with the set of the minimal elements of all strings of his action competence.

Within the description of the action competence of an agent P1 the maximal elements of all strings are identical. This element is the general act-pattern H^*_i (the root), according to which P1 must always act, providing that he is acting at all. This identity makes it evident that the action competence of an agent makes up a connected whole. It is nothing but the partition of H^*_i. The different strings are the alternatives between which P1 can choose for an act. If he does something he has to run through exactly one of those strings. This corresponds to the connection between → and α which was given when introducing α.

NOTES

1. Cf. Louch (1966: 32-6).

2. Cf. Winch (1958: 24-33).

3. This differs from Goldman's distinction between act-token and act-type (Goldman (1970: 10-15)) and above all it is differently justified. The criticism Goldman (1970: 2-10) makes of Davidson (1963) and Davidson (1967) (probably unjustly) does not apply to this distinction.

4. E.g. Davidson (1963: 686). It is very likely that he understands 'description' along the lines of Russell's theory of descriptions. But it should be clear by now that there is not one description or several essential descriptions constitutive of the individual but that there may be various descriptions used at different occasions and by different people speaking about one and the same individual.

5. It may be that what Davidson is getting at involves taking 'description' in the sense of 'describe as. . .'. But it is then not a question of describing as but of seeing as. Cf. Wittgenstein (1953: xi).

6. Kenny (1963: 163) makes a similar observation when criticizing the notion that in sentences of the form 'A does B' the predicate 'does' must be understood as a relation. This is not possible: for, if the sentences are not true, the name of the objects or corresponding definite descriptions could have no referent. Then the relational expression R (A,B) would be meaningless by definition.

7. As phonemes and words are such patterns as well, a description of phonemes as sets of speech events is inadequate.

8. Wittgenstein (1953: 145).

9. Cf. Wittgenstein (1953: § 199); Melden (1970: 94). I have already stressed this property in connection with the discussion of the properties of rules. It is to be observed, though, that we really can produce expressions and make descriptions of patterns which do not hold, owing to the syntactic possibilities of our language.

10. I do not distinguish between different kinds of generation as Goldman (1970: 20-30) does, for these differences do not seem obvious to me. The definition of the causal generation may as well be applied to the cases of the conventional generation, e.g. the result of a certain move in chess, namely that the opponent is check mated, is also what has been caused by the agent's act. The relations of the causal generation are conventional as well, and there too the conditions must be given. For various reasons augmentative generation has been dealt with in different ways, cf. also 2.23. Followers of the assumption that the following of HB is the cause for the following of HA tend to establish the relation the other way round. Since I am not of this opinion, for reasons given in 2.1, 'generates' here can be used in a more general sense, which is related to its mathematical use.

11. The surplus consists in the fact that the following holds: For some x (if x α HA then x α HB) and for some x (if x α HB then x α HA). But in both sentences replacing the existential quantifier by the universal quantifier would not yield true sentences.

12. Cf. 2.5.

13. Another definition of basic acts is given in Danto (1963, 1965). He defines them by arguing that these acts are not caused, which I do not think to be recommendable because of the many uses of 'cause'. However, Danto renders his use more precise; cf. Melden (1961: 65), Goldman (1970: 63-72) and Danto (1973).

14. Cf. Melden (1961: 56-65).

15. We shall introduce other means for the analysis of such cases.

16. Cf. Alston (1964: 39-44).

17. Cf. Kenny (1963: 162). Note that specification does not fill the gap between act and

70

act-pattern. This seems to be assumed by Goldman who does not notice the ambiguity of 'John's mowing his lawn (at t)' as a designation of an act-pattern and sometimes as a designation of an act.

18. This specification was already known to the Scholastics: *obiectum specificat actum*. But it seems as if there are certain differences compared with the adverbial specification, e.g., that KILL is always necessarily KILL (X).

19. By means of ⌐ we can formally describe the regress which results form assuming willing (W) as an action, hence a subpattern of the general act-pattern H*, and assuming for every act:

(i) HX ⌐H* ⇒ (x α HX ⇒ x α W (HX)) for every HX.

(ii) W (HX) ⌐H*.

Let HX ⌐H*, then it holds that

    x α HX ⇒ x α W (HX)   by (i)

    x α W (HX) ⇒ x α W (W(HX))   by (i) and (ii)

    etc.

20. Because of M2 [kill someone in war with intent and premeditation] is not considered as [murder someone], obviously because of the honorable reasons. But 'in war' has to be understood as a necessary specification creating a new institutionalized pattern, for, according to the current notion, one can murder someone in war as well.

21. H* is the general act-pattern according to which one also acts whenever one acts; cf. 2.5.

22. It would seem that these HA need not even be special cases of HFOR.

23. Up to now we confined ourselves to cases with two components in our definitions and introductions. Generalizations to n components could easily be derived.

24. Goldman (1970: 36).

25. 'In N-manner' is not identical with in 'N-form', because the movement of the hand when writing an N does not have the form of an N, only those phases where the recording instrument is pressed onto the paper.

26. Cf. v. Wright (1970): 327).

27. We shall confine ourselves to two partners. Generalizations can easily be made.

28. They need not be subpatterns of HFOR.

29. Austin (1971: 28).

30. Cf. Habermas (1971).

31. Cf. Ryle (1949: 27-32).

32. Roles can only be found in the INTERACT-branch.

3 PRACTICAL SEMANTICS

3.1 FORMS OF SEMANTIC DESCRIPTION

Most often traditional semantic descriptions are of the form (197) or (198) where meanings are associated with signs which are mentioned:

(197) *almost* 'nearly'.
(198) *man* 'featherless biped'.

Here meanings of words are described by other words or syntagms. Scant attention is paid to the structure of sentence-meaning; it has even been assumed that the syntactic structure is independent of meaning.

In semantic descriptions of the form (197) and (198) the claim seems often to have been that the expression between '. . .' is the meaning of the italicized expression. Obviously '. . .' is to be understood as something like an operator which transforms linguistic signs into meanings, subtracting the expression, as it were, and leaving the meaning. In this way one can easily hypostatize meanings and consider the meaning as independent from the expression.[1] But since only the meaning of the italic sign is to be described by (197) or (198), (197) may be phrased as

(199) *almost* means the same as *nearly*.

(197) and (198) are merely deducible from (199) and, in addition, indicate which sign is to be explained by which. But even this is reversible in the end.

Now, if we extend the domain of the relation 'means the same as' to sentences or even to texts, we obtain a form valid for every semantic description of this type:

(200) $R(T_1, T_2)$

where T_1 and T_2 are texts (more exactly: sentences, syntagms, or morphemes) and R is a relation between these texts. The form (200) is already included in the syntagm 'a description of T_1' because every description is a text (T_2).

Within the semantic description above, R is interpreted as synonymy (SN), which leads to difficulties for a clear understanding of SN. We want to show this with the description of the meaning of 'Schlaf haben', starting from our extension of the domain of SN to sentences, interpreting the synonymy of parts of sentences as derived from the synonymy of sentences. A sentence of L_1 like

(201) Ich habe Schlaf (I am sleepy).

cannot be understood by Northern Germans in their language L_2. According to Grimm's dictionary it should mean more or less the same as

(202) Ich bin müde (I am tired).

where (202), it is assumed, belongs to language L_2 which can be understood by Northern Germans, too. It is easy to demonstrate that (202) does not mean the same as (201): One need not be sleepy if one is tired. E.g., if I get up in the morning and do gymnastics I will be tired afterwards, but more often than not I won't be sleepy. Therefore the following sentence from L_2 might be a better description of (201):

(203) Ich bin müde und will schlafen (I am tired and want to sleep).

But this cannot be accepted as a description of the meaning of (201) either. For 'Schlaf haben' does not mean that one wants to sleep. It may well be that one is tired but still wants to remain awake, say, when driving a car or if one wants to watch a film. So (204) might be synonymous with (201):

(204) I am tired and I can remove this fatigue by sleep.

This gives by far the best equivalent of the meaning of (201), though here too, differences might be discovered requiring further qualifications. It is important to note that in a language where (201) does not occur, a sentence like (204) probably won't be as usual as (201) in the other language. Usually the sentence (202) is used instead of (201), though one does not say the same thing with it. From this one can infer that there is a sentence or some sentences in L_2 with which one can explain (201) of L_1, but that, in normal use, there is no sentence which is used in the same way. And further, that there does not exist in all languages a reasonably short[2] synonymous sentence corresponding to a sentence of L_1, a fact which affects this kind of semantic description.

Another difficulty is that one cannot insert only one sign between '. . .' that covers all uses of the italic sign, but one needs different ones, according to the context:

(205)   *wing* 'air-force formation' or 'pinion' or 'part of a building'.

Actually, this would mean that 'wing' is neither synonymous with 'part of a building' nor 'pinion' nor 'air-force formation', but only synonymous with all three of them. One remedies this problem by saying that 'wing' is ambiguous and that one meaning of 'wing' is the same as that of 'air-force formation', a second the same as that of 'pinion', a third one the same as that 'of part of a building', which, of course, is somehow strange, since it is a question of properties of 'wing' in relation to L_2. So within a description by means of an L_3 different from L_2 it might happen that 'wing' is not ambiguous.

Or-connections within a semantic description occur not only when describing so-called ambiguous expressions, but probably always. This can be demonstrated with expressions which denote so-called concrete objects, where such a semantic description still works best. Let us take

(206)   A book is a considerable number of sheets of paper with writing or printing on them.

which can be understood as semantic description according to the form (200). Apart from the difficulty of determining the meaning of 'considerable' (how many pages must a book have at least, how many at most?) and of how to distinguish a book and a note-book, we run up against an *or*-connection yet again.

Our description is unlikely to be complete because I would also call something a book if it is painted or blank, i.e., neither written nor printed. Moreover other petty details are lacking. E.g., if one asks somebody:

(207)   Have you already read this book?

one need not mean whether he has already read this printed work, where by this is meant an object one can take into one's hands. The addressee might answer the question (207) in the affirmative if he had read a different copy. So there is a type-token-ambiguity with 'book' since in this case the type might be intended.

I do not want to consider the necessity of a further lengthening of the description (206). The difficulty with the long descriptions seems to be related

74

to the assumption that the description sentences are to be analytical sentences, namely sentences which are only true because of their meaning, irrespective of the state of the world. One obtains analytical sentences by starting from a tautology, like

(208)   A book is a book.

The second occurrence of 'book' is to be replaced by a synonymous expression, e.g., 'considerable number of sheets of paper with writing or printing on them'. The result

(209)   A book is a considerable number of sheets of paper with writing or printing on them.

would remain an analytical sentence. This procedure explains the relation between synonymy and analyticity[3] and it shows that for analyticity absolute synonymy is required, so that (209) according to our discussion would not be analytical, because it would be wrong under certain circumstances. For artificial languages one can fix the meanings in so-called meaning postulates, which secure the status of a sentence as analytical if the synonymy of the substituting expressions has been stated beforehand.[4] But this is trivial. It is impossible for natural languages, provided that one does not intend to codify them but to describe them. We want to find out what is synonymous with what. Thus, there is absolute analyticity just as little as there is absolute synonymy.[5] One should give up both in favor of weaker features and relations.

The relation R in (200) has not only been interpreted as SN but also as equivalence EQ, which is defined as follows: S1 is equivalent to S2 if and only if S2 is true if S1 is true and vice versa. EQ is weaker than SN in two respects: (i) Equivalence exists only between sentences, not between parts of sentences, for one can only talk of truth and falsity where sentences are concerned. (ii) Equivalence cannot be predicated of all kinds of sentences, because interrogative sentences, for example, cannot be judged to be true or false.

Equivalence, like synonymy, requires a syntactic analysis. Only in this way can one describe the equivalence between the infinite number of sentences and only in this way can one derive something from EQ (S1, S2) for the relation between the parts of sentences which are responsible for equivalence. If it were possible to derive from the equivalence of sentences relations for their parts, this would really be an advantage compared with a theory which provides such relations between parts of sentences from the beginning, because the interdependence of the relations would have been described within this description. But the derivation of relations between parts of sentences from equivalence between sentences is not so simple that one could infer from two equivalent sentences to an equivalence-relation between the parts where they differ from one another.[6] E.g. having inferred from the equivalence of

(210)   He is sleeping.
(211)   He has fallen asleep.

that there is an equivalence-relation between 'sleeping' and 'has fallen asleep', one is not then allowed to conclude that equivalent sentences arise from substitution in every given sentence:

(212)   He has fallen asleep regularly during his tutorial.

For, here, substitution yields sentence (213) which is not equivalent to (212):

(213)   He is sleeping regularly during his tutorial.

In other cases, too, substitution of equivalent parts does not lead to an equivalent sentence:

(214)   A book will always remain a book.
(215)   A book will always remain a considerable number of sheets of paper written or printed.

Further problems, related to those above, result from so-called intensional contexts, where even substitution of equivalent sentences need not lead to equivalent sentences. Nobody is likely to claim that (216) and (217) are equivalent:

(216)   I believe that a man is a featherless biped.
(217)   I believe that two times two makes four.

This is, too, an illustration of the fact that so-called analytical sentences are all to be dealt with in the same way as concerns equivalence. For, since they are supposed to be always true, they must not behave differently as concerns equivalence. The difficulties resulting from (ii) might be removed if discovering equivalences were restricted to propositions and if one explained how the equivalence of the propositions influences different linguistic act-patterns in an additional component of the theory. The result would be a useful extension of truth-functional semantics, as we shall see later.

However, sentences without propositions, like 'good morning', could not be described in this way either.

In any case, a theory of semantics confining itself to equivalence could not adequately describe natural languages, if the semantic description is to represent the function of the language in communication. This becomes clear from the consequence, mentioned above, that all analytical sentences in such a theory would be dealt with in the same way, and hence the use of sentences could not be described by means of equivalence. There are cases where two sentences are equivalent, indeed, but only in such contexts where both can be used. On the other hand, in the case where in a certain context only one sentence can be used without deviation it makes no sense to speak of equivalence. These considerations and our discussion of the use theory suggest another interpretation of R; it may be understood as sameness of use. This would be the widest conception, including all former interpretations. But it seems still rather vague, since we do not know what sameness of use is to mean and more particularly whether there is such a thing at all. A more extensive account will make it necessary to examine the relation more closely and to give up the demand that the describing sentences be analytic. We shall have some suggestions to make about this later.

Let us now turn to the arguments in (200). It is often maintained that there is a relation of object- and meta-language between the italic sign and the expression between '. . .'. This use is not the one known from logical languages, where the convention is that the meaning of a metalinguistic sign of the nth level is a sign of the $(n-1)^{th}$ level; whereas, in our case, the italic sign is not the meaning of the expression between '. . .', rather, the meaning of the italic sign and that of the expression between '. . .' are the same. At best italicizing and the inverted commas-operator are signs belonging to a metalanguage as does an explicit characterization of the relation between the two expressions, 'means the same as', etc. This can be regarded as a strong objection to the very notion of describing meanings. Usually a description consists of stating properties of objects, not in giving equivalents for their designations.

As concerns the relation of the two languages L_1 and L_2, we can classify them according to (i) whether both are identical or not, and (ii) whether a language is natural or artificial. Since cases with artificial L_1 concern logic and mathematics, and since we confine ourselves to natural L_1, we have to discuss the following three possibilities: $L_1 \neq L_2$ and L_2 is artificial; $L_1 \neq L_2$ and L_2 is natural; $L_1 = L_2$. Rapid progress in developing artificial languages and the great success in applying them in many sciences also encouraged linguists to use them for semantic description of the form (200). The best known method for semantic descriptions by means of an artificial language is componential analysis. It is based on the decomposition of meanings of signs, most often morphemes, into components and has the form of traditional semantic descriptions inasmuch as it works in such a way that (i) it produces relations between the signs to be described and the so-called noemes and semes which stand for the components of the meaning of these expressions;[7] (ii) it assumes synonymy as a relation between the (sets of) noemes and the sign to be described, although this is hardly made explicit, because the status of the noemes is not very clear.

Because of (ii) we can expect that componential analysis will come up against the problem set out above. This will be discussed later. The noeme-language L_2 used in componential analysis not only consists of an alphabet of noemes, but admits syntactic constructions. As rules for the constructions of this language I assume the following:[8]

Let n_i be noemes, a_i expressions, then
(i)   all n_i are expressions.
(ii) if a_1 and a_2 are expressions, then $a_1 + a_2$ and $a_1 \vee a_2$ are expressions.
(iii) if a_i is an expression, then $\bar{a_i}$ is an expression.
(iv) these are all expressions.

Heger calls these expressions sememes but his definition of them as sets of noemes is not quite sufficient. These sets should at least be sets ordered under + and V.

However, the interpretation of sememes as sets will not be very useful in this case, because one cannot give truth values to sets as one can to many signs from L_1. In such cases synonymy could not be achieved because the sememe would have different properties than the sentence to be described. For this reason, an interpretation of the noeme-language in the form of the predicate calculus seems to be useful. The noemes are interpreted as one-place predicates, so that

$$(218) \quad (n_1 = n_2) = \text{def } n_1(x) \Leftrightarrow n_2(x).$$

'+', 'V' and the tilde could be defined by the connectives '$\wedge$', 'V' and '$-$':

$$(219) \quad n_1 + n_2 = \text{def } n_1(x) \wedge n_2(x).$$
$$(220) \quad n_1 \vee n_2 = \text{def } n_1(x) \vee n_2(x).$$
$$(221) \quad \bar{n}_1 = \text{def} - n_1(x).$$

Accordingly, it holds that

$$(222) \quad n_1 + n_2 = n_2 + n_1.$$
$$(223) \quad n_1 \text{ V } n_2 = n_2 \text{ V } n_1.$$

In this interpretation the assumption of many-place — at least two-place[9] — noemes suggests itself, so that one could get rid of problems in the description of 'father', 'go', etc. which would be unsolvable with one-place noemes.

The logical interpretation can also solve some problems resulting from the fact that componential analysis does not admit arguments of noemes and thus cannot mark the different arguments of relational noemes. This becomes especially evident when componential analysis has to describe syntactic structures of L_1. Consider a representation of the syntactic structure of

$$(224) \quad \text{He knows her}$$

by bracketing, as $(n_1 + n_2) + (n_3 + n_4) + (n_5 + n_6)$, so that 'he': '$n_1 + n_2$', 'knows': '$n_3 + n_4$', 'her': '$n_5 + n_6$'. But in this way the difference between (225) and (226)

$$(225) \quad \text{He knows himself}$$
$$(226) \quad \text{He knows him}$$

cannot be represented, because there are no referring expressions in the corresponding $(n_1 + n_2) + (n_3 + n_4) + (n_1 + n_2)$ with which one could represent the identity of reference of 'he' and 'himself'.

This example makes it clear that the syntax of this noeme-language would be too simple for the description of a natural language. According to (222), the bracket expression for (224) would be equivalent to

$$(227) \quad (n_5 + n_6) + (n_3 + n_4) + (n_1 + n_2),$$

which would then mean that (224) would be equivalent to

$$(228) \quad \text{She knows him.[10]}$$

One could solve this problem by introducing asymmetrical concatenations of expressions into the noeme-language. But one does not know how to define them. Another possibility would be to introduce relational noemes, so that an asymmetrical relational noeme r_1 in L_2 would correspond to the predicate in (224). But this would necessarily lead to a different representation because the two sememes $n_1 + n_2$ and $n_5 + n_6$ would have to stand directly as arguments of r_1. Otherwise one would run up against troublesome consequences through assuming a relation (or concatenation) between the relational predicate and its arguments.[11] So what could a semantic description with a noeme-language bring us except problems? Three aims of componential analysis which are often put forward are:

(i) The relation between signs from L_1 is to be made clear in the structure of the expressions of L_2.
(ii) The sememe corresponding to a sign from L_1 is to explain this sign.
(iii) The noeme-language is to serve as some sort of super-language with which all natural languages can be described.

The clarity demanded by (i) is to be achieved by keeping the syntax of L_2 extremely simple. Its simplicity forces us to make the implicit paradigmatic relations explicit and syntagmatic. Further, the structure of the noeme-language is given by simple deductive methods allowing us to define most noemes with the help of a certain basic set of noemes, that is, by a recursive procedure. Of course, the underlying idea is that from a part of the noeme-language one can deduce the rest and so too in the natural language to be described. But this idea of deduction involves the question whether there really are synonymous expressions within the noeme-language and whether there is synonymity between expressions from L_2 and from L_1.

The value of aim (ii) depends on the value of the notion of explanation it takes for granted. Usually I explain an expression X to someone by giving him an expression Y which he can understand better. In order to explain X from L_1 to someone by giving him a Y from L_2, one must presuppose that he has mastered L_2. But noone learning his first natural language is likely to be master of this markerese. For the explanation of all natural languages learnt later on in life, the natural language L_1 could be used as well, at least if the condition of synonymy were fulfilled, since signs from L_2 synonymous with those of L_1 would also have synonymous signs in L_3 and, because of the transitivity of synonymy, the signs from L_1 could be explained by means of the synonymous signs from L_3.

But, it will be said, this is a question of a scientific explanation. Now the use of artificial languages in semantic descriptions is open to the following criticism: Since all artificial languages are created by explicit agreement involving an existing language, they rely in the end on natural language. This does not mean that comparing a natural language with any artificial language may not yield worth-while insights. Every comparison of a language with another one yields insights. But it means that an explanation of the second type is not objective and free from circularity.

Aim (iii) is another version of the age-old dream of explaining everything in one coherent system. And it clearly cannot be broached before aims (i) and (ii) have been achieved. One can only decide empirically whether all natural languages can be described with a noeme-language, namely by showing that each one can be so described. But for the time being it is doubtful whether it is possible to describe even German or English in this fashion, as our examples have shown. But even if the proof could be adduced, the noeme-language would still not have the unique status expected by its creators, because the meaning of the artificial noemes would have to be given in some way. Were it to be given by a recursive procedure in L_2 itself, e.g., in such a way that n_1 were defined by n_2 and n_3, n_2 by n_4 and n_5 etc., we would still come to elementary noemes which would have to be explained in an L_3, surely a natural language, if we want to do more than just continue our game. If the elementary noemes are explained with L_1 — a procedure nearly always used in spite of the assertion that L_2 is an independent language — a partial tautology is the result.

There is a further attempt to use artificial languages in the latest development of generative theory. After introducing semantics into generative theory and explicitly laying down that the deep structure is to be a semantic representation of a sentence and the surface structure a phonological one,[12] people essentially ceased to use in the deep structure the natural language to be described or a natural language extended by components which are not well defined. It was believed that the abstractness and universality of the deep structure could only be reached if it were formulated in an artificial, logical language.

It was assumed that all sentences with the same meaning could be reduced to a common deep structure and that to every n-fold ambiguous sentence n deep structures might be attached. Hence one can conclude that here too something like synonymy is postulated between the sentences from L_1 and L_2, though this has not been made explicit. People often contented themselves with so-called cognitive synonymy, which is nothing but equivalence. But most often we find general declarations such as

(229) S_1 can be mapped onto S_2.
(230) S_2 represents S_1.
(231) S_1 corresponds to S_2.

etc., which hardly lend themselves to empirical examination. Certainly the semantic descriptions of generative theory have many points of contact with componential analysis, since they begin with the expansion of such an analysis with features, and nowadays specifications with features are used in all versions. The essential difference is that the main question for generative theory is how to get to a description of the meaning of sentences from the meanings of their parts, or how to deduce the semantic relations between sentences from the semantic relations between their parts. Most generativists do not even go so far as to describe the meaning of the ultimate constituents of a sentence, but introduce them into L_2 without analysis.[13] The aim of description is only to show the so-called logical form of the sentences. Here again we find the well-known hope for a universal language of description, based upon the assumption that a sentence has a logical form, an assumption made at the time of the Tractatus. But now it seems to have been decided that, at best, several logical forms correspond to a sentence, depending on the logic we use.[14]

Now I want to demonstrate with the help of an example how this type of generative theory works and what questions should be put to it. I presuppose a simple generative syntax of German and the logical L_2 used for this.[15] The example deals with the semantic properties of quantifying morphemes 'everybody' or 'all', 'one', 'some', for which '$\forall x$' and '$\exists x$' are used as a proxy in L_2. The two sentences

(232)   Everybody loves somebody.
(233)   Somebody is loved by everybody.

should have the following structure according to our simple syntax:

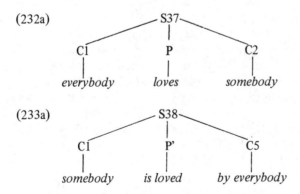

(232a)

C1 — everybody
P — loves
C2 — somebody

S37

(233a)

C1 — somebody
P' — is loved
C5 — by everybody

S38

According to our intuition (232) and (233) are not synonymous, nor even equivalent. This should become evident from the logical versions which would have the following form, if we insert 'L' for 'loves', 'Q' for the syntactic category of quantifiers:[16]

82

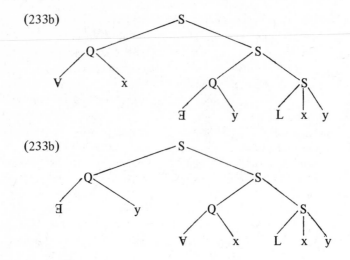

(233b)

(233b)

In the logical tree we can always use the same predicate L, because P and P'
are to be considered converse predicates which can be translated into L_2 by
a simple shift in their arguments. The difference between the meanings of
(232) and (233) is shown by the shift of quantifiers in L_2. Accordingly it is
represented by the difference in the logical structures.

There is, however, an objection to both translations. According to the definition of the existential quantifier '∃x', the b-sentences would also be true
if there were several y's for which (232b) and (233b) were true, yet we would
not assume the same thing for the a-sentences. In a closer translation of (232a)
an addition like ∀z (Lxz → y = z) would be necessary. Such a quantifier has
already been introduced into current logical languages. But in other cases
there is no corresponding quantifier in L_2, e.g., ' ∃ ' cannot be accepted as a
translation of 'some', though often assumed to be one. For (232b) would also be true even if there were only a single y for which ∀xLxy were true.

The sentence

    (234)   Everybody loves a few people.

would then be true. Here one might also think of introducing a new quantifier
into L_2 which includes the condition 'more than one', for example

    (235) $\varsigma x P x$ = def $\exists x_1 \exists x_2 (P x_1 \wedge P x_2 \wedge x_1 \neq x_2)$.

But this does not seem to be enough either, for 'some' does not mean the
same as 'at least two'. Shortly after the beginning of the world it would have

been possible to say:

(236) $\exists x\,(Hx \wedge Gx)$,

where 'H' stands for 'human' and 'G' for 'good', but not

(237) Some humans are good.

because they were only two humans who were good. Obviously the reason is that some people need not be as many as all people, but that $\exists x$ may well be used if there is only one individual of this kind in the universe.

There are similar difficulties in the other direction. For some among ten million is likely to be more than two, a possibility not included in our definition of ς. Of course, one could make up a definition which also postulates more individuals for ς.

(238) $\varsigma xPx = \text{def}\, \exists x_1 \ldots x_n\,(Px_1 \wedge Px_2 \wedge \ldots \wedge Px_n \wedge x_1 \neq x_2 \neq \ldots \neq x_n)$

would allow us to assume different numbers of individuals. But we would always have to give an exact number of n; not so with 'some'. The translation of 'all' and 'some' by quantifiers gives rise to further problems because $<all,\ \forall x>$ and $<some,\ x>$ cannot be assumed to be corresponding pairs. The translations (236) of (239) and (241) of (240) do not only differ as to the quantifiers but also by substitution of a conditional for the conjunction, which shows that the meanings of the quantifiers do not exhaust the meaning of 'all' and 'some'.

(239) Some men are good.
(240) All men are good.
(241) $\forall x\,(Mx \rightarrow Gx)$.

This demonstrates that the translations given do not even meet the condition of intensional isomorphism which might have counted as an explanation for synonymy.[17] For the time being it does not seem to be possible to translate 'some' into a logical L_2 or an extended L_2.

The problems of this application of an artificial language seem to be related to those of componential analysis. They call for an extension of L_2 which is independent of L_1. Now it is doubtful

(i) whether an L_2 is possible, rich enough to be sufficient for the des-

cription of every given L_1 without giving up the preciseness of L_2
(ii) whether the construction of such a rich L_2 is possible independently of a natural language
(iii) whether extension of L_2 will not end in isomorphism of L_1 and L_2, so that the description degenerates into tautologies.

As concerns (i), some extensions of L_2 may be possible, but in such a way that a sufficiently rich extension would have to give up the so-called preciseness which ought to be L_2's justification. In many cases where logical languages have been connected with natural ones, the intention was to avoid difficulties resulting from the use of natural languages for certain purposes. Accordingly such descriptions have always been connected with a normative claim which renders them inappropriate for pure description. Thus one might exaggerate: if an expression from L_1 does not have certain meaning properties which the corresponding expression from L_2 does have, then they cannot be synonymous.

Now to the case where L_2 is also a natural language: this has been much discussed, particularly in theories of translation with very practical aims such as that of obtaining general ideas about the properties of the relation between L_1 and L_2. More often than not two contrary hypotheses have been discussed rather superficially:

(i) Every sentence of every natural language can be translated into every other natural language.
(ii) No sentence of any natural language can be translated into a different natural language.

The controversy here has often been conducted in a rather heavy-handed manner and basic differences glossed over. E.g., 'can be translated' in (ii) means something like 'can be completely translated', since it would be obviously wrong with our normal use of 'translate'. But complete translatability will be closely related to synonymy and would have to be dealt with in this context as well.[18] All semantic theories dealt with up to now are somehow related to translation, for they start from the assumption that the sentences of L_1 are described by sentences of an L_2. In the case where L_2 is an artificial language, the idea may be to use this description for the stimulation of certain parts of a natural language in computers. For this purpose one would not even need a complete description. One might confine oneself to calculating consequences for certain domains or question chains, etc. If L_2 is natural, one might understand semantic theory as a basis for translations, perhaps automatic ones. So, a lot of possibilities for applying such theories can be imagined, but these possibilities differ a great deal from those open to traditional semantic theories (of the $L_1 = L_2$ variety). So, before introducing such a theory, I want to outline in the next section its leading ideas.

3.2 AIMS OF PRACTICAL SEMANTICS

Practical semantics is of the $L_1 = L_2$ variety and differs from the semantic theories dealt with above chiefly in two respects: (i) It does not start from the assumption that there is only one meaning of a sign within a language, nor does it assume a general *must* for the relation between act-patterns and meanings. It rather assumes that most problems of action and communication between individuals arise precisely because different social groups as well as different agents obey different rules. (ii) It does not confine its description of signs to mere description of relations between signs, as for instance EQ or SN, or even to a substitution of certain signs for others, but rather starts with interactions in general, linguistic interactions in particular, and attempts to describe the context of the various act-patterns as well as the use of signs within these interactions.

One consequence of these two points is that practical semantics cannot merely limit itself to the description of meanings. For, even if one succeeded in constructing a perfect formal semantic theory of the kind discussed above, one would not have accomplished much as it would be understood only by a few specialists. The application of such a theory would still remain a communicative problem because it would have to be taught and understood.

Differences between rules of different individuals exist not only in the case of peripheral signs, but also in the use of the most central signs, e.g., 'if', 'true', 'real' and others. Not all people of our culture use signs such as 'if' in the same way. There are differences as to the asymmetry of 'if', e.g., some people use 'if p then q' to conclude as follows:'now q, so p'.

There are also differences as to the speech act going with p, e.g., some people answer 'if p then q' with 'but not p at all', clearly assuming that p is asserted. In consequence, there are also differences in following modus ponens, the paradigm of a logically clear-cut rule.

Perhaps many people will say it is obvious that something here is wrong: Our logical deviant must learn the right use of 'if'. This postulate is suggested by the systematization of 'if' in logic which makes us sure of the correct use, perhaps too sure. I shall not go into detail here, but I believe that one can conclude with the perverted 'if' as well as with the logically respectable 'if'. Even for a person who assumes that it is already settled which use is correct and which is incorrect, the problem arises of how one is to teach the right use.

For it is unlikely that such a person will assume that the incorrect uses do not exist.

The example of 'if' shows how important the differences between the uses of certain words can be for communication. Where P1 and P2 use 'if' differently they will have difficulties in all arguments based on modus ponens. This is an extremely important difference because words like 'if' play an indispensible role in communication: they constitute the relations between sentences and hence are important for learning and finding out meanings. A deviating use of words such as 'true' seems to be still more important. It appears that it is used to define certain mental diseases.

Our example is also interesting as it shows that misunderstandings can consist not only of the fact that P1 uses a word Y where P2 would use another one X. If this were the case, then P2 would only have to assume that when P1 utters Y he actually means X, in which case 'actually' already goes too far in an ideal sense, because P2 supposes that he already knows how to use Y correctly.

In this case both would only have to find the Y they would use for X.[19] As the problem is one of simple substitution, it would lead to a regress in communication since, if P1 uttered Y and P2 'You mean X by Y?', P1 might answer 'You mean Y by X?' or 'You mean Z by X?' and so on. Unfortunately, such simple substitutions are just not enough for the majority of cases, simply because not all uses of Y can be expected to coincide with all uses of X. The problem of synonymy exists for different competences as well as for different languages. The only way to improve the communication is for both to explain their meaning of 'if' and this definitely can neither be achieved by definition — in the case of 'if' this can be shown extremely well because there is no definition of 'if' — nor by such reproaches as: 'But this is not logical!' For the logic, if one should talk of logic here at all, changes with the difference in the use of 'if'.

Explaining the use of a sentence can consist of clarifiying the use of the sentence or of tracing its relation to other sentences. Perhaps, in the course of this one would arrive at sentences which are elementary in the sense that one would not know any more how to come to an understanding if one does not agree upon their use. Even then, knowing which sentences cause the misunderstanding is a gain. Such a sentence could be:

(242)   This is white.

which can be directly verified by sensory perception. This does not mean that the use and the truth of (242) do not depend on other sentences. Nor does it mean that P1 and P2 cannot use a sentence such as (242) differently. They really can. But then we can see that they will have enormous difficulties in understanding each other. Neither the useless request 'Look, it *is* white' nor such assertions as

(243)   This is objectively white.

can be of help. For each can claim the objectivity for himself. We must keep in mind that 'objective' is only used if something is already the subject of controversy. If one asserts that (243), one presupposes that one can argue about the color of the object. This should serve as a warning to those who want to use words such as 'objective' in supporting arguments.

The dispute about the truth of the assertion of (242) makes it clear that problems of truth cannot necessarily be solved within a so-called discourse. Especially in a dispute as basic as the one above, a clarification of the use need not lead to a better understanding or to consent. For in questions of truth the relation between speech and action is concerned. A consensus concerning the truth of the assertion of (242) is reached by past or future common practice. Perhaps P1 will show P2 what it means to him to say that an object is white by playing a simple language-game, for example by classifying colored objects. In such a way they would come to realize how useful the parallel use of words is for this interaction. The meaning of linguistic signs cannot, in the long run, be explained by a discourse but can only be clarified through their use.

The different problems raised by understanding do not somehow come into existence as a result of external linguistic differences. Neither can they be dismissed as failings of our everyday language. They result rather from the fact that there is no uniform language for all speakers and thus no uniform meaning for any given expression. These are not only surface problems, for meaning is closely related to action, to socialization, to the form of life. Therefore logical analysis and criticism of language, which are reductionistic in tendency, cannot be of use here: they prematurely reduce the speakers' worlds, standardize too soon and with the help of questionable assumptions.[20] A semantic theory must not just assume that understanding works well and that a uniform language exists, but it must be able to show how understanding comes about in the first place, how by communication the competence of individual agents and the language of social groups come into existence and can be changed, under which social conditions certain types of communication arise and are obeyed and how the social conditions themselves can be influenced by communication — e.g., how the status or the role of a partner is built up by communication.

Thus, the fundamental aim of practical semantics must be (i) that the agents

88

communicate better and more successfully. This goes for both interacting
partners P1 and P2: P2 has to understand P1 better and P1 has to act reflec-
tively in order to be understood. Learning a set of sentences which admit no
misunderstanding or an ideal language are no ways to achieve this aim because there is no such ideal language and because we live in a particular
world where nobody has the power to disseminate such an artificial language.
Since, on our understanding of science, the agents themselves must have the
possibility of reducing problems of understanding, practical semantics has to
develop a method the internalization of which will enable an agent to recognize misunderstandings, to uncover their roots more quickly and, finally, to
abolish them.

Therefore what the agents have to do is to learn, alongside their normal
competences, methods providing for a clearer view of the relations between
linguistic signs and act-patterns.[21] And practical semantics has the task of
developing such methods and to teach them. In this respect criticism and
analysis of language make sense since they can be regarded as an explanation
of certain of these relations.

Thus we consider the principal aims of practical semantics, which are
derived from (i), to be that agents acquire the ability to: (ii) broaden their
perspective on the context of their own utterances and those of their partner;
(iii) broaden their perspective on the context of their own acts and those of
their partner; (iv) broaden their perspective on the context of their acts and
their utterances.

A context is a set of objects connected by a system of relations. In our
case such objects can be: act-patterns, sentences, events, and the like. Relations can be: is a subpattern of, is a condition for, is of pattern, is the negation of, implies, etc. This will be discussed later. Here we want to make a basic
distinction between three kinds of contexts: the explicit context, the implicit
context, and the historical context. Unlike the historical context the explicit
and the implicit context refer to patterns. For linguistic patterns the explicit
context can be understood in such a way that only those parts which are
represented by linguistic patterns belong to it. E.g., in

(244)   He is coming. I know it.

the first sentence belongs to the explicit context of the second sentence. But

(245)   He can come.

would belong to the implicit context of (244), as well as

(246)   He is moving.

More generally, the explicit context of an act-pattern HX is the ordered set
of the act-patterns remaining in the interaction or interactions where HX
occurs:

(247) MOP_{12} = $ASSERT_1$ (that S1 if S2) † $UTTER_2$ (*yes*) †
         $ASSERT_1$ (that S2) † $UTTER_2$ (*yes*) † $PROVE_1$ (that S1)
         → $UTTER_1$ (*so* S1).
(248) $ASSERT_1$ (that S1 if S2) † $UTTER_2$(*yes*) † . . . † $UTTER_2$
         (*yes*) † $PROVE_1$ (that S1) → $UTTER_1$ (*so* S1).

So (248) would be the explicit context of $ASSERT_1$ (that S2) in (247). Of
course it is doubtful whether the explicit context of an act-pattern can ever
be given completely. Within our general definition of explicit context, the
explicit context of linguistic patterns proves to be a special case, where the
surrounding patterns are restricted to their linguistic specifications.[22]
   Unlike the components of interactions, the subpatterns, conditions, and
possibly the generating patterns of HX belong to the implicit context of HX.
The last assumption will probably lead to counting only basic patterns as
explicit and would then be very problematical.
   The historical context of an act consists of all acts and events relevant to
the act which precede or succeed it. Therefore the historical context is open
in two ways: first, it elongates permanently into the future; second, given
new events and acts, the assignment of an act to a pattern can even be changed.
It is evident that with 'relevant' we refer to a rule because we can compre-
hend acts as well as contexts only by means of rules. Reasons for distinguishing the different kinds of context as well as further explanations of them will
be furnished later.
   Pursuing the aims (ii) − (iv) will not mean that agents are to acquire completely new abilities. On the one hand, the contexts are in a certain sense already known to them. They know them, they have internalized them. On the
other hand, they also have a view over the contexts. But this view often does
not reach far enough to avoid and overcome the problems which arise. An
example which is relevant here is that of the psychoanalyst whose aim is to
detect unconscious parts of the partner's historical context, in order to make
the rules of his action clear to him and to give him a basis for changing these
rules.
   Thus, possession of the broader perspective on different contexts is not a
theoretical ability. The context rather defines the rule and thus belongs to
the rule. If the contexts are different the rules are different. That's why the

knowledge of the context plays such a decisive role in the understanding of action, which is nothing but an assignment of acts to a rule. This shows the interrelations between 'to have a broader perspective on the context' and 'to understand acts better'.

One field of application for practical semantics would be contradictions which are defined by the relation mentioned above 'is a negation of'. Contradictions play a part in many theories: in sociological ones (contradictions in the society), in logical, in psychological as well as in psychoanalytical theories. Everywhere contradictions are things to be removed. It is evident that contradictions have something to do with relations between sentences. In practical semantics and in similar theories we deal essentially with two types of contradictions at present: (i) contradictions which result from the competence of an agent, parts of his competence as it were; (ii) contradictions which arise in interaction with other partners.

Since these contradictions need not be direct, we want to talk of what I will call incompatibility. But it must always be possible to reduce incompatibilities to contradictions. There are above all paradigms for incompatibilities within the competence of an agent: P1 may regard different propositions as true, laws as right, etc., which include elements contradicting one another. From this various conflicts may arise for P1 in certain situations. The other paradigm is that where a contradiction may arise between a law or a norm accepted by P1 and an act which P1 has performed or wants to perform. From this, conflicts arise which are known from psychoanalytical theories about the super-ego. In the special case of linguistic acts, an example would be that P1 lies, but regards lies as bad, or just that P1 asserts something which later turns out to be contradictory to other assertions or assumptions which he regards as true. This suggests that such contradictions may also remain unconscious for P1. But can one seriously assume that there is something in a sentence Y uttered by an agent which he himself does not know, so that he might be forced to regard X as true if he asserts Y? I would say that an agent need not have a view over the relations between his sentences in such a way that he always knows what a sentence includes. For without this assumption a change of context and of competence could not be explained. It seems to me that the value of linguistic communication consists exactly in clarifying the context. Yet, in the end it will not be possible to force someone to concede X if he has asserted Y. At least there is no logical *must* involved. Still we realize the sense of the aim of having a wider view over the contexts. Because in this way many such conflicts can be avoided.

This brings us to our second case, because such incompatibilities are most often revealed by a partner and it is usually a partner who causes one to accept certain connections, to give up others, etc. For (ii) we can again distinguish several cases: Two partners in an interaction may become aware of differences in opinions or norms accepted by them. This may for example come to light if P2 does something which one could not, in P1's opinion, do at all or which one should not do, in P1's opinion, under the circumstances, etc.

The other case is that P1 may do something and wrongly interpret the reaction and understanding of P2 because the pattern of his act pertains to another context. This is a classical case of misunderstanding which, of course, is closely related to our first case. We shall discuss this relationship later in connection with questions of understanding and of the truth of linguistic utterances.

Finally we want to call attention to a related case where a partner P1 performs two acts which he himself regards as incompatible. The point is not that P2 does not understand how P1 can pursue the same aim — although P2 does think this — with the two acts. From this it would not follow that the acts are incompatible. The case in question here only occurs in symbolical acts because no agent can for example laugh and not laugh all at once. But in symbolic acts there is such a thing: A young male P1 takes a female P2 in his arms. P2 whispers "No, no! " but she nestles closer to him. From this a conflict may arise for P1 (double bind).

In all these cases the understanding of both partners is crucial. They have to be able to remove the incompatibility which they can only do if they can discover, identify and perhaps describe contradictions by means of such relations as sub-patterns, implication, etc. This holds for incompatibility in interactions as well as for incompatibility in the competence of an agent.

In order for one to recognize an incompatibility one cannot simply start from one's own competence. For example, if a smoker regards the sentence

(249)   Smoking is extremely dangerous and anti-social.

as true, he still can regard (250) as true:

(250)   I must smoke.

without contradicting himself. For it might be that he simply does not regard as true:

(251)   If something is dangerous for me, I don't do it.

or at least admits certain exceptions to this. Or it might be that the context is not so simple, because he also regards other norms as valid, such as

    (252)   I like smoking.
    (253)   I do everything I like.

which can contradict (249) and (251). But basically one has to be cautious in ascertaining contradictions in the competence of others; perhaps in many cases where there obviously is a contradiction for P2 there is none for P1.

The differences in competence have different effects in life. For example, let us imagine an individual who does not know or follow the current logical rules, say someone, who, as in our example, uses 'if' quite differently. It would have to be proved in action that a system using 'if' according to the rules known to us is somehow superior. The problem of evaluation which we had with logical semantics reappears in this 'somehow superior'.

That one system is superior to another can only be assumed if P1, too, accepts this evaluation which, usually, will not be the case. Imagine for example a rainmaker whose procedure is successful perhaps every tenth time. Yet his fellow tribesmen seem to believe:

    (254)   If the rainmaker goes through with his procedure then there
             will be rain.

In our society we would probably say that this is a very peculiar use of 'if', at least according to our understanding of occidental meteorological theories and of good weather forecasts.[23] It is clear that in such cases the superiority of one use of 'if' over another cannot be proved with the existing principles of evaluation but that the principles of evaluation must be changed as well. For, the idea that principles of evaluation are somehow independent from these contexts cannot be seriously considered.

This is also the reason why practical semantics does not propose ready-made ideal contexts but only wants to improve the chances for the agent to master given situations. The assimilation of contexts as well as that of evaluation principles always remains a communicative process.

In its aims, especially as is shown in this example, practical semantics has a point of contact with some psychoanalytical and psychological theories. I would like to discuss one of them briefly, Festinger's theory of cognitive dissonance. In his theory contradiction plays a central role. It is true that Festinger neither says that it is a question of contradictions resulting from the competence of agents nor that it is a problem of understanding and of language. But his definitions show that consonance and dissonance are relations between sentences:

    (255)   X and Y are dissonant if and only if not-X follows from Y.[24]

(256)   X and Y are consonant if and only if X implies Y or vice versa.

In these definitions some of the semantic relations mentioned above are used (to follow, to imply and to be contradictory) and are to be understood in such a way that their arguments are sentences. Thus here things like opinions, acts, evaluations, etc., occur as well.

Festinger's hypothesis is that all individuals try to reduce dissonances which arise and that not reducing these dissonances gives rise to frustrations. According to Festinger, agents have different capacities for tolerance of dissonance,[25] probably because agents with a great dissonance tolerance interpret the contexts less strictly and perhaps have a more restricted view over them. For a semantic theory the ideal should be for agents to be able to realize the greatest possible consonance. This is not to say the greatest possible conformity, for consonance can also result from an understanding of the reasons for dissonance and the acceptance of their insurmountability. Nor is this to say that complete consonance can ever be reached or even aimed at. For this might result in a historical stand-still. In practice such ideas are useless: it will often be impossible to remove dissonances completely: If X and Y are dissonant and this dissonance can be removed by changing either X or Y, a frequent consequence of this change would be that a new dissonance would arise between the result X' of the change of X and, say, Z which did not exist between X and Z. Nevertheless it seems to be desirable to find a standard for the dissonance and perhaps to develop consonant parts of linguistic competences. Here, it would seem, is a further aim of semantic theories and a possibility for their application, e.g. in the teaching of languages.

In the formulation of our aims (ii) − (iv) we deliberately used the contexts of acts because these abilities must always be seen in their historical context. In doing this, the context of patterns and conditions must be taken into consideration, because understanding acts and contexts of acts consists above all in assigning them to patterns. Interpretation means in fact just this. So, if we assume that two communicating partners are never masters of the same rules, an important basis for the internalization of the abilities mentioned in (ii) − (iv) is the ability to find out the partner's rules, to realize alternative possibilities of assigning acts to rules and to find new rules for this purpose. One should possibly make several hypotheses about the rules obeyed by a partner and one should be able to evaluate the probability of this or that hypothesis according to the historical context. Each rule contains a different part of the historical context, so that choosing alternative possible interpretations always involves the choice of relevant components from the historical context.

Alternative rules as a contrast are apt to give one a better understanding of one's own rules and of their relativity. Here is a point of contact between the ability to realize alternatives and the ability to compare one's own competence with that of one's partner: one of the most important ways to understand and to define a rule is to contrast it with similar ones. For related rules define one another. This holds as well for linguistic patterns as it does for the example of planning or making decisions, which always consists of choosing alternatives. In order to choose one alternative, it is useful to reflect upon the consequences and the conditions of this choice, which consists at least partly of relating sentences. Similar considerations seem to play a part in the assigning of a partner's act to a rule. The contrasting of alternatives provides a useful basis for the evaluation of rules, which starts from a good understanding of competing rules. For only if one contrasts alternatives does pluralism seem to be guaranteed, in that one perhaps acknowledges that the rule of the other person is the better rule or that it cannot be decided which one is the better, instead of always naively assuming that one's own rule is the best or even the only one that would or should be obeyed in a given historical context. If openness of communication between two partners in such questions is to be advanced, the partners will first have to learn to realize and tolerate deviations.

A question arises when one compares the aim of practical semantics with the use to which Wittgenstein put his philosophical method. Are formalization and practical semantics not contradictory? Wittgenstein did not want to formalize his method, probably because he

(i) wanted to avoid its being related to questions of preciseness, which is always ascribed to formal languages in contrast to natural ones;
(ii) thought a formal and thus closed representation of his method to be impossible in view of his theory of learning (in every process of learning, being shown how to do something and imitating, thus action and understanding, are important; descriptions are only instruments of learning and are often misleading);
(iii) realized the danger of regarding a formal language as an objective standard or ideal and so allowing it to escape criticism.

As concerns practical semantics, it has to be noted that only very simple formal means are used and that their expressions are closely related to the expressions of the agent's language, for example German. The act-patterns themselves are even gathered from the agent's language, since we take them from infinitive expressions of his language. This is the use of the square bracket operator which we have so far only used and not explained: it helps us to form names of act-patterns out of linguistic signs. So we succeed in talking about act-patterns without talking about signs though we get the patterns only be means of signs.

Therefore the relations between the patterns are finally determined by the relations between signs.

Thus, a claim is satisfied which must be fulfilled by every semantic theory: that it is reflexive, i.e., can be applied to itself. Since practical semantics satisfies this claim the Wittgensteinian objections (i) − (iii) do not apply to it. For its formal means of description basically do not have a status different from the signs of a natural language and, more particularly, can be criticized and changed in a similar way. Their only purpose is to make the description clearer.

The description of acts and act-patterns in practical semantics consists above all of

(i) giving the conditions under which an act according to a certain pattern can be performed, or norms determining when it can, may or must not be performed;
(ii) giving generations and partitions of patterns with the conditions required;
(iii) describing acts and act-patterns in relation to interactions.

However, it is not intended to make detailed descriptions of acts and contexts of social groups in a linguistic theory. This would be an undertaking that could hardly be realized; the examples we give later are so complex that a complete description of this kind cannot be imagined. It would also be impossible to enumerate all conditions of a generation. One might perhaps succeed in saying which conditions have been infringed if a partner believes an infringement of a rule to have occurred. A complete description is also unimaginable because these contexts are not fixed but can always be changed and are permanently changed by agents. Because of this and because the normative force of such descriptions has to be avoided, it is the aim of practical semantics that the agents themselves be masters of this method, so that they can, if necessary, make such descriptions not in a contemplative sense, but where certain problems are to be overcome.

Thus practical semantics is not intended merely to be a description that leaves everything as it is.[26] It rather seeks to provide the necessary basis for the agent to recognize existing connections and to construct and to test alternatives to them. In this context ideals like symmetry of roles and competence, symmetry of status and their relation with ideal forms of life have to be clarified.

In addition it may well be a task of practical semantics to make constructive proposals for interactions and communications, starting from the description of occurring interactions, in order to provide a basis for a detailed discussion of the ideals mentioned. Therefore these proposals will concern

96

general abilities important for communication. Such general abilities would
be: to find out the rules according to which people have acted; to form hypotheses concerning the relations between acts of the partner; to make assumptions about alternative rules and to test them in the context; to find new rules;
to recognize and to tolerate deviations.

Since it is important here as well as elsewhere to understand how to introduce and carry out this method, the constructive proposals must above all be
of use for the learning and practicing of the necessary abilities. The communication games which we shall come to talk about later have to be evaluated
with this in mind. In their formal presentation they can only be described
and examined by specialists, later, perhaps, in order to be applied in the teaching of languages, but their use will have to be shown for every single agent.

This need not be done in a formal way. The reader will probably know of
such games from his own experience and will be able to evaluate corresponding strategies without needing a formal description. Thus, the formal description is conceived of only for certain purposes, say in order to calculate and
optimize utility, using different variables. But the description is irrelevant to
questions about what utility really is. The purpose of constructive proposals
for the teaching of languages would above all be to show the contexts of
such communications by describing them and thus, on the basis of a theory,
to make decisions possible on didactic methods, e.g., decisions as to how to
acquire communicative abilities.

3. 3 COMMUNICATION

3.3.1 *Linguistic action*

The uttering (UTT) of linguistic signs plays an important part in human action. But UTT is only one part of linguistic action. If a parrot produces certain
squawks, similar to the sounds of a language, we do not assume that he is
communicating with us. We do not give him serious answers. This is related to
the fact that UTT occurs only as generated in human communication: I
assert (ASS) something or I ask (ASK) something or I order (ORD) something,
etc., by uttering something. This can be described in the following generations:

(257)   ASS (X) → UTT (Y).
(258)   ASK (X) → UTT (Y).
(259)   ORD (X) → UTT (Y).

Even in cases which we would intuitively classify differently from (257), (258), or (259), UTT is generated; for example, if I just utter something in order to test a microphone or to make phonetic exercises:

(260)   TEST (Z) → UTT (*la la la*).
(261)   PRACT (SPEAK A) → UTT (*Haste makes waste*).

The difference between these cases and (257), (258), and (259) will be discussed later.

Further on we restrict UTT to those phonetic acts which are of use for communication. In addition to phonetic acts we shall admit written utterances, but we shall leave codings in flag-languages, etc., alone. In the generations (257), (258), (259) we provided specifications for what someone utters, asserts, etc. In addition, other specifications would have to be introduced here, as for instance for a partner who has to be present if I want to ask or assert something that makes sense. In the last analysis this arises from the number of places the verb 'communicate', which would occur on the left in a detailed generation, would have. We shall not expand on these generalities here; we only want to go into the particulars of the generations given and discuss the status of the specifications of these patterns.

The domain of specifications of UTT is the set of linguistic expressions, usually within one language, say German. Such expressions may be single phonemes, morpheme-expressions, word-expressions, syntagm-expressions, sentence-expressions, or whole text-expressions comprising not only the phonematic representation but also intonation and syntactic structure. The meanings of the expressions concerned are largely described by the expressions on the left of '→UTT'. Since UTT with its specifications is a pattern and the specifications concerned form new subpatterns, the specifying expression is also a unit of the *langue,* as we supposed before. So we write it in italics to emphasize that it occurs in each pattern as mentioned, not used. A more differentiated description would afford phonematic and syntactic descriptions. This status of Y makes clear why and how far linguistic expressions can be regarded as patterns for their realization: they are parts of different rules UTT (Y), UTT (Z), etc.

Certainly there will be further restrictions on the domain of specification of UTT in certain generations, which is one of the effects of the fact that generations concern meaning. Thus in our generations (257), (258) and (259), only a sentence-expression could stand as a specification of UTT, otherwise the generation is deviant. If we characterize deviating generations with an asterisk, so that it operates on the innermost deviating expression, we get for instance

$$(262) \quad * (ASS (X) \rightarrow UTT (was)).$$

Generations such as (257), (258), and (259) provide us with the basis for defining the concept of sentence: only expressions specifying UTT which may occur in non-deviant generations of the form (257), (258), and (259) can be sentences. Syntactically deviant sentences are just those expressions which cannot occur in any generation, so that the following holds in general:

$$(263) \quad * \begin{Bmatrix} ASS\,(X) \\ ORD\,(X) \end{Bmatrix} \rightarrow UTT\,(*S)).$$

Clearly in order to narrow the defined set to the set of sentences we have to specify which generations are of the form (257), (258), and (259), since deviant sentences can certainly occur in other generations as specifications of UTT, e.g. deviant sentences can be cited (CIT):

$$(264) \quad CIT\,(*S) \rightarrow UTT\,(*S).$$

Since such a narrowing down seems to be possible within the description of linguistic interactions, the proposed sentence-definition could solve certain problems with ellipses which have traditionally worried linguists. E.g. 'Fred' is not normally regarded as a sentence and it could not be inserted for Y in a generation like (257). But in the context of a communication such a generation actually could occur:

$$(265) \quad ASK_1\,(Z) \rightarrow UTT_1\,(who\ did\ it?\,) \dagger ANS_2 \rightarrow ASS_2\,(X) \rightarrow$$
$$UTT_2\,(Fred).$$

To talk of an ellipsis would not be very useful here; for nothing is left out. P2 asserted with his utterance that it was Fred. This belongs to the rules of the English language. On the other hand, the unrestricted generation of the form (257) with 'Fred' as specification of UTT would be deviant, which shows that 'Fred' must not be regarded as a sentence but, in a certain context, can function as a sentence. We could arrive in this fashion at a better sentence definition, not excluding ellipses, minor sentences, etc., but taking their use into account and providing a precise description of their meaning. We could also provide for a clear concept of deviation by creating a scale from syntactically deviant expressions at one end to falsely used sentences at the other end.

In our generations (257), (258), and (259) only certain subsets of S are respectively possible as specifications of UTT. Certain difficulties arise because these subsets overlap and the hearer has to grasp from the utterance just which pattern in fact generates UTT. Because there is no one-one mapping between these subsets and the generating patterns, it is not always clear how the utterance of a sentence has to be understood. The utterance of

(266)   You are going.

can occur in all three generations if intonation is left out of consideration. In other cases intonation does not help either. By uttering

(267)   Don't drink Coca Cola!

one can order something, give some advice, beg somebody, etc. A solution can be achieved in part by indicating the conditions of the generation: e.g., a condition of ordering is that P1 possesses the corresponding position within an order-hierarchy.

In part, the question as to which generation is in fact present is answered by indicating the alternatives to preceding or succeeding components of the communication. Or perhaps only the historical context of the utterance shows how the utterance was meant; it may even not become evident at all, so that P2 must check back: "Was that an order?", etc.

The rough distinction between kinds of sentences which, in part, might be conceived for the purpose of differentiating alternative generations will not suffice for the description of all differences; on the one hand, because there are many more than three linguistic patterns generating UTT (S), so that the distinction between declarative, interrogative, and imperative sentences will not do; on the other hand, because these kinds of sentences do not correlate with the generating linguistic patterns. For I can describe, tell, and assert with a declarative sentence. If we are not able to establish subsets of sentences in term of syntax, which I suppose we cannot, then the description has to be achieved by alternative generations and conditions. But for certain purposes we can make syntactic simplifications by choosing, instead of sentence-chains, so-called sentence-forms as specifications of UTT where the position of the morphemes is not yet taken into consideration. Then we define certain operators — say Q, which generates th order of morphemes and the intonation of an interrogative sentence — which give rise to certain restrictions on the sentence form (for imperative sentences, second person, subject deletion, etc.).

These operators prove to be cognate with certain transformations. In addition they indicate a semantic relation, since they can be used as specifications of UTT only in certain generations; for instance Q cannot be used in (257).

The traditional classification into kinds of sentences would then, it seems likely, prove to be useless. Probably further restrictions of this kind can be introduced into the conditions of the generation by more detailed syntactic descriptions of S.

On the other hand, deviations within the generations (257), (258), and (259) need not be caused by a deviation of UTT (S). Often deviation is due to a deviation of ASS (X), ASK (X), etc. Examples for this are:

(268)   *ASK (that you lend me some money).
(269)   *ASS (to ask you for some money).
(270)   *ORD (that I return the money to you).

More specific deviations would be:

(271)   *ORD (that it is raining).
(272)   *ORD (that you have laughed).

In all these examples the deviation of the whole generation is due only to the deviation of the left part of the generation and it is this which has to be described. This directs our attention to the relation of these act-patterns to the domain of their specifications and in the end to the status of X.

As instances of X we have two types of expressions; first, complement clauses (CS) for what we assert, ask, suggest, order, etc. and second, expressions such as 'this', 'that', with which we refer to what we assert, ask, etc. We regard things which we assert, ask, etc. as objects and we refer to them with 'this', 'that' and indefinitely with 'what' as we refer to other objects. What should be noticed is: (i) that we do not refer with *that*-clauses to these objects; rather, we express them. Therefore what we assert, ask, etc. is a special sort of object which can be expressed; (ii) that these objects only have existence in so far as they are expressible. For what is a command that cannot be expressed or a statement that cannot be expressed? It is not a command at all, and it is not a statement at all.

The linguistic form of the complement clauses occurring in the place of X can easily be given: they are introduced with 'that', 'whether' or a zero morpheme:

(273)   ASS (that everything is all right).
(274)   ASK (whether everything is all right).
(275)   ASS (everything would be all right).

Other kinds of complement clauses, in particular definite or indefinite descriptions (which are used to refer), are not admitted in most patterns:[27]

(276)   *ASS (whom I wish).

This type of complement clause can be eliminated by a definition in syntactic terms.[28] There is also some sort of distributional variation in the act-patterns, e.g. 'that' is not possible in ASK, 'whether' is not possible in ASS, etc.

The restriction of the scope of X to CS does not allow decomposition into sequences for the generating patterns, which is possible for UTT. E.g., if S consists of n words W_i, hence $S = W_1 \; W_2 \; \ldots \; W_n$, then it is possible to utter S at one go, but also as an articulated HFOR:

(277)   UTT (W_1) † UTT (W_2) † ... † UTT (W_n).

UTT (S) might be considered as a subpattern of this sequence pattern. But the corresponding decomposition is not possible with ASS, because a word cannot be asserted. This has certain consequences for the distribution of the patterns over sentence-coordinations. For

(278)   I am laughing.
(279)   I am not laughing.

we can distribute UTT ((278) and (279)) yielding UTT (278) ⌐UTT (279) and also to UTT (278) † UTT (279). For a generating ASS (that (278) and (279)) ASS (278)⌐ASS (279) is admissible; ASS (278) † ASS (279), however, is not,because different rules are valid for succeeding assertions. Whereas ASS (278)⌐ASS (279) would be a contradiction, ASS (278) † ASS (279) might not be one. In the meantime the agent might have stopped laughing or changed his mind and normally that is what will be assumed by his partner. Thus the two patterns would behave differently in communication. The *or*-coordination of (278) and (279) would again behave differently. Here UTT would be distributive in a special sense because 'or' must also be uttered: UTT (278) † UTT (*or*) † UTT (279), while distribution over ASS is not possible at all, because none of the corresponding complement clauses is asserted. Such distribution rules also include much discussed examples like

(280)   Either you will be quiet or I'll turn you out.

where only 'that you be quiet' stands as a specification of ORD and the second part of the sentence would occur in the specification of another pattern, say WARN or THREAT. By slightly changing the example this becomes clear because

(281)   *ORD (that I'll turn you out).

is deviating in the way (270) is. This is related to the fact that P2 and not P1 occurs as a further specification of ORD.

Until now we have assumed that expressions specifying UTT are sentences and that they are mentioned in UTT (. . .). But this seems not to be true for X: although we utter sentences and we assert something by uttering sentences we do not assert sentences, or ask sentences. The objects 'X' stands for are not sentences. But then, what are they? Would the candidates for X which possess the properties required so far not be the propositions of logical semantics? Propositions not in the sense of some object in the heads of the agents which would be individual, or ideal objects which tend to resist description, but propositions in the sense of Frege's thoughts, which he wants to distinguish from such psychological objects.[29]

Unlike Searle who wants to explain propositions by propositional acts and their components, the act of referring and the act of predicating, Frege gives more of a holistic definition, though he also identifies parts corresponding to the act of referring and the act of predicating. In one of the introductions of the notion of a thought, Frege says that a thought is what is common to interrogative and declarative sentences.[30] He therefore dissects declarative sentences into acts which are related to the parts of our form ASS (CS), namely the assertion ASS and (the conceiving of) the thought, and as a third component the acknowledgement of the truth of the thought, since thoughts are what can be taken into consideration as concerns truth or falsity. The relation with our CS can be easily recognized in expressions like

(282)   The assertion that. . .
(283)   A thinks that. . .
(284)   The thought that. . .
(285)   It is true that. . .

where it is the complement with which we express thoughts. And Frege, too, realizes the close relation between *that*-clauses and thoughts, inasmuch as he uses the expression 'the thought that. . .' as a name for a thought.

Differing from this case is the normal declarative sentence where, for Frege, the thought is the sense of the sentence. Frege explains this difference by arguing that the *that*-clause[31] in the expression 'the thought that. . .' is used obliquely so that its meaning (in Frege's sense) coincides with its sense in direct speech. Since we shall not discuss the distinction between sense and meaning made by Frege, we shall not take up this idea, though the following discussion touches it sometimes.

As long as Frege sticks to complete sentences, the assumption that the senses of imperative sentences are not thoughts is justified. But as soon as he realizes the similarity between the sense of declarative and interrogative sentences on the basis of an analysis corresponding to ASS (X) and ASK (X), it is only one step to assume such transformations for imperative sentences and others as well. Frege does not speak of thoughts here, but he makes it clear that an order, a request, etc., though not being thoughts, are on a level with thoughts.[32] This may well have something to do with the fact that reference is made both to a thought and to the linguistic act-pattern in expressions like 'assertion', 'question', 'order', 'request'. This reappears analogously in the indefinite descriptions 'what he asserts', 'what he asks', 'what he orders', where the reference to thoughts may be secured by explicit use of *that*-clauses, as in

(286)   What he asserts is that. . .
(287)   What he orders is that. . .

Here it doesn't seem to make sense to say that a thought is expressed only with the *that*-clause in (286) but not in (287).

Thus we can assume that Frege intended to make a restriction here because, as a logician, he laid particular stress upon assertion, and that it will be more useful for our adoption of Frege's line of thought to emphasize the similarity.[33]

So, can we say that thoughts or propositions are the same as certain complement clauses? Hardly. We shall hardly be ready to concede that a thought is a linguistic sign, for then two agents with different languages would never be able to conceive the same thought. Nor is a linguistic sign what can be true or false or a sentence what can be asserted. We rather assume that we can express with sentences something which can be true or false,[34] and that this is the same as what is asserted, etc. Is this, then, the meaning of the sentence? [35] This solution could be suggested by the way of speaking that a *that*-clause expresses a proposition, tempting us to assume that the same proposition could be expressed by synonymous *that*-clauses. But don't we get into a circle if we assume that the sentences must be synonymous? Not absolutely, at least not if we do not want to explain the synonymy of two sentences, as some people do, by saying that they have as their meanings the same proposition and if we make clear that this condition does not work the other way round, i.e., that synonymous sentences do not always express the same propositions.

The identification of propositions with the meaning of sentences, however, leaves out of account at least two things: (i) the same sentence can be used to express different propositions without being ambiguous; (ii) the same proposition can be expressed with different sentences which are not synonymous. As to the first objection, it is clear that two people uttering (288), and by this asserting something, do not assert the same thing:

(288)   I did it yesterday.

But all the same it would not be advisable to take this for a question of ambiguity. The second objection was already seen by Frege. If we want to say the same thing today which we said with (289) yesterday, we would have to use (290):

(289)   What did you do today?
(290)   What did you do yesterday?

But hardly anybody will assume synonymy for (289) and (290), and within the use theory of meaning one could easily show that the rules of use for both are not the same.

Frege handled this problem by admitting different transformations of sentences which preserve the thought. But just what sort of criterion allows us to decide whether a transformation is admissible? Obviously it has something to do with the meaning of the sentences.

In our examples (289) and (290) we have already said that by uttering one sentence under conditions C1 you can assert the same thing as by uttering the other one under condition C2. This is to say that with some but not all utterances of one sentence the same can be asserted as with some utterances of the other sentence, and this is clearly a question concerning the relation of sentence to sentence utterance: (i) To assert the same thing is not something the sentences do but something done by agents. (ii) Not the sentence goes with a certain command, etc. but the utterances of the sentence. This is analogous to the case of referring expressions like 'the house', where one does not refer with all uses to the same house, as sometimes assumed in the case of proper names, but this time to this house, another time to that one.

Surely all this is an affair of the rule of use for the sentences in question, and a description of the rule must provide for the decision whether the sentences can be used in these circumstances to say the same as another

105

sentence in other circumstances. This must be seen within the conditions of application.

Before considering the relation between sentence and sentence utterance in detail in section 3.3.2, we want to discuss a radical solution of the problem which starts from the idea of creating exactly one sentence as a name for every proposition, so that reference would be made to the same proposition in all its uses, provided that its meaning does not change.

This solution was already outlined by Frege.[36] It is extended by Quine, whose procedure is to fill out utterances of sentences into so-called eternal sentences. E.g., an utterance of (291) might correspond to (292):

(291)   I hear a noise.
(292)   H. J. H. hears a noise on March 3rd, 1971.

Unlike (291), the sentence (292) has a truth value fixed once and for ever. If it is true today it will be true tomorrow. Quine's program — and, following him, the program of certain formal linguists — is to eliminate all index words such as 'I', 'it', 'now', 'here', etc. in favor of " absolute expressions" thus creating sentences expressing one and only one proposition. But is this possible without loss? Could we really express in a language containing only absolute expressions instead of index words all that we can express in a language containing index words?

I suspect that if I were to say (292) instead of (291) to my wife she would be bewildered, since this is no longer human speech. It resembles the speech of the behaviorist observer, the inhuman element being the attitude of speaking of me as if I were observing myself and then reporting what I observed. Usually I do not observe my feelings and sensations, I have them. And usually I do not report them in a biographical third-person statement but I express them. The method of verification of (291) and (292) is therefore very different.

A cognate phenomenon is that we could not imagine performative utterances in a language without 'I'. In uttering

(293)   A asserts that S.

the utterer does not assert that S but in uttering

(294)   I assert that S.

in its performative use the utterer asserts that S. Sometimes speaking in the non-indexical mode turns into the speech of schizophrenics:

(295)   P1: Tom Brown is happy at t.
(296)   P2: Who is Tom Brown?
(297)   P1: Tom Brown is Tom Brown.

Normally (297) does not count as an answer but as a refusal to answer (296). But what could our restricted P1 have answered to P2's question? There are several alternative ways of continuing this strange dialogue:

(297a)   P1: Tom Brown is the one standing before P2.
(297b)   P1: Tom Brown is the one standing before P2 now.
(297c)   P1: Tom Brown is the one standing before P2 at t.
(297d)   P1: Tom Brown is the one speaking to you.
(298c)   P2: What time is it now?
(299c)   P1: At t it is t o'clock.

Here we have enough material to raise some questions about the very possibility of filling out every statement into an eternal sentence as Quine proposes.[37]

First, we see that there are contexts where the pronouns cannot be replaced by proper names. In order to understand (295) in contrast to (300),

(300)   I am happy.

the hearer must know (i) who has the name Tom Brown; (ii) where Tom Brown comes from or where Tom Brown lives; (ii) is necessary because there are many Tom Browns and in order to understand which one is meant one must be able to single out Tom Brown from Chicago or Tom Brown from Toledo so that the speaker has to use an improved version of (295) containing definite descriptions, e.g.,

(295a)   Tom Brown from 1 is happy at t.

Since it would be a very strong and obviously false assumption that there are proper names for all things in our world, replacement of all index words by proper names would be impossible. Also it would be impossible for the speakers to memorize all these names.

Second, the way out might be (297a) which, unlike (297), could be an answer to the question (296). Here a so-called definite description is used instead of the proper name. I do not want to go into this delicate matter here but only discuss two problems which arise with definite descriptions. The first problem is that definite descriptions must be given a unique reference within the whole universe, but that in normal life neither the speaker nor the hearer can achieve this.[38] Nobody can single out every object among all other objects, past, present, and future. This would require an omniscient agent and a preestablished universe. The second problem is that it will be impossible to find uniquely referring descriptions not containing proper names. I suspect that in every definite description of this type one comes across a proper name (or an index word) in the end. If this is correct, as is suggested by the appearance of 'P2' in (297 a), then the problem of proper names is resurrected. A more revealing theory of definite descriptions and of proper names would prove that both derive from the use of indexical expressions. For we cannot imagine how somebody can teach us the use of definite NPs without using 'this'.

It seems that when teaching the use of such NPs we have to utter sentences like

(301)   This is an N.

where parts of the definite description appear in predicative position. The same holds for all reference-fixing acts, especially in the case of proper names. Since here the possibility of referring to a certain person with a proper name goes back historically to an act of fixing the reference we would come in the end to heavily indexical acts of uttering sentences such as

(302)   I baptize you with the name of. . .

Third, a more exotic problem. In his most "absolute" answer (297c) P1 makes reference to a certain time, and so this cannot necessarily be regarded as an equivalent for (297b) because one does not know whether one has to give a point of time or a period of time. And questions like 'How long does *now* last?' do not make much sense. So if P2 does not know what time it is now P1 cannot tell this to him. He can only utter trivialities like (299c). P2 has to go around with his own watch like all the inhabitants of this strange world. And their watches have to be extremely exact. One can only hope that their watches have and keep the same time and that they still manage t say something while staring ceaselessly at their watches.

After all, Quine's procedure may be adequate for certain technical usses, but it is not — and was not intended — for the description of ordinary languages. When transferred to ordinary language it resembles the premature standardizations which have been dealt with in 3.2. Therefore the program for semantics which consists in operating with so-called indexes containing several coordinates[39] and aiming at an integration of the historical context of the act by a reformulation in eternal sentences suffers from, at least, two deficiencies: (i) It is by no means sure that non-indexical descriptions may be found for the respective coordinates. Usually we find phrases like 'a 1962 Volkswagen' which is not non-indexical at all; (ii) These theories cannot explain or describe the rules of referring. Reformulation is regarded as an unexplained capacity of the semanticist who is able to pick out the relevant parts out of the historical context and knows what is meant by the speakers. Questions of how it can be known what P1 said by uttering S and other communicative problems are ignored. The superscholar has solved all this for himself since he has absolute command of the language.

That eliminating index words in the interests of semantic closure is premature standardization can also be observed if we look at the two basic conditions not discussed yet, (i) that the truth value of eternal sentences does not change and (ii) that their meaning does not change. Now even in the extreme case of an anlytical sentence like

(303)   The square root of 16 is 4.

one has to think about the meaning of 'is always true'. There may have been a time when the truth of a sentence like (303) was not known and the sentence even could not have been asserted. For the people of that time with their language it cannot have been true. In our language we use the sentence as if it were always true. We cannot imagine that something that is true may once have been untrue. Another doubtful example would be a future sentence: Was (292) already true in 1963? As everybody knows, answering this question in the affirmative can give rise to difficulties.[40] It presumes that the world is somehow determined, a strong presumption to start with in linguistic research.

It seems as if Quine intended to avoid such problems by the restriction that the language or the meaning must not change. If the truth value of an eternal sentence changes, the language or the meaning must have changed. If so, two questions which are important for us remain unanswered: (i) We do assume that what someone has said cannot change its truth value. But since we basically do not know the truth value but only think this to be true today and false tomorrow, such an assumption is optimistic in a certain way. If one assumes that the truth value is fixed once and for all one should rather concentrate upon what we think to be true; (ii) what someone assumes, asserts, etc. is only accessible for us by means of sentences and thus only by means of meanings. So if something that someone says is thought to be true today and false tomorrow, the stipulation of constancy of meaning only makes sense if the meaning is not affected by our judgement concerning the truth of what has been said. Accordingly the postulate of constancy of meaning

would not allow the change of the truth value to depend on the strength
of the relation between meaning and possible truth. But since we do change
our judgement of the truth, the postulate of constancy of meaning cannot
make sense.

For Quine's aims it may be appropriate to keep the problem of change
aside by postulating constancy of meaning. But then questions of how truth
values of eternal sentences can change, how the agents can have different
opinions about the truth of eternal sentences, and how such utterances are
related to changes of meaning, are ignored.

Let us turn now to the relationship of X and Y, i.e. CS and S. The representation we have used so far has illustrated that CS in ASS (CS) has a
status different from that of S in UTT (S). While S was mentioned, and
could be described in a relatively reliable way, CS gives rise to a general
problem of understanding. Since P1 only utters S and does not comment
upon his act, his partner P2 has to grasp the meaning of what P1 uttered, i.e.
he has to understand that P1 asserted CS by uttering S. This holds equally
for CS and for ASS itself. As for the relationship of CS to S there are two
extreme possibilities: (i) CS could be a translation for S, if the languages of
the partners were different, as for instance French and English in

(304)   ASS (that he is coming) → UTT (*Il vient*).

Though this case is not normal, it raises most of the questions arising in normal communication between partners of the same language. Since the competences of English-speaking partners are not completely identical, the problems
are here analogous to those of translation. However, speaking of translation
here too would not be a happy use of 'translation'. (ii) The other extreme
is to assume that the relation between CS and S is describable in purely syntactic terms, e.g., by transformation or by saying that S is a part of CS:

(305)

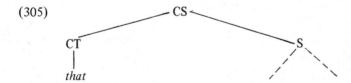

Often such an assumption would indeed be useful, e.g., if someone swears,
the wording of the oath will be decisive; likewise if someone asserts something.
But this rigidity only puts the communicative problem to one side, for P1
does not swear for himself. P1 does not assert anything for himself. And inas-

much as his act is part of a communication he depends on the understanding of a partner. Yet the assumption of the rigid relation might have a hygienic advantage, because it would always remind P2 of the fact that his interpretation can be doubted.

The assumption of a rigid relation as in (305) would involve certain problems, for example with the use of pronouns. If P1 orders with sentence (267), the corresponding generating pattern could be: ORD_1 (that I should not drink Coca Cola) hence the pronouns have to be changed. But this can only be done correctly by someone who understands (267). Besides, one should not introduce a one-one correspondence if one wants to describe the meaning of S by means of generations, if giving the various generations is intended to be a description of the meaning. Then it should be represented in the description that the same thing can be asserted with the utterance of (278) and that of (306):

(306)   I am the one who is laughing.

Of course, that this is not complete synonymy could be shown by an extensive description of the whole generation and of the possible embedding in communications, as well as by the necessary extension to more (all?) partners of a linguistic community and their consent as concerns this relation. I suppose that a number of transformations in generative theory have their place in the interrelation of X and Y. Maybe Y would belong to the surface structure and X to the deep structure. If this is true, the generative theory could be established within a more comprehensive theory of communication and the status of such transformations could be made clearer. And it could be shown that some problems of understanding would be suppressed in the theory if X is assumed to belong to a universal language, say an artificial logical language. On the other hand, the advantage of such a theory would be obvious if one could succeed in establishing a one-many correspondence between X and Y and in preventing it from becoming a many-many correspondence.

The problems left out in the two extreme possibilities of translation and transformation are, on the one hand, that the relation between CS and S does not in fact concern sentences (hence patterns) but the acts, and, on the other hand, that stating the relation is a third act, a kind of higher order act, in addition to the uttering of the sentence or the assertion of something. Since our partner's competence will never be completely known to us, we will have to assume that we can never determine the specification of a generating pattern for UTT(Y) with certainty. We can do so only as far as we have the same rules. But surely any approximation can be reached by explaining the explicit and implicit context. But this is a matter of communication itself.

The problem of understanding becomes even more complicated by the fact that he who describes is in the same position as P1 and P2: He can only explain his own understanding of UTT(S) by using a CS from his own language. This complication however, is caused rather by the fact that three people are in communication, so that P3 can make a description of what he thinks P1 said and then of what he believes P2 understood. Within the communicative application of practical semantics this problem disappears in part, because P2 and P3 are identical. If these considerations justify the sort of representation we have used so far, which was based on the assumption that the specification of ASS etc. does not occur as mentioned, because it is a complement clause used within the description, namely a complement clause of the language of the describing person, then we must accept that the problem of eliciting the appropriate CS is not only a problem of description but occurs as the main problem in every communication. To get an idea of the theoretical status of what we say and understand in its relation to what we utter and the practical consequences, as well, we have to give some sort of recursive analysis of 'communicate' which develops the places of meaning and understanding there

3.3.2 *Meaning and understanding*

When we deal with problems of communication we have to know to a certain extent what takes place in communication and how problems of communication may arise. A coherent view of communication is to be given by an analysis of the fundamental description which applies to every communication:

(307)   P1 communicates with P2.

In the course of this recursive analysis we shall touch upon fundamental problems of meaning and understanding and, at the same time, understand how they arise.

We begin developing the implications of (307) by giving a set of necessary, though not sufficient conditions for the truth of an assertion of instances of (307). The first condition is:

(i)   P1 acts.

Although this condition is not very illuminating since it includes all cases of action, it excludes some cases where people have thought that communication takes place. For instance the so-called axiom that one cannot not communicate is ruled out. If P1 is not doing anything and sitting in a room with P2 who thinks that P1 is indicating by his silence that he is angry or is rebuffing him, etc. then P1 will not have communicated because (i) is not fulfilled. Here P2 thinks that P1's not-doing anything is an act of omission, and if it really is, then P1 acted and we might have a case of communication. But the criterion for this is that P1 really did something and not only that P2 thinks so. Otherwise every agent would be dependent in his acts on the belief of one or more partners and it could happen that he would be rightly held responsible for something that he did not do. We have to bear in mind our principle (148) which states that not every case where P1 does not act positively is a negative act, an omission. For otherwise, when acting according to one pattern we should simultaneously omit to act according to all other existing patterns and hence perform an infinite number of acts.

Usually we would not say that always when P1 acts and P2 is present or concerned we have an instance of communication. We have to incorporate a more special condition implying (i):

(ii)   P1 acts symbolically.

and a third one imposed on P2:

(iii)   P2 understands P1.

But then, of course, it remains to be spelled out what it is to act symbolically. If we had a clear understanding of what a symbol is we could give as a first tentative explication that someone acts symbolically if he uses a symbol. When you are lost in the forest you may take a column of smoke as an indication of habitation or you may yourself produce smoke in order to make your presence known. Somebody looking out for you may see the smoke produced by you and take it as an indication of your presence. Now, communication is not involved in either case: the inhabitants would not have communicated with you and you would not have communicated with the person looking for you. But the reasons in the two cases are different: in the first, the inhabitants did not use the smoke as a symbol for their being there, and in the second, the searcher did not take the smoke as a symbol produced by you as a symbol. What is decisive here is not to define what we mean with the expression 'symbol' and its close relatives,[41] but to formulate what goes on in communication and to give the different conditions for the different cases.

The most clear-cut examples of communication are when P1 utters a linguistic sign. As we have seen at the beginning of 3.3.1, he must not always communicate by this but usually he does. The decisive characteristic here is that P1 means his uttering Y as something else. E.g., he means his utterance of Y as an assertion of X. If someone uttered something without meaning something he has not performed a symbolic act. All this obviously applies to cases other than those where linguistic signs are uttered. If P1 yawns in order to express ennui we would speak of a symbolic act as well. The characteristic here seems to be that he performs, so to say, an act of two patterns built in a complex pattern: he means his yawning as an expression of ennui. Therefore we introduce as the main feature of symbolic action the condition

(iv)   P1 means y as x.

where 'y' ranges over acts. In the special case where P1 utters a sign Y the act is his utterance of Y. Descriptions of this would be

(308)   P1 means his utterance of Y as x.
(309)   P1 means x with his utterance of Y.

Here somebody might object to this analysis because it replaces or explains unfamiliar or unclear expressions by other unfamiliar or unclear expressions. I do not take such objections too seriously because this is just the situation in which we must live. I can only give you other expressions for the expressions you do not understand or I can teach you their use. The essence of the analysis lies in the fact that this interrelation is developed and that one expression casts light on the other one.

   For the practical use of condition (iv) we have to scrutinize problems arising in everyday life with this condition. In order to do that we start by looking at the use of questions like

(310)   How did you mean this?

When we ask this we refer with 'this' to an act of P1 and therefore we must be able to identify this act, hence be able to assign it to a pattern, e.g. to HY. But this is not the whole story. We may, for example, want to know P1's motive or what P1 wanted to achieve by his act. We want to understand better what P1 did. Therefore P1 can answer our question (310) by uttering:

(311)   I meant it as an act of HX-ing.
(312)   I did it because S.
(313)   I intended to HX.
(314)   I wanted to bring it about that not-R.

All these answers seem to be related, insofar as we can understand them as pursuing the generation of P1's act, to the left thus giving more detailed knowledge of his act. In the case of (311) and (313) P1 tells P2 that he wanted to act according to HX → HY. In the case of (312) he gives the state of affairs before his act, implying that he acted in order to create a new state of affairs comprising not-S or having not-S as a consequence. Not-S is to be the result or consequence of his act and specifies its pattern because in most patterns results are built in. So if HS is a pattern with the result not-S, P1 says nothing other than that what he wanted to do was to act according to HS → HY. We are concerned with a kind of backward-looking motive here whereas in (314) we have a forward-looking motive because here the state of affairs aimed at is given.[42] Therefore with (314) P1 says only that he wanted to act according to HR → HY.

That P1 wanted to act according to HR → HY is, of course, no guarantee that he did so. Intending to do x is not yet doing x. Though the question (310) aims at the same answers as does

(315)   What did you intend?

it is not the same question. In my answer to (310) I would usually pursue the generation to the left, but the pattern to the left is SAY or patterns on a par with it. And here I can fail in different ways. But in meaning it as an act of HX-ing I cannot fail. In this we have a special trait of symbolic acts for only here does the question (310) apply. But as the answers (312) to (314) show, it plays a role here cognate to the role of questions about motives in general.

We continue our analysis of 'mean' by the differentiation of two cognate uses of 'mean' well known from other semantic theories.[43] The first use is exemplified by (316) and is the one in our condition (iv):

(316)   P1 means y as x (or x with y).

The second use of 'mean' is exemplified by

(317)   Y means Z.

From here on these are differentiated by writing the first — the one in (316) — with a capital. Differences between 'Mean' and 'mean' are: first, 'means' is a two-place predicate, 'Means' a three-place predicate. Subjects of 'Means' are names of agents such that P1 ranges over human beings. Subjects of 'means' are names of linguistic signs, hence signs between '. . .' or equivalent operators.

For this reason (318) is odd and (319) is normal:

(318)   What do you mean?

(319)   Whom/what do you Mean?

Similarly (320) and (321) are odd and (322) is normal:

(320)   What does Y in German Mean?

(321)   What does 'lazy' Mean in this text?

(322)   What does P1 Mean with 'lazy' in this text?

Second, Y in (317) and y in (316) do not range over the same objects. Mixing up these two kinds of objects would lead to a common ambiguity. The acts referred to with y are on the level of the *parole* whereas the Y stands for units of the *langue*. This is not to say that there is no relation between y and Y. Consider the special case where P1 uses a linguistic sign in his act y such that y is the utterance of Y. The formulation shows that use is made of the pattern here. Avoiding the ambiguity, we might find it more adequate to say (324) instead of (323):

(323)   What does Goethe's sentence Y mean?

(324)   What does Goethe Mean with the utterance of Y?

Sentences as units of the *langue* cannot be possessed or produced by individual agents. Though when speaking of Goethe's idiolect it would be correct to say:

(325)   What does Y mean in Goethe's competence?

From our analysis and formulation of condition (iv) it is clear that we have to write the 'mean' in (iv) with a capital and to concentrate now on this use. Analyses of what 'Mean' means have been given by Grice and Schiffer. I do not want to repeat and to discuss too much what has been said there. Where I differ from their opinion will, I hope, become clear through the present work. But I think that Grice and Schiffer concentrate too much on problems of meaning theory and do sometimes not pay attention to the use of 'Mean' in English. Since Grice and Schiffer are native speakers of English, I am aware that I could be wrong in my analysis because speakers need no evidence for what they say in their language. However, I want to draw attention to the fact that analysts are exposed to two dangers: The first is that they could be mistaken in their theoretical assumptions about what they say about their language. And the second is that in scrutinizing language to get a coherent theory about the use of expressions, one often overgeneralizes certain features and changes the language in the stream of theorizing just as we are always in the process of changing our own language. Grounds for both phenomena lie in the fact that we are apt to change our language in the way it seems useful to us and that our partners can easily grasp what we Mean in our transformed language.

From Schiffer's analysis one could get the impression that 'Mean' is an act-pattern although this is not clearly stated. Schiffer states only that if Seymour Meant something then it is most likely that Seymour did something.[44] Clearly this is not stating that Meaning something is doing something and there are in fact a lot of indications which show Meaning not to be an act-pattern. First of all you cannot order someone to Mean something:

(326)   *Mean y as x!

There is more evidence for this in the deviation of:

(327)   *For what purpose did you Mean x?
(328)   *How do you Mean y as x?
(329)   *Where do I Mean?

A corollary of (328) is that Meaning cannot generate act-patterns, whence the oddness of (330):

(330)   I Mean x by HY-ing.

Clearly a sentence like (330) is not deviant in every use, but it is if 'by' is understood in the sense of the *by*-relation of action theory.[45] A cognate phenomenon is that it is impossible to combine 'Mean' with manner adverbials whereas combination with sentence adverbials such as 'normally' etc. is possible.[46] Other pointers to the fact that 'Mean' is not an expression of an act-pattern are the following deviations:

(331)   *I am Meaning x.
(332)   *How long did it take to Mean x?

They exhibit the peculiar relations of Meaning with tense. 'Mean' is a static verb in the definition of Kenny since Meaning does not take time.[47] Nor is it possible to Mean for a long time or to Mean quickly. Therefore Meaning cannot be an activity since all activities are non-static.

The distinctions between Meaning and a related act-pattern can be shown in the special case of Meaning with the utterance of NP where NP is a part of a sentence uttered and is used to refer. E.g. we can talk, with the NP in

(333)   The king of France has retired,

of different persons and we can Mean different persons in different utterances of it. Therefore one says that one can refer to different objects with 'the king of France'. 'Refer' does not mean the same as 'denote'. For one talks of denoting in connection with signs, usually terms: a term P denotes an object O if and only if one can truly assert P of O. Since one has to refer to O in order to be able to truly assert something of O, referring is a precondition for denoting. There is an analogy between the subject of 'refer' and 'denote' on the one hand, and 'Mean' and 'mean' on the other hand, so that we have as a standard form for 'refer':

(334)   P1 refers with NP to O.

A further analogy between Meaning and referring is that (i) one can refer to the same object with different NP's, (ii) one can refer with one NP to different objects. E.g., one can refer to the king of France with 'he' as well as with 'the king of France' and in different utterances to different kings of France. The limit is set by the meaning of the NP. For usually one cannot refer with 'he' to a female person: "Usually" — this means that one in fact can do so if the historical context allows my partner to understand whom I am referring to, or if I am referring deviantly and my partner understands me all the same. There is one further difference to be dealt with: in the case described, Meaning and referring are quite different. I can Mean O but refer to Q, if I refer deviantly.

When one refers, a partner is somehow involved: referring is (i) an act-pattern REF and (ii) a linguistic act-pattern. For this reason Meaning is somehow the basis of referring. One really can refer deviantly or one can fail to refer, but one can neither Mean deviantly nor fail to Mean. One just Means what one Means. In Meaning I am not dependent on my partner: I Mean, first of all, just for myself, no matter whether I am understood or not.[48] Hence the deviation of

(335)   *P1 Meant to/for P2. . .

Since REF is an act-pattern, it will also generate other act-patterns: I can refer to O by pointing to O etc. But this does not apply to Meaning as we have seen with (330). As with all act-patterns, there are happiness-conditions for REF. In work on logical semantics it has been assumed that such a condition

118

is the existence of the object which is referred to. This could be accepted, if one knew exactly what 'existence' meant without bringing in normative restrictions such as Frege or Russell had in mind. At any rate, imagined objects would have to exist as well, because one can refer to imagined objects.[49] E.g., the referent of 'the green bottle' might only exist within a fairy-tale. We have to be careful not to mix up referring to imagined objects with failing to refer or deviant referring. Thus one can see from the famous NP 'the king of France' that one can refer even if there is no king of France.[50]

There is a widespread tendency to explain Meaning with the help of intending, which could turn out to be a very risky undertaking because the latter is unclear at least to the same degree as the former.[51] There seems however to be a chance for such an analysis since intending seems to be a *genus proximum* for Meaning in some cases. For example the questions

(336)   How did you intend y?
(337)   What did you intend with y?

are on a par with the question

(338)   How did you Mean y?

except that the latter applies only when presupposing that y was a symbolic act, where (336) and (337) apply to acts in general. In both cases direct answers develop the string of generation of the pattern of y to the left.[52]

The analogy between 'Mean' and 'intend' can be taken further. The deviation of the following examples show that 'intend' is like 'Mean' in not being an act-pattern:

(339)   *Intend y as x!
(340)   *Intend x!
(341)   *For what purpose did you intend x?
(342)   *How did you intend y as x?
(343)   *Where do you intend x?
(344)   *I intend x by HY-ing.

But the matter is more complicated. For example it is possible to use (341) and (344) without deviation when they are used to say that I intended to HX for the purpose of. . . or that I intended to HX by HY-ing. It is obvious that there are differences between 'intend y as x', 'intend something', 'intend to HX' which are relevant for the analysis.[53] Since it seems impossible to me to explain 'Mean' with 'intend', I do not want to give an analysis of 'intend' here which would have to start from considering the different objects of both verbs. I only want to point out some important differences between 'Mean' and 'intend'. In part this can be done by the rest of our deviant *Mean*-senten-ces, which are not absolutely deviant when 'intend' replaces 'Mean':

(345)   I am intending x.
(346)   How long did it take to intend x?
(347)   How long did you intend ..?

Another difference between 'Mean' and 'intend' is that Meaning accompanies, so to speak, the act of uttering and is not possible without it,[54] whereas in-tending can precede the act and is relatively autonomous. When I answer your question (337) with

(348)   I intended to HX by HY-ing.

it is not implied that I really did HX, I may have failed to do it. But, on the contrary, I cannot have failed to do what I Meant although P2 may not un-derstand what I Meant. Insofar as Meaning goes with the act, successful sym-bolic action is bound to Meaning.

An agent is relatively free in what he intends. He can intend to do nearly everything by HY-ing, although he cannot be sure that he will achieve it or it may not even be very sensible to intend something which is impossible or which he is very unlikely to be able to perform. On the other hand, since he is limited by the language game, he does not have anything like unconditioned freedom to Mean whatever he wants. If, for example, you encode sentences by replacing each word by a number, you can interpret a chain of numbers as a certain chain of words by decoding. But you need a lot of practice in the use of this symbolic system in order to be able to Mean something with the chain of numbers. A condition of arriving at Meaning something with '1 2 3' would be a use of this language independent of mere encoding and decoding. And even then you cannot Mean everything you want with the numbers be-cause they have a fixed meaning.

How is it then possible to Mean y as x? Since P1 is bound — as we have seen — to a language in his Meaning, the fact that he can Mean x with an ut-terance of Y seems to be closely related to the meaning of Y. The Meaning of the utterance of Y has to remain somehow within the scope of the mean-ing of Y. Since the meaning seems to be more general than the Meaning, one might assume that the Meaning is the product of restricting the meaning in a certain context. But how can this be accomplished? A widely given answer to this is that the Meaning results from the *langue*-context of the word or sentence in question. Just as it has been assumed that the meaning of a word would be restricted by the other words in the sentence.

During the controversy arising from this assumption in linguistic semantics, the question has often been discussed whether a word has meaning without context, that is without co-occurrent signs within a chain of the *langue*. Here, at least two questions are mixed up: The first is whether a word can be isolated at all, the second whether contexts alter the meaning of a word. The first question is not especially semantic. It can be answered as follows: We speak in sentences, and therefore the linguist should begin his work with sentences. But since the number of sentences is so large, we have to describe them by analysis. When analysing sentences one obtains parts, maybe words, which have existence only as parts of sentences and their meanings have existence only as contributions to the sentence meaning.

The statement that an isolated word has no meaning turns out to be superfluous. If one regards the meaning of a word as what we can achieve by it in communication, then an isolated word has no meaning in this sense since isolated words do not occur in communication. But since a word contributes to the meaning of a sentence, which alone can occur as an independent unit in communication, the meaning of a word must be defined as a potential contribution to the meaning of a sentence. Meaning in this sense can certainly be isolated in the linguistic description.

The second question now is: Can a word in different contexts make different contributions to the sentence meaning? In a certain sense this question can be answered straight away in the affirmative, namely if the word occurs in different syntactic positions or belongs to different syntactic categories. So we can render our second question more precise: Can a word in different contexts, without change of the syntactic category, make different contributions to the sentence meaning? Obviously this is assumed by those who say that the context alters the meaning. Let us assume that the meaning of a linguistic unit Y is B1 in the context C1, B2 in the context C2, etc. From this it follows that every linguistic unit can have an infinite number of meanings since the number of its contexts is infinite. For this reason such a concept of meaning is useless for linguistics.

If the meaning B of a linguistic unit is defined as its constant contribution to all possible contexts, the statement "the context restricts the meaning" becomes contradictory. Let B1 be the contribution of Y to C1, B2 to C2, Bn to Cn, then B has to be at least as special as any given Bi and it is impossible to obtain Bi from B by restriction. For one cannot restrict something special to get something less special.

The so-called contextual restriction has been discussed in particular in connection with cases of so-called polysemy which are of more systematic interest. We want to argue by means of an example that the restriction does not work here either:

(349)   He discovered a red seal.

It is said that 'seal' in this context may have two meanings: the first B1 = 'piece of wax', the second B2 = 'fish-eating sea animal'. In

(350)   I found the best seals at the circus.

'seal' can only mean B2. People talk of restricting or cancelling out the poly-semy by the context. Another kind of restriction of the meaning of 'seal' is said to take place in

(351)   My seal has got three young ones.

Here, too, only B2 is in question, and in particular female seals, that is from the set of seals only certain have been chosen. Against this the following arguments can be put forward: (i) If something is restricted here it is not the meaning of 'seal' as we understand it, otherwise I would have changed the meaning and hence the *langue*. (ii) It is unreasonable to distinguish two kinds of restrictions, for in

(352)   I bought a red seal.

'seal' would be restricted to all red things called seal. This could be under-stood as a cancelling out of a polysemy 1) 'red seal', 2) 'not red seal'. But that 'red seal' has the meaning 'red seal' is trivial. (iii) Adding further context gives reason to believe that the context actually does not cause a restriction of meaning:

(353)   I found the best seals at the circus. Among them the one John
          used at the signing of the Magna Charta.

There is no general correlation between the addition of context and the re-striction of meaning, and we cannot hope to explain the Meaning of an utter-ance of Y as a restricted meaning of Y.

Perhaps one could assume that a word has a meaning only as an isolated unit of the *langue*. As soon as it is within a context the meaning would be restricted to the Meaning. But this cannot be the relation between meaning and Meaning in our sense, either. For, since we only use words in contexts when speaking, we would never get to know the meaning but only the Meanings or the restricted meaning of a sign. But if we did not get to know the meaning we cannot know the Meaning. For one cannot restrict something which one does not know and thus obtain something which one does know.

The principal mistake in the theory of contextual restriction is the inadmissible reduction when it explains the relation between meaning and Meaning as abstraction or inversely as restriction, where in fact it is a matter of rule and the following of a rule. And this relation cannot, as we saw, be understood in such a way that the rule is an abstraction from instances of its being followed and even less from all such instances. We cannot go behind the relation of the rule to the following of the rule. But how is the rule involved in Meaning y as x? It is involved insofar as it is a condition for Meaning y as x that it is usual to Mean y as x in this situation, in other words that y counts as x. Here different parts of the rule enter the scene. First, what y is and what x is can only be known by assigning the acts to patterns. Second, the statement that y counts as x states that the pattern of the latter generates the pattern of the former. It describes one aspect of the rule.[55]

Returning to our analysis of (307), we may ask whether we have to incorprate y's counting as x into the set of conditions. But for this it seems too weak. Since, in order for P1 to communicate, it is not sufficient that y counts as x; P1 must know this. He cannot follow a rule which he does not know. On the other hand, incorporating the condition that P1 knows that y counts as x would go too far since it presupposes that the one who states this knows it too, and thus P1 would be dependent in his acts on the knowledge of an agent who describes his acts. This is the general difficulty which arises with the factive verb 'know', that it commits us to assert what is known by ourselves. So could we formulate the condition as follows: P1 believes that y counts as x? I think this would be falling into the other extreme since in ordinary speech this often implies that the one who asserts this does not believe it, i.e. he implies that P1 does not know it. The way out of this seems to be the formulation:

(v) P1 could honestly say: 'I know that y counts as x (in this situation)'.

This is rather clumsy but it does the job.[56] To avoid clumsiness I generally use 'believes' or 'knows' in the following and hope the reader will make the necessary qualifications.

Before having a look at our condition (iii), which we have disregarded so far, we have to add another condition on the P1-side. We are told by historians that in the *conquista* of Peru the *conquistadores* were obliged by the *requirimiento* to urge the native *indios,* before attacking them, to convert to Christianity and to submit themselves to the Spanish crown. The *conquistadores* discharged themselves of this duty by reading out the *requirimiento* in the middle of the night in front of the villagers' doors. Clearly, this was not a case of communication, because they did not want the *indios* to understand them. Therefore we have to add the condition:

(vi) P1 wants P2 to understand him,

by which we avoid accepting manipulation as an instance of communication.

Now we can pass over to the P2-side and go back to condition (iii). The formulation given in (iii) is patently too wide because understanding someone usually means that one considers his act as correct, even approves of it, or that one is in agreement with P2. Though this could turn out to be the right analysis, it seems to be asking too much here. A sufficient condition for a particular communication would be that P2 understands what P1 does or that P2 understands what P1 Means, e.g. that P1 Means y as x. Here 'Mean' and 'understand' correspond and this is reflected in several facts. First, 'understand' does not designate an act-pattern, just as little as 'Mean' does, though, unlike the latter, it passes several act and process tests:

    (354)   Understand y as x!
    (355)   I am understanding y as x.
    (356)   Suddenly, I understood y as x.

But it does not pass them all:

    (357)   *Where do I understand y as x?
    (358)   I understood y as x intentionally.

The sentence (358) is used to say that I really did not understand y as x but intentionally interpreted it as x although I understood it as something else: I faked. I think this can be explained by assuming two related uses of 'understand', one akin to the act-pattern INTERPRET and a second one decisive in communication.[57] (354) has to be understood as the request to interpret y as x, as for instance with our encoded sentence '1 2 3' where it must be understood as the key for interpretation. But what is done in decoding or interpreting is not normal understanding. Understanding happens to us, it is not done by us. We cannot even avoid understanding. Therefore P2, unlike P1, need not act in order to make an assertion of (307) true.

Second, we have a far-reaching symmetry of objects in the use of 'understand' and the use of 'Mean' such that we can bring out analogous standard-forms:

    (359)   P2 understands y as x.
    (360)   P2 understands the utterance of Y as x.

But 'understand' also covers 'mean', since the object of the latter may reappear as object of the former:

(361)   P2 understands Y.

In the case of communicating by uttering linguistic signs, P2 can understand that P1 Means x with his utterance of Y because P2 knows that the utterance of Y counts as x in that situation, i.e. because he knows the rule. But this is only one aspect of the affair. The condition for understanding need not always be that P2 knows that y counts as x, it is possible that P2 only knows that P1 knows or believes that y counts as x. This is to say that sometimes P2 believes that it is not a common rule which P1 is following but only that P1 thinks he is following a rule.

Of course, these formulations suffer from the same shortcomings as did condition (v). Since we would not be likely to assume that P2 in his understanding is dependent on the knowledge of a describing observer or partner, we formulate the two alternative conditions in the following way:

(vii)   P2 could honestly say: 'I know that y counts as x (in this situation)'.
(vii') P2 could honestly say: 'I know that (v)'.

These alternatives are not alternatives to be discussed theoretically with the aim of getting rid of one of them. They are alternatives which describe different ways of communicating in real life. Naive communication and sceptical communication – so we might baptize them – are the Scylla and Charybdis between which we have to sail in communication.[58] An optimistic or even naive P2 trusts in three things: (i) that P1 thinks he is in the same situation as P2 thinks he is in; (ii) that P1 would Mean with an utterance of Y the same as he would; (iii) that P1 assumes that P2 trusts in (i) and (ii). Hence this P2 assumes that P1 follows the same rule as he does. A reflective or sceptical P2, however, could have doubts about all this. And therefore sceptical communication may turn into mutism or psychotic communication. Primarily because of the last assumption: If P1 really assumes that P2 does not assume that P1 assumes that P2 trusts in (i) and (ii), then P1 will be disturbed in acting according to his own rules. He is likely to assume (i) that he must detect what the situation is for P2; (ii) that he must detect what P2 would Mean with the utterance of Y in this situation. In this way we enter into the infinite regress well known from competitive games, since P2 could always take P1's way out into account in his own considerations and the same holds for P1 and so on.

The cure for this is not naive communication, but reflective communication which is naive up to a certain point but pricks up its ears at misunderstandings. The central ability of a reflective P2 would be to detect when he misunderstands P1, a very difficult task indeed because (363) is implied by (359) as it is by (362), so that P2's experiences are not different when he understands what P1 Means and when he understands him differently:

(362)   P2 understands y as z.
(363)   P2 understands y.

This shows that P2 can understand y also in the case where he understands y as z. But then sometimes we would say that he misunderstands P1. 'Sometimes' here means that when we become aware of it and when we see consequences worth mentioning then we speak of misunderstanding. It is important to notice that misunderstanding is a special case of understanding and that both together are the contradictory of not-understanding.

Another problem could be seen in the question about criteria for the truth of (363). Though P2 can be sure whether he understands y or not because he has direct experience of his understanding, for somebody stating (363) it may be difficult to give the criteria. There is no objective referee who can decide on this because anybody else would be in the same position as P2 is, relying himself on his own understanding.[59]

Mostly we detect misunderstanding through the action of P2 when we see that he acts differently from the way we would have expected if he had understood y as x. Take the example of a request by P1 and assume that P2 is supposed to HX. If he HX-es then — we would say — P1 has perfect evidence that he was understood. The criterion for understanding is the common practice in which the communication is embedded. Understanding is a juncture for interaction. P1 can force P2 to act provided the latter understands, since he has either to HX or to omit to HX. Notice, however, that the fact that P2 HX-es is only a criterion for P1 if he, on his side, understands P2's act.

If P2 HX-ed he need not have grasped everything that P1 Meant. E.g., before fulfilling the request he may have reflected on the consequences of fulfilling it or not fulfilling it. He had to know what P1 was likely to do if he refrained from fulfilling it, i.e. he had to understand what a request is for P1, how strongly he Means it, etc. And for this he could only get evidence were he to refrain from acting. The dilemma for P2 is that, since he cannot fulfill the request and refrain from it at the same time, he needs some precedent, which is never absolutely reliable because it is never certain that it is the exact precedent.

This problem of understanding can be demonstrated with conditions as another part of the rule: it appears with (vii) and (vii') in the phrase 'in this situation'. As an example I choose ironic communication where, on the classical definition, P1 Means y as something different from what he usually would Mean (in most cases the contrary), e.g. uttering 'John is a fine fellow' but Meaning that he is not a fine fellow at all. Since this is a case of communication the general conditions for communication must hold, in particular that P1 Means with his utterance of Y that John is not a fine fellow at all and that P2 understands it as this. In addition, the conditions that P1 could honestly say 'I know that y counts as saying that John is not a fine fellow at all in this situation' and that P2 could honestly say that he knew this must hold.

And since ironic communication is a special case of communication, further conditions must hold. The most important of them seems to me that it is part of the situation as conceived by P1 that P1 does not believe that John is a fine fellow. In order to understand y correctly, P2 now has to recognize that this. But where can he know this from? It is not made explicit in the communication. It is a kind of activated belief which must be recognized by P2 in order to understand what P1 Meant. Although we would speak of misunderstanding here if P2 did not recognize this, the example suggests that the parts of history and knowledge activated on each side always differ somewhat and that this is one reason for the fact that perfect understanding is impossible. The reason for this is that both partners may judge the situation differently, as belonging to different types of situations, depending on their rules (for doing this) and on their knowledge of history.

Before tracing back the problem of common knowledge and assumptions, we shall extract one more condition for communication from our example of ironic communication. If the conditions that P1 does not believe that John is a fine fellow and that P2 knows this are fulfilled, we have not necessarily got an instance of ironic communication before us; it might be a detected lie.[60] Ironic communication requires that P1 knows that P2 knows that P1 does not believe that. . . (John is a fine fellow). Combined with condition (vi) this leads us to the assumption that P2 has to have or to recognize this knowledge of P1 and to the condition for communication in general that
(viii) P2 recognizes that (vi).

If in (ironic) communication P2 does not recognize that P1 knows that P2 knows that P1 does not believe that. . . then we would say that condition (viii) is not fulfilled although P2 believes it to be fulfilled. He will understand P1's act as a detected lie. And since this would be a (possibly unnoticed) misunderstanding, the communication would not have been a successful communication (for us, who know that condition (viii) is not fulfilled, *ex hypothesi*). Misunderstanding is only noticed if it is noticed that something has gone wrong or, to speak as we did in 3.2, if dissonance is felt. This could also be the case when P1 asserted something that P2 does not hold to be true, as will be seen in the next section.

We have assumed that perfect understanding is really not possible. One reason for this is that it is impossible for P2 to know or to recognize just the relevant parts of the historical context, i.e. the condition-fulfilling parts which are held relevant by P1. Perhaps the situation is such that condition (vii) never obtains and we are always in position (vii') so that we can never rely on complete resemblance of our rules. How could this unfortunate situation be explained? It simply arises from the fact that our rules grow up in history and that the historical contexts of two person's learning and following a rule are never identical.

The meaning of Y is that of which nearly *all* members of a group could honestly say 'I know that y counts as x'. But we have to emphasize that meaning in this sense is a sedimentation of what people have Meant and that our analysis of communication provides for the possibility of Meaning in a productive manner and of changing the meaning of the expressions in a language.[61]

The point is not to concentrate overmuch on the case where what I Mean lies within a given framework of idealized meanings but, rather, to turn to the creative aspect of understanding and ask how I can possibly come closer to what P1 Means, i.e. how I can come to a better understanding.[62]

Here some people would object that understanding, like truth, cannot be divided or graded: What is only half true, is untrue and what is only half understood, is not understood at all. So far, so good. But if you adhere to this position you must also claim that there is no understanding and no successful communication and you are in conflict with our normal attitude to understanding where it seems perfectly clear that we can improve our understanding.

But how can this be achieved? There is a method, wide-spread in literary criticism, for understanding a text better: you have to analyze the meaning of Y, perhaps you consider the historical development of the meaning of Y. This may sometimes lead to a better understanding of what P1 Meant in uttering Y, for it can cast some light on the use P1 makes of Y, on his rule and on the genesis of the sedimentary Y. But obviously this is working too much on the lines of condition (vii). If you want to understand P1 better you have to be open to beliefs and assumptions of your partner's that differ from your own — and, in order to achieve this, you have to be ready to challenge your own beliefs and assumptions—and you must try to find out the relevant beliefs and assumptions of your partner. For this you have to inquire into the personal history of P1. Sometimes knowing something about P1's acquisition of his rule will do, sometimes you have to get some precedent, you have to remember some occasion where P1 acted in such and such a way.[63] Clearly

128

you cannot do this without rules, you must always go back to your own rules but you have the possibility of observing and learning new rules and of changing your own rules.

Here we also see the innovative aspect of Meaning. Every agent has a licence to deviate from rules, e.g. in order to propose a new rule by his act. One limitation he is subject to is that he can hope to be understood, i.e. that his partner can grasp his use and the new rule. Another limitation would be that his own history will not allow him to Mean anything whatsoever with some act.

Bearing in mind some of the important reformulations discussed above, we can summarize our analysis by giving the following set of necessary conditions for (307):

(i)   P1 acts.
(ii)   P1 acts symbolically.
(iii) P2 understands y.
(iv)   P1 Means y as x.
(v)   P1 could honestly say: 'I know that y counts as x (in this situation)'.
(vi)   P1 wants P2 to understand y.
(vii) P2 could honestly say: 'I know that y counts as z (in this situation)'.
(vii') P2 could honestly say: 'I know that P1 could honestly say: 'I know that y counts as z (in this situation)''.
(viii) P2 recognizes that (vi).

3.3.3 *Meaning and truth*

The connection between the topics of this section might be seen less easily than that between the corresponding pair 'meaning' and 'understanding'. People acquainted with theories of logical semantics, however, will be familiar with treating meaning and truth together as it is done in a theory which says that to know the meaning of a sentence is to know what would be the case if it were true. This seems to be the point of the old neopositivistic assumption that meaning is the method of verification as it is of the approach derived from Tarski's definition of truth which applies to semantics by way of

(364)   S is true if and only if p,

where 'S' is a variable for names of sentences, i.e. quoted sentences, and 'p' for the corresponding sentence itself, yielding the trivial-sounding result:

'Snow is white' is true if and only if snow is white. The apparent triviality of this account as a semantic method for the description of natural language may partly disappear if we have a closer view as to how it can be used in communication, e.g. in order to verify something asserted by a speaker. But before doing this we have to point to some defects which — at least partially — can be remedied within practical semantics.

First, theories based on the slogan "No semantics without truth conditions" are too narrow because they can only deal with declarative sentences when they are used to make assertions and therefore could only be considered as one component of a theory based on the slogan "No semantics without use conditions". If a sentence is e.g. used to give a definition, there is no sense in speaking of truth conditions since it is stipulated that what is said is true. This is one reason for assuming that truth conditions do not go with sentences but at best with generations of the form 'ASS(CS) → UTT(S)'.

Second, if a theory of linguistic action has to start from basic generations as we treated them in 3.3.1, questions of truth do not apply to the S-level but rather to the CS-level, since normally we do not speak of the truth of a sentence in a language but of the truth of what someone asserts, believes, says, etc. If this is correct, debating whether what someone asserted is true only makes sense if what has been asserted is understood.

Third, from this, problems with indexical sentences have originated, and have led some people to try to get rid of them: A linguist willing to describe the meaning of (291) by stating

(365)   'I hear a noise' is true if and only if I hear a noise.

would provide us with a very strange theory of meaning since the meaning of (291) should not be thought of as dependent on the semanticist's hearing a noise. This does not show that an account in the form of object- and metalanguage is not adequate but suggests that reference plays a part in truth conditions. When I comment on the truth of what someone asserted I have to understand what he referred to and when I give truth-functional relations between sentences I must account for the rules of referring.

Some of these points may be exemplified by a pseudo-juridical case where in the court testimony it is said that

(366)   The defendant was insulted by the victim.

Since not too much is known about the story of the criminal act except that Mrs. Mellow flogged Mr. Jones, the judge P2 wants to find out whether what the witness P1 says is true. Could this be the motive for Mrs. Mellow deed?

In order to worm this out of P1 the judge asks him whether Jones did this before the flogging or after it. P1 seems embarrassed by this question and he points out that he did not assert that Jones did this but the victim, who was Jones' brother. This considerably diminishes P2's interest in the verification of the assertion of (366). Nevertheless, he wants to find out whether it was actually the case. Perhaps the belief was justified that P1 related (366) because it had something to do with the case. So he continues by asking how Mrs. Mellow was insulted and is informed that

(367)   The victim said: "Your father is a duck."

When asked how he knows this, P1 answers:

(368)   I heard the victim saying: "Your father is a duck".

This is interesting because it requires an ear-witness; it could be doubtful whether 'is a duck' or 'is a dog', etc. is what was said. But seeing is here what would be decisive: it is crucial that the defendant was the one insulted and this is only the case if he was the addressee of the utterance. Therefore the judge asks to whom the victim referred and P1 answers:

(369)   The victim addressed his utterance to the defendant.

Here we may stop the story. We are now in a position to discuss some of the problems in the area of the topic of truth conditions. From the first misunderstanding we learn that when the question of truth is to be settled, then one must first get the references clear. Here various problems may arise, e.g. the partners may not know the same things (in our example the judge did not know that Mrs. Mellow was only punishing Jones for tormenting his brother and therefore cannot understand the act of referring as it was Meant) or P1 could use an NP differently from P2, e.g. P1 could refer with the 'defendant' to the lawyer defending Mrs. Mellow. Surely, then, he would refer deviantly, but there are many cases where reference to different people or things is possible without deviation, e.g. many people refer with 'Champagne' to Californian sparkling wine.
When references are clear, scrutinizing the necessary conditions may begin. For an assertion of (366) to be true it seems to be sufficient according to P1's competence that (367). I am not sure if this would be the criterion the judge would apply or accept. Perhaps he will reject this because you cannot insult somebody by saying something about his father. If this is correct then searching for truth conditions or implications is something which is done to find out

what people can Mean with the utterance of a sentence, to find out something about their rules, and here no rule of use is privileged. Of course, in court what P1 said may turn out to be irrelevant when it is correctly understood but this is not to say that he did not use the sentence correctly.

The standardized use of 'insult' in the jurist's language is only one among others and need not be the basic one (even if the pretense is often maintained). At any rate, P1 is in good company with his use of 'insult': there is an interesting article about ritual insults by W. Labov where 'insult' is used in this way.[64]

So questions of truth and questions of meaning are closely related: if P1 and P2 dispute about the truth of what was said, this actually only makes sense when P2 understands what P1 Meant, since if P1 Meant Y as X and P2 understood it as Z there would be no reason for dispute because P1 thinks X to be true and P2 thinks Z to be false, and $X \neq Z$. On the other hand, if P2 understands just what P1 Meant it would be astonishing if one of them were to think what was said was true and the other to think it was not, at least if both have the same understanding of 'true'.

People working with truth conditions and verification often seem to assume that they could arrive by this method at sentences which would be easily verifiable by scientific methods, e.g. the so-called *Protokollsätze*. Our example yields a good argument against a generalized assumption of this: What the victim uttered could be crucial for deciding the question whether (366) was true or not. But there is — so far — no physical method or machine capable of rewriting what was uttered into a phonematic representation. Only one who is master of the phonematic rules of the language can decide what was uttered. He must have mastered the phonematic oppositions and contrasts to be capable of deciding whether it was 'duck', 'dog', 'tug', 'doc', or 'dock' that the victim uttered.

Though the insult example serves to illustrate the methods of practical semantics and its application in everyday or someday life and how the Meaning of what someone has uttered may be got at, it does not solve the problem of truth. Perhaps by giving truth conditions one arrives at propositions where truth can be more easily decided upon or where truth is more likely, but this is not a solution of the connection between truth and meaning. The status of the implied sentences is not different from the status of the original sentences and the truth of one assertion cannot consist of the truth of other assertions. This is not the way out: we had to discuss the truth of (367), (368) and (369) in the same way. Neither could one explain how anybody could learn the meaning of (366) if in order to manage this he first had to learn the meaning of (367), (368), and so on.

Though our example gave an impression of how truth conditions may be related to meaning and to what was Meant it does not really show what truth consists of. To clarify this question we can advance by considering what we can say about truth and on what occasions we speak of truth. The basic form of sentences usually uttered when the truth of something is discussed is

(370)   CS is true.

Scrutinizing this sentence-form is promising, because here we are walking on firm and familiar linguistic ground and so are in a better position to avoid missing the point of the problem, which is not the case with the form (364) where 'is true' is considered as a predicate of the metalanguage,[65] thus introducing a host of technical problems and solutions which cannot be considered as communicative problems and solutions for communicative problems. However, sentences of the form (370) and sentences akin to it are usually used when the question of truth crops up and therefore could give us a fundamentally misleading picture of the role of truth because most often the predicate 'is true' is, in some way or other, built into other expressions such as 'believe', 'right', etc. or such innocent looking and familiar acts as those of ASS, AGREE, etc. To get a clearer view of this I shall proceed in two steps: First, we shall consider the communicative methods we follow when the question of truth arises by going back to our insult example; second, we shall develop out of these considerations the important role which is played by tacit truth as the ground of common action.

There is a well-known *dictum* about the relation of 'is true' to ASS in logical semantics[66] which says that 'is true' adds nothing to the assertion. Sentences such as

(371)   Mao shines in our hearts.
(372)   It is true that Mao shines in our hearts.

are said to be synonymous, or in a weaker version:[67] If one asserts (371) one asserts the same as when one asserts (372). This seems to be correct as far as truth conditions are concerned but does not take into consideration the fact that both sentences have basically different uses: e.g. (371) can be used as an answer to the questions:

(373)   Who shines in our hearts?
(374)   Does Mao shine in our hearts?

which (372) cannot. (372) is only used in contexts where something is uncertain or is open to question. Consider the curious effect of a story in which every sentence begins 'it is true that'. Oddness may arise from the fact that the ordinary narrator does not always claim the truth of what he relates and does not even want the question of truth to be raised in the normal sense.

A good narrator would not constantly insinuate that the truth of what he relates has been questioned. The conspicuous use of sentences of the form (370) and of their negations is to corroborate, to confirm, to deny, to contradict, etc. and all this will only be done when truth is at issue. In this sort of communication sheer corroboration, etc. will usually not do. People require verification, e.g. in the way illustrated by our insult example, intended not as a method of improving understanding, but as a means of deciding about the truth of what is at issue. And this is required for CS and its implications as well.

A wide-spread view on the matter of meaning and truth is expressed in a quotation from Danto:[68] "To know what a sentence *means* demands only the powers the mastery of language engages, but to know which of the sentences we understand are *true* (or bear the positive semantical value for sentences) demands a turn from language to the world, and calls upon other powers." So, for the truth of a CS you have to look at the facts because

(375)   CS is true if it corresponds to the facts.

Obviously this goes too far, for we do not want to assume that CS would have to correspond to all the facts. Rather, we think that there is exactly one fact that secures the truth of CS and therefore we must give preference to (376) rather than (375):

(376)   CS is true if CS is a fact.

Here we have arrived at another point of contact between language and the world. For facts are part of the world (or are the world), and sentences provide us with our only access to what can be true or false. Certainly we do not assume that facts exist only because of our sentences; what is true is true, no matter whether we know or say it. Only if we realize facts or talk about them do we need complement clauses which we insert for CS. And presumably it is just those facts that are important. But is (376) really an explanation that leads us further? Hardly. For the relation between 'true' and 'fact' is so close that one cannot explain the one with the other: (i) (376) already includes the same CS on both sides. This also becomes evident in 'it is true that. . .' and 'the fact that. . .' where exactly the same *that*-clauses may appear. (ii) 'true' is already included in 'fact' so that one can strengthen (376) to:

(377)   CS is true if and only if CS is a fact.

Thus it is clear that one cannot give an explanation of 'is true' in this way.[69]

A different interpretation of (376) is based upon the assumption that facts, in one way or other, are of a different nature than propositions: The truth of a proposition would lie in its correspondence with a fact. But if both are of a different nature they certainly cannot totally correspond, and if only some of their properties or parts are to correspond such properties or parts would have to be isolated first of all. Which parts could these be? The criterion for their choice, which is necessary to decide whether the proposition is in accordance with a fact or not, remains in the dark.[70]

Therefore we have to give up the misleading picture representing truth as the missing link between language and the world. Language, truth, and the world are not separated in the simple way assumed in this theory. It is not sufficient simply to look at the world in order to give an answer to the question 'Is CS true? '; I have to know where I must look, how I must look, what I need to see in order to decide, etc. All this is part of my ability to follow the rule of the sentence just as the method of verification is part of the language game because we do these things, in our form of life, in order to verify something, and what counts as a verification is determined by our rules. So, we should not engage in the discussion of some absolute or philosophical truth but continue the discussion from a communicative point of view.

As I have stated, analyzing only the use of the explicit 'is true' may be misleading about the general question of truth since 'is true' is built into many other expressions. I want to consider some of them briefly. From our Mao example we got one relation between 'assert' and 'true' which was that if someone asserts that CS is true he asserts CS, where 'assert' is used in a very wide sense including corroboration, confirmation, etc. But we all know that from neither of these CS follows: it could have been falsely asserted. Only when CS is truly asserted does CS follow from the assertion of CS. So we want to look a little closer at 'assert CS truly'. This is patently the designation of a specified act-pattern and it is a subpattern of ASS (CS). Unfortunately, it seems that true assertions cannot be considered as the only real assertions where all happiness conditions are fulfilled without the argument becoming circular, since we had to adopt CS as a condition for this pattern. Nevertheless it might be an advance to get the CS into the condition, because then the coherence of truth with action becomes clearer and, at the same time, the relation between 'true' and 'right', which is the predicate for evaluating acts and could eventually come out to be prior to 'true'; this hypothesis is also supported by the fact that in language acquisition we learn first the notions of right and wrong and later those of true and false, a fact which is mirrored in the fact that children learn the forbidding use of 'no' before the denying use.

So, is it a condition for asserting CS that one believes CS to be true, which would lead us indirectly to the truth of CS? Not at all, since one can assert CS and all the same not believe CS if one is insincere. But what would be the indirect way to CS from 'P1 believes CS'? Normally, in the first person, when I believe something I believe it to be true. It is impossible for me to assume not-CS and believe CS. That is what is so striking about Moore's paradox 'It is raining but I don't believe it'; someone who hears this could only assume that the speaker is so mistaken that he is not employing the words in their normal sense or that he is being so obviously insincere that nobody could believe him. But from my believing CS it does not follow CS. Even if all the people I know believe CS then CS would not follow. And if someone were to ask me if not-CS were possible I would answer in the affirmative but add that I see no reason to doubt it. Everything or nearly everything speaks for CS, and nothing, or very little, speaks against it.

This reduces the value of the question whether CS is true in the absolute sense considerably and makes us turn our eyes from absolute truth to the things we are convinced of. We easily fail to notice that we are never concerned with the naked sentence or the naked proposition but always with the asserted, believed, etc. proposition.

This accords with our basic form (370) as well as with the fact that CS appears in a condition of an act where it is only part of an if-then-assertion and within the range of ASS. I think that this is one reason why there cannot be some sort of absolute truth independent of action or mental activity. Here is the place of the prominent role of ASS: it does not function simply as a way of telling the truth but rather for an agent who wants a partner to believe the asserted CS.

It is just for this reason that contradicting is a reasonable response when one believes not-CS. Then the interesting case is present where we want to find out whether CS is true or want to argue about it. Truth results from argumentation and from action in general. And although statements about the genesis of truth are not equivalent to statements about what truth is, the invariably essentialist answers to the latter question invariably prevent us from seeing the importance of the former question.

So I want to concentrate now on the function of truth in interaction and in communication in order to show that here not absolute truth is decisive but rather what the partners believe to be true or what they believe is commonly believed to be true. Let us begin with an example of action in general: Jones' buying gold. One condition for a true assertion of

(378)   Jones bought some gold.

is that

(379)   There was some gold.

But is the sublime or absolute truth in play here? I don't think so. If somebody, say Jones after buying the gold, were to verify that it was not gold but
only fool's gold that he had bought, nobody who knew this would then say
that Jones bought gold, the reason being that what he bought was not gold.
But anyone who does not know this could honestly assert that (378). Only
I, who know that it was not gold, know also that this assertion could not be
true. But usually we are not in the situation where one can be sure of having
knowledge of absolute truth. We only assume that what is true could be
otherwise or will possibly become otherwise in the future. As long as we do
not know that it is false we have every right to say that we truly asserted that
(378), notwithstanding the fact that in the near or distant future it will turn
out to be different. If knowledge is as crucial as is suggested here, we possibly
have to differentiate between knowledge of the agent and knowledge of the
partner, e.g. one who describes P1's act. It seems to be sufficient for Jones'
act that he believed that it was gold that he bought. But this is apparently
not the case since he may be mistaken without noticing it. All seems to be in
order if we assume as the condition for (378) that

(380)   Jones knew that there was some gold.

which presupposes (379). But would this not be too strong, as was condition
(vi) in 3.3.2? In some respects it is, since other people cannot be dependent
in their acts on what I know. This can be illustrated by considering members
of other, e.g. primitive, societies who presuppose in their acts that there are
witches influencing the members of the society.[71] But the remedy cannot be
a formulation like the one we gave in 3.3.2. It is not sufficient that Jones
could honestly say 'I know that there was some gold' since if he could and
there was no gold, he just could not have acted as (378) would have us believe. Truth and action, not even in the degree of Meaning, are not subjective.
An error or a misbelief concerning the condition for acting according to a
pattern has the consequence that the act could not be performed.

Now assume the following course of events: Jones bought some gold which
he knows to have been treated by an old alchemist. It is real gold and everybody holds it to be real gold. One day it turns out to have an atomic weight
not that of normal gold. What then? Would we say that it is another kind of
gold and maintain (378) or would we say that it was not real gold and refute
(378)? In my opinion it could continue in both ways but without further

qualifications we would say that it was not real gold. So is atomic weight the decisive criterion? No. We could discover one day that we are mistaken in our assumptions that gold has the atomic weight 197.2 and then we would continue to take this metal as gold. It would remain gold just as it was before anybody knew the atomic weight.

This suggests that certain features decisive for something being gold at one time may not be decisive at another time. Therefore a semantic theory based on the definition or description by *genus et differentia* could not handle this case.

We have seen something of the role of knowledge or belief in communication when discussing the conditions (v) and (vii) in 3.3.2 where it was explained how P1 could Mean y as x in this situation and how P2 could understand y as x in this situation. In naive communication and in naive theories of communication it is assumed that both partners follow the same rules and evaluate the situation analogously and that therefore understanding is secured or it is even assumed that the truth of certain propositions and knowledge of them is crucial for communication. In contrast to this, it seems necessary to me to reflect on the role of knowledge and belief in understanding communicative acts.

Let us imagine another example: Our P1, say Jones, is sitting at the table with his wife P2 Claire and is uttering:

(381)   You prepared tournedos Rossini.

As what could he have Meant his utterance of (381) in this situation? An answer to this depends largely on what P1 believes and an understanding of his act depends widely on the P2-side knowledge. Jones, who is a great admirer of tournedos Rossini made with real goose liver knows that his wife knows this but he also remembers that she prepared tournedos Rossini for him once before made with *mousse de foie gras*. From this he concluded this was her mode of cooking it and (i) P1 does not like P2 to prepare tournedos Rossini. Therefore he could have Meant his utterance of (381) as a reproach if another condition were to hold, namely that (ii) P1 believes that P2 knows that (i).

Otherwise he cannot reasonably hope that Claire could understand the utterance of (381) as a reproach. Claire, on the other hand, knows that Jones is an admirer of tournedos Rossini because he often told her of the old times in France when he savoured succulent and tender tournedos Rossini. Therefore (iii) P2 believes that P1 is pleased by her preparing tournedos Rossini. And since it also holds true that (iv) P2 believes that P1 recognizes that (iii), Claire understands Jones' utterance (381) as praise. We have an instance of misunderstanding which is due to the differing views of the situation. These problems do not arise and cannot be solved by remarking that both partners may be mistaken in their beliefs and that mistaken belief is the reason for misunderstanding. It is only our description which insinuates that there is an objective standpoint of one who knows everything that is said here. But even the omniscient observer is subject to the vagaries of belief; he has no knowledge guaranteeing absolute truth in these matters. Neither could the problem be solved by the remark that both partners make a different use of 'tournedos Rossini', which is correct, but is only another way of stating the misunderstanding.

If the theorist — as a third partner — enters on the scene, raises the question of how tournedos Rossini ought really to be prepared and gives a widely accepted answer to this, he may settle the problem, but what he has done, among other things, is to teach his own language to the partners. And if I were Jones I would show this theorist that his question was a silly one, the question of somebody who does not know very much about cooking.

Let us draw some general consequences from the example. If we include in a situation everything which is the case at a certain time, and if we assume that no agent is omniscient and knows everything that is the case, we must concentrate on the situation as P1 conceives it, which is all that P1 believes to be true at this time. This includes both past and present and future events which he expects. If we describe the situation in which communication takes place we formulate it in terms of what the partners believe, i.e. we assert that certain things are the case. To describe the communication we would say: P1 believes that the tournedos are made with *mousse de foie* but he himself would say that the tournedos are made with *mousse de foie*. Nonetheless our own assertions within the description of a factual communication do not have a different status from the belief of P1 or P2. They are only assertions claimed to be true but not of absolute truth. If the partners in a communication want to come to a better understanding they must come to a better knowledge of what their partner believes and not — as we, counterfactually, mostly do — assume that they have enough knowledge in common. E.g. Jones appears very careless. He knows from precedent that (iii) and, since there is no counterevidence to (iv), together with (i) he must realize that something must go wrong with his act; he performs it in full knowledge of its ambivalence and of the resulting misunderstanding on P2's side. Perhaps he puts up with the misunderstanding, he does not want to hurt Claire's feelings. But he must fear repetition or that he must give up his standard for tournedos Rossini.

One reason for the fact that perfect understanding is impossible is that there are no two agents who believe exactly the same things or who have exactly the same knowledge. Another reason would be that having exactly the same knowledge may not secure perfect understanding. Up to now in our formulations of belief-conditions we have not made clear how 'believe' is to be understood here. Usually we use the verb as an expression for a state of the mind which e.g. survives sleeping. Therefore it is not reasonable to say that believing stops or that I do not believe what I believe during sleep. We do not recapitulate the things we believe every moment and that's why the formulations given up to now are not precisely given. Although 'believe' is less static than 'know', which allows no progressive form and reacts positively to nearly all static verb tests, it is too static to formulate these conditions precisely. It is not sufficient that P1 and P2 know or believe the things we postulated but that both have them in mind at the respective moment.[72]

If P1 acts in a certain way he appeals to the relevant conditions for his act and he must trust that his partner can pick out the relevant conditions; this is another source of the impossibility of perfect understanding: It is impossible for P2 to be aware of just those parts of the historical context which are held to be relevant by P1.

I hope that this discussion has shown the value of common knowledge for action in general and especially for communication: perfect understanding could only be possible if exact common knowledge existed and communicative acts are only understood as far as relevant common knowledge goes. Though I do not want to give a definition of common knowledge, I want to point to the fact that there could be different types of belief-conditions ranging from knowledge of a historical fact, e.g. of the biography of one of the partners, to the implicit common knowledge which defines the form of life of a society. This knowledge of mine does not consist of propositions once verified in a so-called scientific manner but is socially derived: my parents, my teachers, and my friends handed it on to me and I believed it. It is the most certain sort of knowledge for me because it was never verified and never questioned. I have not been told that my hands won't disappear while I am sleeping but I rely upon it constantly.

3.3.4 *Illocutionary and perlocutionary patterns*

The connection between linguistic action and action in general lies not only in the fact that speaking is also action, that speaking consists in uttering sentences, hence in acting in accordance with to certain patterns, and that, besides mere uttering, there are such speech acts as asserting, describing, and arguing. The relation between the two in its entirety is likely to become clearer if we consider the position of communicative acts within the rest of action.

When accepting the fact that the rules of action probably cannot be learnt without language, we have already supposed an influence of speech upon action in general, an influence in one direction. One can silently understand acts, but whether acts can be understood without any language is dubious; it does not even make sense to ask such a question. For how could this be decided? We do interpret the acts of a child who cannot speak (for we have a language), but does the child act with the intentions we attribute to him? Every theory of action, then, depends upon a theory of meaning.

As to the influence in the opposite direction, we already find a close connection in those relatively action-free ways of using language upon which linguists have concentrated most of their efforts in the past. E.g. when P1 tells P2 what he saw on holiday in Italy and P2 listens quietly mumbling affirmatively every now and then, etc. Here there is indeed no direct action involved; still there may be consequences involving actions. P2 herself will be on her guard against the papagalli in Italy, etc.

In the following I want to discuss in a somewhat more systematic framework three typical examples which illustrate the relation of speaking to acting. A classification may be given of the occurrence of act-patterns in partitions and generations as follows.

There are act-patterns in the partitions and generations of which (i) only non-linguistic patterns occur; (ii) linguistic and non-linguistic pattern occur, where UTT (Y) is taken as a paradigm for a linguistic act-pattern; (iii) only linguistic act-patterns occur. Since I see no reason for counting act-patterns of type (i) as linguistic act-patterns and I do not know of any example where someone has asserted this, let us begin with an order ORD which seems to be of type (ii) and where action is involved in a twofold way: first, because of the act which the partner is to perform as a reaction to the order, second, because of the reference made to this act in the imperative sentence.

The shortest possible order interaction could, then, have the following form:

(382) ORD_1 (CS) † HX_2,

where CS is such that the pattern HX is included in it. For a syntactic analysis we might have:

(383)

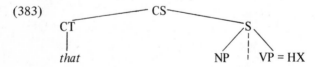

A condition for an adequate reaction by P2 is that he understands what P1 wants him to do. For this purpose he must understand the CS and know what it means to act according to HX. We should understand 'understand' so broadly that P2 could also act according to -HX if he has understood P1. For omitting HX presupposes, according to our definition, that P2 has understood what has to be done. Thus, understanding really leaves the partner alternatives and is different from the case where an act is a causal or conditioned response to understanding. The examples make it clear that understanding can only be guaranteed by common practice. The unconcerned observer renounces understanding, common action, from the beginning. But this does not mean that some sort of perfect and sublime understanding is required either: P2 may very well have understood something different, e.g. he might think that P1 has asked a question. This is uninteresting for P1 as long as P2 acts as he expected him to, say according to HX.

Our second type (ii) example, for the link between linguistic action and action in general, is those act-patterns which are, amazingly enough, not usually regarded as linguistic although they can generate linguistic patterns. An example of this would be

(384)   OFFEND → UTT (*idiot*)

That OFFEND is regarded as a non-linguistic pattern seems to amount to saying that not only linguistic patterns occur in its generation. For I can also offend somebody with gestures.

Our third example, which illustrates type (iii), is the best-known example of the relation between linguistic action and action in general. By uttering so-called performative sentences like

(385)   I swear it.

one can act according to SWEAR which is usually not regarded as linguistic, but which is supposed to bring out the relation between linguistic and non-linguistic action particularly clearly, because the uttered sentence includes an expression for the act-pattern according to which one can act by uttering the sentence. From the classification above it should be clear that I cannot see the point of this statement. For me performative sentences are the very paradigm of purely linguistic action. I hope that this will become intelligible from my definition.

Performative sentences SP cannot be completely defined by their syntactic form because like other sentences they can be used in different generations. SP is to be a performative sentence if and only if

(i)   HX → UTT (SP)

(ii)   SP has the following form:

(386)

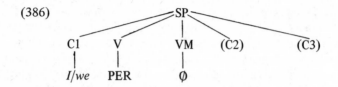

where PER represents a verb from the category of so-called performative verbs. But this holds only if PER is the uppermost verb within a syntactic structure, e.g. it is not valid for 'ask' in

(387) I assert that I ask whether. . .

(iii) PER = HX. In other words, the performative verb itself has to designate the generating pattern. For this reason 'swim' cannot be a performative verb for

(388) *(SWIM → UTT (*I am swimming*)).

The part of the tree beneath SP without the complements in brackets is called a performative. The C2 in the structure (386) can recur as a specification in HX.

I do not want to introduce further restrictions on the pattern HX, though it certainly does not seem to make sense to call such patterns non-linguistic.

Sometimes the mere uttering of SP is not sufficient for the generation. Other acts have to be added. This would look like

$$(389) \quad HX \rightarrow \begin{bmatrix} UTT\ (SP) \\ HY \\ \cdot \\ \cdot \\ \cdot \end{bmatrix}$$

According to our definition of the arrow, HX need not directly generate UTT (SP) in (i). We can imagine connecting links as in the examples (390) and (391) which may be tentatively described by (392) and (393) if it is not assumed that there is simply a subpattern-relation between ACKNOW-LEDGE or DECLARE and ASS:

(390) I acknowledge the receipt of your letter (=that I received your letter).

(391) I declare that I did it.

(392)   ACKNOWLEDGE → ASS → UTT (390)

(393)   DECLARE → ASS → UTT (391)

Performative sentences are useful in communication because they remove, at least partially, doubts concerning the generating pattern; as when, for example, it is clear that the sentence uttered is a performative one and not, say, a biographical one. If I utter

(394)   I assert that my horse can fly.

and I do not give any commentary or the like, the generation will be

(395)   ASS (CS) → UTT (*I assert* CS).

The simple

(396)   My horse can fly.,

however, can occur in quite different patterns. E.g., I can narrate a part of a yarn by uttering (396). To that extent our generation (395) is incomplete because it is probably presupposed that the generation could be debatable or, in the case of the simple utterance of (396), unclear. And this shows that performative sentences have a more special use than the sentence forming part of the CS.[73] In other cases the performative can be a kind of stereotype which is necessary for the act according to the generating HX, say with BAPTIZE.

Further important restrictions for SP are that there can be no sentence-negation in (386);[74] as a temporal adverbial only 'now', as a locative only 'here' are admitted. It should be noted that there is a three-fold identity of reference in performative sentences: the agent of HX, according to (i), is identical with that of UTT, which is again identical with the referent of 'I', according to the meaning of 'I'.

The utterance of performative sentences, like other acts, cannot be adjudged true or false.[75] Even in the case of 'assert', which is regarded as a paradigm for truth-functionality, this is not possible. It does not make sense, if A utters

(397)   I assert that S

to ask whether the uttering of (397) is true,[76] unless what is Meant is whether the assertion that S is true. If (397) is a performative sentence one always makes an assertion by uttering (397), unless this utterance is deviant for some reason.

Our definition of performative sentences is essentially based upon the form of the specification of UTT. Thus we set narrow limits without disregarding that here too there is a gradation. E.g., 'yes' can be uttered as a performative sentence in a certain sense, or 'I should like to ask you for . . .' and the like. The similarities and differences would become evident within a detailed description.

The belief that performatives are not full-blown linguistic act-patterns may derive from our mode of speaking about performative acts: E.g., if somebody has related something which we now want to report, we use sentences like 'he said. . .', 'he told. . .', etc. where we go back to illocutionary patterns or to UTT. Not so with performatives. Here what is considered important is not saying something but, as with all acts, the generating HX: 'that he christened the ship', not: 'he said that he would christen the ship', etc.[77] With this expression one would not refer to an act of baptizing but to a purely linguistic act: what he uttered, asserted, etc. For this reason, what he said can be true or false here, but not so in the former case. If someone understands the utterance of a performative sentence as a report or autobiographically and not as generated by HX, then it becomes an idle ceremony.

The differentiation we made with our three types of action may be brought together with Austin's famous distinction between illocutionary act-patterns ILLOC and perlocutionary patterns PERLOC though it seems not quite clear to me and I suggest that it cannot be made clear in the way Austin proceeded.[78] Here I only want to make the distinction a little more precise, which naturally involves some modification of the two concepts, without criticizing previous definitions and taking up all criteria provided by earlier attempts.

I start from our classification in to three types of act-patterns and provisionally assume that patterns of the third type are instances of ILLOC, those of the second type instances of PERLOC. Can this assumption be justified by further differences?

According to our previous examples of ILLOC in 3.3.1, only CS and infinitive constructions which can be regarded as special cases of CS will be possible as specifications of all instances of ILLOC. This is related to the fact that acts according to ILLOC always concern propositions; this, again, is the reason why expressions with which one refers to propositions, such as 'this', 'it' etc.[79] are likewise admitted. Instances of PERLOC, however, also allow other specifications, say

(398) $GREET_1 (P2) \rightarrow UTT_1$ (*hello*).

The example shows that this is not only caused by the fact that PERLOC can also generate non-linguistic patterns. For even in the case that they generate linguistic patterns they do not need a CS as specification. Another example where both are again possible would be WARN: we can warn somebody to do something, using a propositional specification, but we can also warn someone of the dog.

A third criterion for the distinction between ILLOC and PERLOC might be that ILLOC can be generated by PERLOC, but not vice versa:

(399)   PERLOC → ILLOC → UTT
(400)   * (ILLOC → PERLOC → UTT)

E.g. one can warn somebody by telling him or by asserting that there is a snappish dog around, but I did not find examples for the opposite; probably because ILLOC is purely linguistic and one can hardly imagine how to express a proposition without acting linguistically. This criterion corresponds very well to a criterion given by Searle,[80] who states that perlocutionary acts have something to do with the effects illocutionary acts have. In terms of action theory this amounts to saying that patterns like CONVINCE or PERSUADE generate illocutionary patterns such as, for instance, ARGUE.

The other criterion for the distinction between ILLOC and PERLOC which is often mentioned, namely that the success of an act of PERLOC cannot be up to P1 alone, seems to me problematical without further qualification. The distinction seems to upset the previous distinction between ILLOC and PERLOC, since it applies to all types of act-patterns. Perhaps this is related to the interactional character of the patterns, e.g., that it is not always clear whether or not I have forced someone to HX, that is whether or not I have succeeded in forcing him. But this applies also to instances of ILLOC like WARN.[81] At least it seems to me to be questionable whether I warned someone if he did not realize it, as well as whether I proved something to someone if he did not understand it. I have similar hesitations with other examples of ILLOC such as ARGUE, which is related to the partner in a similar way as is CONVINCE. Such uncertainties about just which patterns belong to PERLOC and which to ILLOC should prevent us from overrating the distinction. It seems to me to be of more importance to describe single patterns than to find rough distinctions. For distinctions are the by-product of extensive descriptions. It would even be astonishing if all cases could be classified in such an accurate way.

Since, by our definition, every illocutionary act involves a proposition in one way or another, we may classify illocutionary acts on the basis of a further analysis of propositions.[82] The most prominent components we get are reference, predication, and truth value, which is essentially Frege's anal-

146

ysis into argument, funtional, and truth value. The act of asserting consists —
for example, in Frege's analysis — of the conceiving of the thought, which is
nothing other than reference and predication, and the proposal to accept the
truth value True for it. Here the reference to O and predicating P of O are
assumed to be given and stress is laid upon the truth of the proposition. But
this is only so with ASS and cognate patterns. There are other possibilities
which can be stressed: The truth and predicate may be given whereas the O
of which the predicate is true is what is wanted, which is the case in *wh*-
questions. As a third possibility we have as given truth and reference and
stress is laid upon the predicate. This is the case of defining. When I define P
by uttering the sentence 'O is P' I refer to O and stipulate the truth (since
every definition is true) and I give a meaning to the predicate.

Most illocutionary act-patterns seem to be of the first group, e.g. PROVE,
INFER, ASK (yes-no-questions), ANSWER, whereas in the second I have
found only ASK and SET A RIDDLE and in the third DEFINE and DE-
SCRIBE.

Before concluding this section, one type of illocutionary act-patterns remains to be discussed which gives an important part of the implicit context,
presupposing. A presupposition X of CS was said to be a proposition which
had to be true so that CS can be true or false. If X is false CS can be neither
true nor false. Therefore presupposition traditionally has been regarded as
a relation between propositions and has been strictly separated from implication, which was necessary because contraposition takes us from the implication 'If CS then X' to 'If not X then not CS'.But in the case of presuppposi-
tion this does not hold, by definition, for X should be true whether CS or
not CS is true, that is in both cases. In order to avoid presupposing all analytical sentences with every given proposition, the relation between X and
CS has to be strengthened by, say, the addition of 'necessary condition'
which postulates a meaning-relation between X and CS.[83]

The fact that 'assert' and 'is true' both occur frequently in the course
of discussion within logics and linguistics about presuppositions suggests
that our former considerations may be relevant. It has been argued that
Strawson, indeed the whole discussion, vacillates between the two opinions
that X is a condition for CS's being true or false and that X is a condition for
the asserting of CS.[84] Although there may be doubts about this as far as
Strawson is concerned, the problem has to be settled, since there is no need
for presuppositions if they simply amount to necessary conditions to be
fulfilled in order that a linguistic act may be performed. Then we could use
Occam's razor to cut them off. Can we really understand X as a condition for
acting according to certain patterns? For instance:

(401)   ASS (CS) if X → UTT (Y).

such that one could not act according to this generation if X is not true. This
seems to be supported by the fact that presuppositions are not restricted to
acts of ASS and therefore do not only have reference to truth or falsity: there
must be a king of France at the moment in order to be able to ask whether
the present king of France is bald, just as much as with the case where we
want to assert that he is or is not bald.

This holds not only for ASK but also for ORD, etc.[85] But what does an infringement of the condition bring about? Sometimes Strawson seems to
assume that no assertion at all is then made because the speaker failed to say
anything true or false.[86] But that is going too far, as can be seen from the possible reaction of P2 who might call P1's attention to the fact that it is not
right to assert CS and who may contradict him by saying that not X. But to
contradict only makes sense if something has been asserted. On the other
hand, the assertion of CS may have failed, and all the same P2 may have
grasped P1's intention to assert CS, the communicative act going wrong
because P1 thinks the condition is fulfilled and P2 does not. Therefore a more
detailed description would have to consider the conditions on both sides.

A further defect of (401) is that it gives the impression that X must be
true. But, as our description shows, it is sufficient that the partners of communication think X to be true. And even this is still going too far because
P1, at least, need not believe X: he can pretend to think that X is true, i.e.,
lie. E.g., P1 can utter (402) in order to make P2 believe that Paul had found
the solution:

(402)   Paul concealed from me that he has found the solution.

If P1 asserts that (402) he commits himself to the truth of (403). But there
is actually a relation of presupposition between (402) and (403), because
(403) would also have to be true for the truth of (404):

(403)   Paul has found the solution.
(404)   Paul did not conceal from me that he has found the solution.

This gives us an argument against listing X as a simple condition or as a belief-
condition: We have to assume that P1 has done something else besides acting
according to (401), because what P1 thinks to be true without uttering it
must not be known to P2 and because P1, in this context, can only pretend
that he thinks X to be true. Only in this way can it be understood that P2
knows something besides CS that he must not have known before (namely

that P1 believes that P2 believes X to be true) and that P1 can now be made responsible for his thinking X to be true after having acted according to (401). Since thinking something to be true or believing something is no act-pattern and even less a communicative pattern, and since our previous description shows great similarity with ASS, we can assume that P1 has still asserted[87] something else together with his act of asserting CS, namely X. This second act we call presupposing, and the corresponding pattern is PRES. The difference between PRES and normal ASS, both of which cover the same specifications, may be seen in the fact that presupposing is never explicit, such that between the presupposed X and the sentence uttered the relation stated in (305) could hold although it is not implicit in such a way that it could not be made explicit: everything which can be presupposed can be (explicitly, however this may be) asserted.

The most striking difference between PRES and ASS lies usually in informative power. Whereas for ASS(CS) the following two conditions hold: (i) P1 does not know whether P2 does know or believe CS and (ii) P2 believes that (i), in the case of PRES (X), X is usually not the topic of conversation: (iii) P1 believes that P2 believes X, (iv) P2 believes X, and (v) P2 believes that (iii). Hence if P1 does not believe that P2 believes X but all the same P2 believes that (iii) then P1 may use presupposing to inform P2 that X without asserting it in the normal sense. And if P1 is mistaken in his belief that P2 believes X then an act of PRES may turn out to be very cognate to one of ASS. Presupposing may be used in a very sophisticated manner in communication to make someone believe something.

PRES is a subpattern of ILLOC which is due to the CS specifying other instances of ILLOC and it can only occur together with other instances of ILLOC. Therefore the form of every illocutionary act (except PRES) may be given as

$$(405) \quad \begin{bmatrix} \text{ILLOC (CS)} \\ \text{PRES (X)} \\ \cdot \\ \cdot \\ \cdot \end{bmatrix} \rightarrow \text{UTT (Y)}$$

Here the problems of contraposition do not arise mainly because of the fact that it is not directly a question of relations between sentences and propositions but between act-patterns. For example, let HX be the act-pattern which corresponds to ASS in the wider sense and which includes our ASS together with PRES, then it is not a contradiction that PRES (CS) $\sqsubset$ HX (CS1) and PRES (CS) $\sqsubset$ HX (not CS1) but a tautology. For HX (not CS) must not be confounded with -HX (CS) which, indeed, cannot be followed together with HX (CS).

General rules for ASS, which are transferable to PRES, prove correct in just the same way. If asserting CS1 is a subpattern of asserting CS2 the same will hold for PRES. So if one asserts with the assertions of (403) that Paul has known the solution at some time, this would also be presupposed via (403) when asserting (402). As a rule this could be formulated as follows:

$$(406) \quad \frac{\text{ASS (CS1)} \sqsubset \text{ASS (CS2)}}{x \ \alpha \ \text{PRES (CS1)}}$$
$$x \ \alpha \ \text{PRES (CS2)}$$

And just the same holds for PRES. Thus, since when asserting (403) it is pre-supposed that there is a solution, this is also presupposed when asserting (402).

Since presupposing goes with all illocutionary acts we cannot communicate without presupposing. This is, besides common knowledge, another instance of tacit agreement in communication, though, as we have described it, it may appear somewhat less tacit than common knowledge. But it cannot be removed, e.g. by a request that all presuppositions be made clear and explicit. This would mean that, in a communication between P1 and P2, P1 would only be allowed to presuppose something which has been asserted and accepted by P1 or P2 before hand. But since this assertion involves its own presuppositions, communication could never begin, and the principle turns out to be unsuitable. It is, of course, useful for the partners to improve their understanding so that they are aware of the presuppositions involved and, where something one does not believe is presupposed, to assert and to deny this explicitly.

3.4 SEMANTIC RELATIONS

An important part of the implicit context of a pattern is its being a subpattern of other patterns and its having subpatterns itself. For the illocutionary patterns these contexts are largely determined by the specifying CS. For instance, if someone asserted that (407) we could assume that he also asserted that (408):

(407)   Jack is human.
(408)   Jack is an animal.

150

This can be thought of as a consequence of the fact that

(409)   ASS (that (407)) ⊏ ASS (that (408)).

And an agent acting according to ASS (that (407)) may not be considered as performing a second act at the same time, but the act of ASS (that (408)) is implicit in the act of ASS (that (407)), hence it is only one act according to a complex pattern. Since the assertion of (408) is not explicit in his utterance in the same way as the assertion of (407) there may be doubt whether he really asserted that (408). As with inconsistent belief there may be an apparent inconsistency in his assertion. But there is not necessarily an inconsistency in the assertion if someone asserting that (407) were to say that he did not assert that (408), since this depends on the rule of use for sentence (407) which we assume to be such that (408) is implied when making an assertion by an utterance of (407). Our rule intervenes in such a way that we understand both (407) and (408) to be asserted and since we believe this to be the normal rule, we would hold P1 responsible for having asserted that (408). Therefore we would formulate as a kind of norm:

(410)   Always if someone asserts that (407) he also has to assert that (408).

So, we may ask

(411)   Would you also assert that (408)?

if doubts existed about this, and we could commit him — on the strength of our rule — to having asserted this. Following our rules it seems absolutely certain that someone who asserted that (407) also asserted that (408) but this works on the CS-level where my understanding is formulated in my language and understanding has taken place. If the agent uses the sentences so that the subpattern-relation stated in (409) does not hold for the patterns generating UTT (S) then he could not have Meant the utterance as an assertion of (408). Therefore we cannot explain (409) directly by the meaning of (407) and (408) in the sense that (409) must hold because of the meaning of (407) and (408). But we can say that the relation holds in my language; there utterances of (407) and (408) may be generated by ASS (that (407)) and ASS (that (408)).

So we can derive from (409) a relation between the specifying CS's which we call entrenchment (ENT) and define by

(412)   ASS (CS1) ⊏ ASS (CS2) if and only if ENT (CS1, CS2).

Entrenchment[88] differs from normal logical relations or functions in several respects: First, it is different from the logical conditional as well as from logical implication. The conditional produces sentences from L_1, if its arguments are sentences from L_1. E.g. instances of 'p → q' are logical sentences of the same level as instances of 'p' and instances of 'q'. In expressions with ENT the sentences of L_1 only occur indirectly, in connection with CS, and are accordingly only mentioned. Underlinings or italics in specifications of UTT are operators which transform sentences into names for these sentences.[89] The other difference is that the conditional is a truth function but for ENT the question of the truth of its arguments is secondary. This is, as well, the difference between ENT and logical implication, which are similar with respect to the status of their arguments. But even in the restricted case when CS's related by ENT occur in ASS, the logical implication is still weaker, insofar as contradictory sentences imply every given sentence (*ex falso sequitur quodlibet*) and analytical sentences are implied by every given sentence. Obviously this is not so with ENT, for one would hardly say that for

(413)   Two divided by three is six.
(414)   Two divided by two is one.
(415)   That does not work.

it holds that ASS (that (415)) ⊏ ASS (that (413)) or that ASS (that (414)) ⊏ ASS (that (413)). Therefore we postulate a stronger relation for the meanings of the specifying CS's.[90]

Second, CS's tied together with ENT may behave analogously when specifying other instances of ILLOC besides ASS. When I order somebody to buy a horse I also order him to buy an animal. Therefore the following holds:

(416)   ORD (CS1) ⊏ ORD (CS2) if and only if ENT (CS1, CS2).

This may, however, not be stretched to all instances of ILLOC: in the case of ASK it would yield strange consequences, for example, the questioner asking whether (407) might already have known that Jack is an animal and for this reason did not ask whether (408). But he has to believe that (408) if he believes that (407) after the communication

(417) ASK_1 (whether (407)) ⊦ ANS_2 (that (407)).

This is only due to the properties of ANS which here resemble those of ASS.[91]

In my opinion, this demonstrates that limiting the ENT-relations to CS's would be of limited use. You cannot infer from ENT (CS1, CS2) that ASK (CS1) $\sqsubset$ ASK (CS2) where a proposition is usually held to be involved just as it is in ASS. But deriving ENT from subpatterns secures applicability to all kinds of illocutionary act-patterns and, via generation, to all kinds of sentences and renounces the limitation to declarative sentences which goes with truth functions.[92]

Third, there seems to be a postulate concerning logical implication and its progeny in linguistics, namely that for all p and q: if $p \Rightarrow q$, there is an r such that $(q \wedge r) \Leftrightarrow p$. This postulate just says that an implication can be filled out to an equivalence. In linguistic description this enters as the doctrine that meaning can be given by *genus et differentia* and that this description is complete. E.g., the meaning of the predicate 'is human' can be given by the essential features 'is rational' and 'is an animal'. This may work for a definition, because of the jobs this has to do, but it does not work as a description of the meaning of 'is human'. If it did I would have contradicted myself in holding that (407) together with

(418)   Jack is Mongoloid.

which clearly is not the case. The reason for this lies in the so-called vagueness or openness of natural languages which has to be dealt with more extensively.

Before doing this I want to formulate some constraints on our explication (410) and our definition (412): From the last example we can conclude that the formulation (410) is too wide since one must not always assert that Jack is rational if one asserts that Jack is human. Instead of (410) it would be preferable to give the conditions under which one would have to assert that Jack is rational and one could insert an 'under normal circumstances' into (410), claiming that the dropping of the entrenchment between (407) and

(419)   Jack is rational.

is not normal. Nevertheless, the principle associated with logical implication, namely that CS together with a formulation of the circumstances cannot survive in the case of entrenchment since there is no short way of stating this. The problem with vagueness crops up here again.

From definition (412) it follows that the act done by uttering (407) may be described in the degenerated generation:

(420)   ASS (that (408)) → ASS (that (407)) → UTT (407).

From this it becomes obvious that essential parts have been left out. The most essential, which is not dealt with in logic because it is generally presupposed there, is that references are kept constant; if I refer with 'Jack' in (408) to a horse named Jack and with 'Jack' in (407) to my friend then usually the subpattern-relation will not hold. An amended form of (420) therefore would be:

$$(421) \quad \begin{bmatrix} \text{ASS (that (408))} \\ \\ \text{REF (G, H,. . .)} \end{bmatrix} \rightarrow \begin{bmatrix} \text{ASS (that (407))} \\ \\ \text{REF (G, H,. . .)} \end{bmatrix} \rightarrow \text{UTT (407)}$$

Now back to so-called vagueness, which is not intended here to cover the case where it is not laid down in the meaning of 'book' how many pages it must consist of (obviously only counting is considered to be precise) nor where different speakers may have and follow different rules for one expression. This is how it is sometimes treated by Russell who explains it as a consequence of the fact that every speaker learns the use of the expression in the presence of only some of the different objects the expression is applicable to, in Kripke's terms we would day that the reference is fixed in different circumstances with the help of different paradigms. The vagueness or openness which we are concerned with here has to cope with the fact that entrenchment between CS's does not hold homogeneously but can be dropped (under certain cirumstances) without the assumption of polysemy being suitable.

An example is the verb 'know', so important for the considerations in 3.3.3. There we said that asserting that

(422)   A knows that S.

commits one to that S. And this was nothing else than the assumption of a subpattern-relation between ASS (that S) and ASS (that A knows that S). But strong as this entrenchment may be it can be dropped, as, for instance, a scholar drops it when asserting that the Azande know that witchcraft can occur at any time of the day and night, so shocking his readers in order to point out that the Azande's beliefs are as certain for them as are ours for us. The scholar is not thereby committed to the assertion that he himself believes in witchcraft.

An adequate picture of entrenchment therefore could be one of an open family as in

$$(423)\left\{\begin{bmatrix}\text{ASS (CS1)}\\\text{ASS (CS2)}\\\cdot\\\cdot\\\cdot\end{bmatrix}\\\begin{bmatrix}\text{ASS (CS1)}\\\text{ASS (CS3)}\\\cdot\\\cdot\\\cdot\end{bmatrix}\\\cdot\\\cdot\\\cdot\end{bmatrix}\right\}\quad\text{[ASS (CS)}$$

in which no CSi necessarily occurs in all members. This cannot be filled out so that a form like (424) results:

$$(424)\quad\begin{bmatrix}\text{ILLOC (CS1)}\\\text{ILLOC (CS2)}\\\text{ILLOC (CS3)}\end{bmatrix}\quad=\text{ILLOC (CS)}$$

This form is misleading because every entrenchment may be cancelled and because such a list necessarily remains open.

Within the open family entrenchments may be stressed or may be dropped and new entrenchments may be introduced. With (407) stress may be put upon the entrenchment that Jack is featherless or that Jack is a biped, which naturally can also be dropped. The entrenchment in (407) of

(425)   Jack has a soul.

may be under discussion, e.g. at a time when it was a relevant question whether negroes had a soul or not. Sometimes this may even seem to be a question of fact and not a question of facts of language. The distinction is often question-begging because it presupposes that it is possible to crystallize certain entrenchments as neccessary or essential, others only as accidental.[93] To hold to this distinction, a criterion had to be introduced differentiating the entrenchments between essential and accidental ones, or between necessarily holding and accidentally holding entrenchments. This was always ill founded and arbitrary. In my opinion, there must not even be essential entrenchments in the sense that there must be some all-in or paradigm use where at least these entrenchments hold.

The open list of subpatterns given in (423) is in a sense weaker than definition by *genus et differentia* but on the other hand, even if it were possible to
find something common to all uses, this is not more useful for empirical description of meaning since it does not only rely on two features. It provides
for the wide range of subpattern-relations which normally hold and for different applications of the sentences where entrenchments may be dropped. So
we could say that when something is human it is normally an animal and
biped, etc. The current argument against complex description, that one has to
assume that the defining list is closed and that some entrenchments hold necessarily otherwise one could not make simple descriptions,[94] can be refuted
simply by pointing out that simplicity is not our highest objective.

Open families of entrenchments are due to the openness of the rules of
language and make possible the description of the historical openness of rules.
An example here is metaphorical use, which is perhaps at the bottom of
every change of meaning. So if we refer with 'Jack' to a certain man and
assert that

(426)   Jack is a gorilla.

we easily understand that Jack is not a human being is not entrenched. We
cancel this element in the meaning of 'gorilla' and we understand the assertion as saying that he is a member of a bodyguard or even that he is very
strong, so stressing another entrenchment due to the meaning of 'is a gorilla'.
This possibility depends on the nets of entrenchments of the partners for the
expression in use: a speaker who uses a sentence metaphorically can only
hope to be understood if he believes that the partner would know and stress
the same entrenchments. Notice that dropping entrenchments within the CS
takes place in both predicate and referring expressions and it extends from
frequent everyday cancellation at one extreme to innovative (accidental)
cancellation at the other. If someone does not acknowledge at least one of
my entrenchments I cannot communicate with him.

We shall distill another semantic relation from the following conversation,
a piece of so-called opposite speech:[95]

(427)	P1:	. . .who invented the airplane?	(a)
	P2:	I do know.	(b)
	P1:	You mean, you don't know.	(c)
	P2:	I do know.	(d)
	P1:	You do know.	(e)
	P2:	Yes, I do.	(f)
	P1:	If you do know, can you tell me?	(g)
	P2:	If I do know, how can I tell you? I could.	(h)

156

P1:	You sure could. Okay, can you tell me now who invented the airplane?	(i)
P2:	Yes, because I do know. I do know. I do know, ah, who invented the airplane.	(j)
P1:	You do know.	(k)
P2:	Yes I know.	(l)
P1:	What you mean to say is that you don't know.	(m)
P2:	I do know. If I don't know, I, I, I, I wouldn't be able to tell you.	(n)

The example is from a conversation between a schizophrenic P2 and his doctor P1, the deviation of course being charged to P2. The diagnosis is that there is on the P2 side a reversal of yes-no discrimination and, in consequence, of other corresponding discriminations such as 'I do not know' for 'I know' and so on of which P2 is said to be unaware. But this seems to be very unlikely because if it is really correct that P2 says 'I do know' and Means thereby that he does not know then at least it is clear from the example that he knows that this is not how P1 uses the expression since it would not make sense to understand (c) in his own way and then insist on what he said before.[96] Similarly, if P2 understood (e) as 'You do not know' then it would not make sense to answer 'yes' which amounts to 'no' in his language because P1 would have asserted the same in (e) as P2 did in (d) and consequently P2 had to consent with (f), which cannot be done by saying 'no'. P2 seems to me to have a wider competence than P1 since he knows the rules followed by P1 and his own; at least, he is more communicative than is P1 since P1 does not accept the rule of P2 though he documents by uttering (c) that he knows it. In the end, what P2 does is to give up the usual fictitious assumption that a partner in my place would act according to the same rules as I do but admits that the partners are following different rules and provokes the recognition of that fact.

But is this a reliable diagnosis? I think it is not since, in my opinion, if somebody reverses 'yes' and 'no' throughout and all other expressions correspondingly we could not notice this in mere conversation. Perhaps we would find P2 very impolite for he must infringe upon norms of etiquette and we, not knowing about the reversal, would understand his act otherwise. For instance, (f) as it stands sounds like simple consent to what P1 said with (e). But if P2 Means by uttering it the same as we would Mean by uttering 'No, I do not know' then, in the first part, it would be a refutation of the assertion of P1 and, in the second part P2 would be insisting on what he said in (d).

But is this really all? Do we not find a perplexing deviation within the conversation without knowing anything about other acts of P2? I think we do.

We can find certain inconsistencies in the conversation, for instance the following: With (g) our P1 makes a conditional request. He wants P2 to answer if he can. If P2 understands this correctly, which we assume, he must, in compliance with all he has said, reject the request since the condition is not fulfilled. The more so if he assumes that P1 understands him correctly because he has told P1 three times that he cannot. But what does he do? He utters (h) which amounts (with 'you' unstressed) in his language to either (i) if I do not know it how can I then omit to answer you or (ii) if I do not know it how should I be unable to answer you.

Before discussing this I have to point out that there is a simple interpretation of (h) if P2 did not perform the reversal in the question and does Mean it as it stands. Then he only informs P1 that the request is out of order and together with this reproves P1 because he should have known this from the preceding conversation. This would be a perfectly understandable course of action under the assumption that P2 follows the mentioned rule only in the *if*-clause. But if he is consistent.or, in other words, if the diagnosis is correct, what then?

In the alternative (i) we are close to the conversational principle that it is superfluous to request someone not to give the answer when he does not know it. But this alternative is excluded if we stick to the general formulation of the rule since the alternative is not based on sentence-negation but on the negation of 'tell' only: 'How can I not-tell you? ' Besides it would affect coherence of the conversation as there seems to be no reason for P2 to react in this way.

In the second alternative P2's act is out of place since P1 has not presupposed that P2 is not able to give the answer, but exactly the contrary. So, if P2 nevertheless acts in this way and if he does it honestly his act is bound to the following inconsistency: Since P2 understands the utterance of P1 as the request to give the answer (i) P2 believes that P1 requested him to give the answer. And since P2 rebukes P1 because of saying that he is unable to give the answer (ii) P2 believes that P1 requested him not to give the answer. But (i) and (ii) are obviously incompatible beliefs.

In order to cope with cases of inconsistent assertion, belief, and so on as well as with problems of dissonance mentioned in 3.2, we introduce the semantic relation of incompatibility INC which we define as follows:

(428)   INC (CS1, CS2) if and only if * ASS (CS1 and CS2)
          under the condition that neither *ASS (CS1) nor * ASS(CS2).

We restrict our definition to ASS though other instances of ILLOC behave analogously.

Our example of opposite speech shows too that INC must operate like other semantic relations on the CS-level. I think that its importance does not lie in the fact that agents really Mean incompatible things but that in communication incompatibility functions as a symptom of incorrect understanding. If I think somebody has said something incompatible I would have to improve my understanding. I would have to begin to worm out what he really Meant with the help of communicative methods, e.g. following up the entrenchments. The main reason for apparent incompatibilities seems to be that agents do not fully survey the entrenchments of what they say. When the net of entrenchments is developed and an agent made aware of it, he may see himself that what he said was incompatible in the end. This is one example among the objectives of practical semantics of what we called obtaining a more adequate perspective on the context.

But the fact that there need not necessarily be any incompatibility for an agent who utters without deviating elsewhere a sentence or sentences we find contradictory reminds us that it is not sufficient to define the semantic relations between the CS's specifying ILLOC, but that a transfer to the S's specifying UTT has to be made. Certainly this transfer can easily be made where there is a conventional relation between the CS and S in question. In cases we have to live with the problems of understanding, problems which beset the linguist as well.

In logic incompatibility has often been dealt with.[97] It resembles the sense-relation of incompatibility discussed by Lyons, which is to be defined by the contradictoriness of sentences.[98] Here certain problems arise which are solved in our description, as for instance the preservation of the reference of referring expressions. For, if one refers in asserting that (407) and that not (408) with 'Jack' to different individuals, ASS (that (407) and that not (408)) certainly is not deviant (with emphasized 'Jack').

One more problem is avoided in our definition. Since in logical investigations neither the difference between sentence and sentence utterance nor the succession of the acts of uttering are taken into account, there never appeared to be a problem in defining 'contradictory' there. There never seems to be a problem about having to utter two contradictory sentences at the same time. So logicians are able to define two sentences as contradictory if and only if one is the negation of the other one, or as incompatible if and only if both cannot be true together. But for natural languages this won't do, because, e.g., if INC (CS1, CS2) it is quite possible to act on

$$(429) \quad \text{ILLOC}_1 \, (\text{CS1}) \dagger \text{ILLOC}_1 \, (\text{CS2}).$$

For instance, if (429) is a subpattern of HFOR and if P1 changed his mind after having performed ILLOC (CS1). If this were not possible one could never cause someone to change his mind. This is one of the differences between 'true' in logic and 'true' in normal communication.

INC and ENT are related to one another since

(430) INC (CS1, not CS2) if and only if ENT (CS1, CS2) or ENT (CS2, CS1).

Contrary to ENT, INC is symmetrical:

(431) INC (CS1, CS2) if and only if INC (CS2, CS1).

If, as we assumed, our P2 in the airplane example knows that P1 acts normally and if P2 really follows the rule as it is stated in the diagnosis, i.e. he negates not only whole sentences but also clauses, then the example demonstrates how complicated it would be to follow this rule and to give up all community with your partners. Either our P2 does not fully reach this or he does not act throughout according to the mentioned rule.

By uttering (i) P1 presupposes that somebody invented the airplane. P2, reacting with (j), would answer in his language that he does not know who did not invent the airplane and therein also presupposes that somebody invented the airplane. Even in the case where P2 does not reverse throughout and answers only that he does not know who invented the airplane he must presuppose that somebody invented the airplane. Otherwise he would have to react differently. It seems that the implicit presupposition cannot be encoded in the way assertions are.

This shows that P2, in opposing the rules of his partners, succeeds in achieving all the consequences intended, such as reversal of entrenchments etc. but that he cannot cancel normal presuppositions because presuppositions are immune to reversal of 'yes' and 'no'. To reverse 'yes' and 'no' in presuppositions as well would be a very complicated matter because communication is likely to become incoherent then.

That one proposition is presupposed when another is expressed is due to the meaning of the former and to a special semantic relation which, though akin to entrenchment, is not identical with it. Entrenchments are affected by negation, presuppositions are not. Therefore we introduce semantic relation PRE responsible for the fact that a certain illocutionary act is always bound to a certain presuppositional act.

We define this relation through the possibilities of acting:

(432) PRE (CS1, CS2) if and only if it is impossible to act according

to ILLOC (CS1) without acting according to PRES (CS2)
and to act according to ILLOC (not CS1) without acting
according to PRES (CS2).

This reflects the fact that every agent acting according to ASS (CS1) must perform two acts together and among them one of PRES (CS2), which may be represented in a complex illocutionary pattern:

$$(433) \quad \begin{bmatrix} \text{ASS (CS1)} \\ \text{PRES (CS2)} \end{bmatrix}$$

The whole act may go wrong if one of the two goes wrong. And there are various ways of going wrong, which are given by the different courses of interaction succeeding the act and can be described by the corresponding conditions as we stated them in 3.3.4. The most discussed case is where condition (iv) that P2 believes CS2 is not fulfilled. Then the act of presupposing must go wrong and consequently the whole complex act. But after P2's denying that CS2 and the discussion whether CS2 is true (believed by both) or not, which is necessary because P1 is committed to believing CS2 although this is not a condition for presupposing CS2, the interaction, depending on the result of the discussion, may continue in either way whether the whole act was correct or has gone wrong.

Other ways it can fail arise from the other conditions, e.g. if condition (iii) that P1 believes that P2 believes CS2 is not fulfilled then we don't have a normal act of presupposing but a half-breed act between PRES and ASS because P1 may use the presupposition to inform P2 of CS2. Or, if condition (v) is not fulfilled then P2 may question the right of P1 to presuppose CS2. All this touches on the question of sincerity and shows that sincerity here plays another role than with ASS where it is not a constitutive condition at all for the act to be successful. With PRES, however, the act oscillates between various mixtures of PRES and ASS, which may be described by the different combinations of conditions resulting from the alternative sequences of the interaction.

Besides the differences there are a lot of analogies between PRE and ENT and between PRES and ASS. Though one cannot assert something incompatible directly via PRE (parallel to ENT) one can do it indirectly by explicitly asserting something incompatible with something one has presupposed before. Since the assertion has to be a second act, it must be assumed for incompatibility that the agent did not change his mind.

One proposition may presuppose several propositions directly but also indirectly. There are two ways this may come about which may be characterized by the following rules:

$$(434) \quad \text{If PRE (CS1, CS2) then} \quad \begin{bmatrix} \text{ASS (CS)} \\ \text{PRES (CS1)} \end{bmatrix} \subset \begin{bmatrix} \text{ASS (CS)} \\ \text{PRES (CS2)} \end{bmatrix}$$

$$(435) \quad \text{If ENT (CS1, CS2) then} \quad \begin{bmatrix} \text{ASS (CS)} \\ \text{PRES (CS1)} \end{bmatrix} \subset \begin{bmatrix} \text{ASS (CS)} \\ \text{PRES (CS2)} \end{bmatrix}$$

(434) amounts to saying that the presuppositions of a presupposed proposition are also presupposed and (435) to saying that propositions entrenched by presuppositions are also presupposed. However, this is not to say that the speaker must remember all the indirect presuppositions or actually have them in mind but only that he is committed to the truth of them as well as to the truth of the entrenchments such that they may be discussed within further communication.

Finally, because of the restriction of semantic relations to the CS-level, we want to discuss the consequences for the specifications of UTT and especially the position of a syntactic theory within practical semantics. A condition for the description of how to use sentences in communication is the segmentation of sentences. Since it is impossible to segment all sentences in one step into minimal units (e.g., morphemes or phonemes), difficulties arise about where to segment the sentence and about the order in which the segmentation has to be executed. We do not want to deal with these syntactic problems but shall presuppose a useful segmentation.

Generally, two relations between parts of sentences are distinguished: the syntagmatic relation SYN exists between two parts if and only if both occur within one text or one sentence, e.g. 'everybody' and 'somebody' in

(436)   Everybody needs somebody.

The paradigmatic relation PAR exists between two parts if and only if one can be substituted for the other one within a sentence, such that a new sentence is the result. E.g. 'nobody' and 'everybody',

(437)   Nobody needs somebody.

We do not want to give more precise definitions because they would demand a more explicit theory and a clear distinction between the type and occurrence of parts.

In a certain sense SYN and PAR are not semantic relations. But the semantic relations between propositions can be understood as subrelations of PAR and SYN. This becomes especially evident by a restriction of the <S1, S2>-pairs of two alternative generations, so that S2 results from S1 by substituting one part. Then a part of the meaning of the parts standing in paradigmatic relation is yielded by the semantic relation in question. According to a principle which has been developed in structuralism and holds in the theory of information in a similar form, a part can only have meaning if it stands in paradigmatic relations. For the meaning of a part is only given in the context of a language and that is in opposition to other parts. For this reason one cannot attach meaning to parts like 'to' in

    (438)   Nobody has to recognize somebody.

They are redundant.[99] Still, this principle must be applied cautiously because there are certain parts in sentences which can only be substituted together with other parts. Here PAR and SYN interlock.

By way of PAR and SYN one can arrive at a syntactic theory where all elements are associated to syntactic categories and the structures of sentences can be represented in trees with vertices labelled with these categories. But for this purpose one already needs the semantic relations between the generating CS's. For, (i) whether or not S is deviant must be gathered from the generations ILLOC(CS) → UTT (S); this will, for instance, be the case if there is no such generation at all for the corresponding chain specifying UTT;[100] (ii) the regular differences in meaning which are the basis for the assignment of S-parts to syntactic categories have to be gathered from the regular change of the semantic relations between the corresponding CS's. Here, too, we recognize that such a syntactic theory is only possible and reasonable within the scope of a semantic theory.

3.5 COMMUNICATION PATTERNS

Within this section I shall give as an example the description of a communication pattern which is taken from our ordinary question and answer possibilities and can be understood as a basis for the methodical learning of this sort of communication. Because it is a normative proposal our inquiry is naturally subject to the different hazards besetting normative interventions, including penalties. I premise some general remarks on questions and answers.

3.5.1 *Questions*

The ability to ask questions is generally appreciated as an important linguistic ability. Asking questions is basic to human communication. One can hardly imagine a society where asking questions does not exist, where one can only learn something from other persons if they begin to talk, as it were, of
their own free-will. To learn something special from a partner in a controlled
manner would be impossible without questions. For the aim of asking a question is to find out definite things, to learn something which one did not know
before. From this follows the relation between questions, tasks and problems.

But asking is not only important in order to find out some facts or a partner's opinions, asking is just one part of interactions where the understanding of the partner is improved. By learning something about my partner's
opinion and its context I learn, at the same time, the meaning of the signs
he uses to express it. Thus asking and answering is a way of following up and
discovering meaning relations consciously. The questions continually posed
by children allow them to extend their competence on their own initiative
and can be classified here. Hence the ability to ask questions is one of the
abilities which have to be examined and perhaps systematized in practical semantics so that the agents can acquire this ability as quickly as possible and
can use it to follow up the aims formulated in 3.2.

Asking is always a part of an interaction and even in the extreme case of
putting questions to oneself when reasoning it is incomplete till an answer is
given. Questions must be completed by a partner's answer. Not to answer a
question would be an omission. Therefore the simplest form of a question-
communication is:

$$(439) \quad ASK_1 (X) \dagger \left\{ \begin{matrix} ANS_2 (Y) \\ -ANS_2 \end{matrix} \right\}$$

The specifications of ASK and ANS are not independent of one another but
there is a special relation which we want to call the question-answer-relation
QA, assuming that QA holds between propositions, just like other semantic
relations. A transfer of QA to the sentences uttered is only possible via generation through an expansion of our basic form (439) to (440):

$$(440) \quad (ASK_1 (X) \rightarrow UTT_1 (W) \dagger \left\{ \begin{matrix} ANS_2 (Y) \rightarrow UTT_2 (Z) \\ -ANS_2 \end{matrix} \right\}) \text{ if } QA(X,Y)$$

As has been said the conjunctions of the CS's inserted for X and Y vary distri-
butionally with the respective act-patterns; e.g. with ASK only 'whether' and
$\emptyset$ occur. This suggests that they should not be classed with that part of the
complement clause which expresses the proposition remaining the same in

ASK- and ANS-specifications, say the part beyond the brackets in

(441)   (whether/that) this makes sense.

Still, such a propositional expression is not a sentence but incomplete, as is shown by its semantic properties and word order in German. Since we shall often need such expressions, we introduce (x') as a name for the propositional expression corresponding to the sentence referred to by (x), a convention we shall use only in this section. A question, which we ask in an act of ASK (X) and which we express by the complement clause inserted for X, is distinguished from an assertion by the fact that it cannot be considered true or false. One might say the question Q_1 would be true (or false) if its answer A_1 is true (or false). But this leads to some strange consequences since every question has at least two answers, one of which may be true, the other one false. Let A_{11} and A_{12} be answers to Q_1 and A_{11} = not A_{12}, then it could not be decided whether Q_1 is true or false. For if A_{11} were true, A_{12} would be false. There would be a contradiction since Q_1 would be a true and a false question at the same time.

The attempt has often been made to reduce ASK to other linguistic act-patterns. One of these attempts was suggested by the development of logical semantics: the reduction of ASK to ASS.[101] People thought that one could say (443) instead of asking (442):

(442)   Does such a theory make sense?
(443)   I want to know (from you) whether such a theory makes sense.

Apart from the fact that in some languages additional sentences would have to be used instead of (443) so that a whole family would have to be substituted for UTT (442) in the generation, the behavior of (443) in normal communication still differs from that of (442). A reaction to (443) might be the utterance of

(444)   Indeed?
(445)   Oh, I see.
(446)   So do I.

As answers to (442) the use of these sentences would be deviant,[102] probably because the QA-relation does not hold here. That makes it quite clear that ASK (CS) with its partitions generally stands in quite different contexts of interaction from those of ASS (CS) with its partitions.

Another attempt is to reduce ASK to some ORD- or REQUEST-patterns, which has usually been done by changing the formulation of the specification of UTT, i.e. introducing so-called imperative sentences like (447) for (442):[103]

(447)   Tell me whether such a theory makes sense!

The generation in this case should have the form: REQUEST (that (447'))
→ UTT (447), whereas a generation for ASK should have the following form:
ASK (whether (442')) → UTT (442). It should be noticed that the specification of ASK whether (442') occurs within the specification of REQUEST as
well. I suppose that the former is more elementary and that explaining a propositional expression of the form 'whether S' will not be possible without re-
course to ASK. I do not want to go into details here.

The whole attempt can be criticized in an analogous way to the first one.
P2 can react to the utterance of (447) with

(448)   I can't.

But (448) as an answer to (442) is odd:

(449) $* (UTT_1 (442) \dagger UTT_2 (448))$

P2 might react to the utterance of (442) by uttering

(450)   I do not know.
(451)   No.

Opposite assignments seem to be possible here but only in different generations, at least as concerns (451), the utterance of which as a reaction to the
utterance of (447) would be a refusal to obey the request. Thus it would not be
the negative answer to the question whether (442'). The difference comes
out in the corresponding description:[104]

(452) $UTT_1 (442) \dagger ANS_2 (that not (442')) \rightarrow UTT_2 (no)$

(453) $UTT_1 (447) \dagger \begin{bmatrix} SAY_2 \text{ (that not (447'))} \\ \text{-}SAY_2 \text{ (whether (442'))} \end{bmatrix} \rightarrow UTT_2 (no)$

Bearing these considerations in mind, it does not seem to be advisable to try
to reduce ASK to other patterns when beginning a description but rather to
begin with the representation of the place of ASK in interactions, its partitions, etc.[105] Then the relation to other patterns will be displayed as a by-
product.

By virtue of the separation of act-pattern and proposition we don't have to choose any more between the reduction of ASK to ASS and the loss of the semantic relations established for assertoric sentences.[106] Since semantic relations operate on the CS-level, we can profit from the relations established on ASS (CS) in other instances of ILLOC as far as propositions are concerned. And we can easily establish the corresponding relations for other patterns, e.g. for ASK.

An essential feature of ASK as of other instances of ILLOC is the specification which is a complement clause. Other means of description will be the generations and especially the specifications of the generated UTT (W), the specifications of which are linguistic expressions as well, although with the somewhat different status mentioned above.[107] To unfold the relation between X and W we have to start form the generation ASK (X)→ UTT (W). The traditional account included a classification of the interrogative sentences which stand for W according to their syntactic form, which was of course always inadequate because the same sentence can occur in different generations, e.g. (454) can occur in ASK (CS) → UTT (454) as well as in ASS (CS) → UTT (454):

(454)   He sailed.

Certainly a syntactic classification of S is important, but we want to follow up another possibility: a classification and description of ASK from the point of view of its communicative functions. For this purpose we shall return to our basic form (439) and extend it by additions to the partition of the components, the conditions of generation, the specifications and their contexts.

So-called rhetorical questions, where P1 does not expect an answer from P2 and P2 can dispense with the answer, prove to be a curtailment of the communication. P1 pretends to ask P2 something to get his agreement — he excludes contradiction in any case — but already presumes P2's agreement. Accordingly rhetorical questions would be a special case of leading questions with which P1 urges an agreement upon P2 without leaving him the possibility of contradiction. Since P1 normally allows P2 alternative possible answers and since the sense of an answer consists exactly in making a choice among finite or infinite alternatives, P1 curtails some possibilities of action with these questions. And this leads naturally enough to arguments against communications of this sort.

As an elementary generation of ASK_1 (X) we have already introduced: ASK_1 (X) → UTT_1 (W), where certainly current alternatives such as WRITE or certain codings in flag-languages would have to be added to the family of UTT. In analogy to the generation of ASK, we assumed ANS_2 (Y) → UTT_2 (Z) and the corresponding family of UTT.

But here the additional question arises whether an intermediate like ASS would have to be introduced. For if P2 gives an answer such as 'no' or the like, he commits himself to the truth of what he has said. But this commitment does not seem to be exactly the same as with ASS. E.g. if somebody asks me what time it is, and I tell him: 'It's three o'clock', I might have made a mistake or told a lie, just as with ASS. Still I was not subject to the same obligation as if I had asserted, rather than answered, that it is three o'clock. Therefore I shall not consider myself obliged to produce evidence. If P1 does not believe me I might say: 'Leave me alone', where it is not a matter of my avoiding proof. The question is whether we use ASS like 'assert' in English, or whether we want to follow the contexts which are similar in both cases and which are more in evidence in logical ways of using 'assert'. Because of our aims we shall opt for the first alternative and so we might think that the features corresponding to ASS are subsumed under ANS without an intermediate member being introduced into the generation. But in this we restrict the normal use of 'answer' in ANS. This use of 'answer', for example, admits the utterance of

(455)   Leave me alone.

as an answer to the question whether (442') and often it is used as widely as REACT: 'he answers with a box on the ear'. In other cases 'answer' is used in a way something like SAY, so that it is specified by 'no', 'yes', etc. without the generating UTT (*no*) etc. separately. Certainly one could take ANS to be as wide as this and represent these differences by a partition as

$$(456) \qquad \text{ANS} \;\rightarrow\; \left\{ \begin{array}{l} \text{STRIKE} \\ \text{UTT (Z)} \\ \cdot \\ \cdot \\ \cdot \end{array} \right\}$$

But we shall assume the restricted use of ANS where ANS is an instance of ILLOC, specified by CS. For this reason reactions like (455) in addition to ANS should be introduced into (440) as a component. In this way we provide for a use of the QA-relation that makes sense.

In order to enable somebody to act according to our basic form (439), certain conditions must be fulfilled, as is the case for all acts. In addition to general conditions, valid for other instances of ILLOC as well, an important condition for ASK_1 (X) is:

(457)   P1 does not know X.

This condition holds for every given specification that could be inserted for X. Apparent infringements of the condition (457) are so-called test questions which are asked in a quiz or often during lessons. For here P1 may know the answer to the question and therefore would possibly have no reason to ask the question.

The fact that he asks it all the same indicates that this is not an infringement of the condition (457) but that P1 actually wants to know something different, i.e. that he asks something different, namely whether P2 knows X. This case would have to be represented as a special case of asking:

(458) ASK_1 (whether P2 knows X) if P1 does not know whether
         P2 knows X.

It is important that this asking generate exactly the same patterns as normal asking, so that it cannot be recognized from the sentence uttered whether it is a normal question or a test question. One has to understand the generations with their conditions and one can only understand the act correctly if one believes the conditions to be fulfilled.

An interaction with test questions is asymmetrical. P1 only has the right to ask such questions on account of his role, e.g., because he is a teacher. This role also gives him the right to other acts, e.g., to decide on the correctness of the answer, to give a mark to P2, etc. Test questions are closely related to orders. For P2 hardly has any alternative: he will be penalized by P1 if he does not give an answer. Certainly this communication does not help to extend the knowledge of P2; for this reason it should be used as rarely as possible in teaching, and test questions must be distinguished from other communication where (457) is not fulfilled either, where so-called didactic questions are used. Here P1 assumes that P2 will find an answer and the act of ASK_1 (CS) is to help P2 to find out something different by the answer.

If one wants to distinguish sincere from insincere questions it should be noted that so-called sincere questions can occur in a perverted manner, e.g. if P1 saw that P2's possible answers were very limited. Thus the teacher can ask a sincere question with

(459)   What shall we do today?

But it is clear from the beginning that an answer will only be accepted which lies within the range of doing French. Here, again, it becomes evident that this communication is asymmetrical, since one of the partners has the right to decide on the acceptability of the answer. But normally the relation between X and Y is given by the linguistic rules of a social group, that is as a part of the rules for ASK.

In addition to the conditions for ASK_1 (X) and those for ANS_2 (Y), which we do not want to discuss further, the assumptions and presuppositions of both partners are relevant. A general assumption made by both partners is that

(i) There is a least one direct answer to the question X,

where 'direct answer' has to be understood as a Y with which, if it is the answer of P2, P1 learns what he wanted to know, neither more nor less.[108] E.g. (460) would be a direct answer to (442), whereas (461) would "over-answer" and (462) "under-answer":

> (460) Such a theory makes (does not make) sense.
> (461) Such a theory always makes sense.
> (462) Such a theory can be readily applied.

V is an over-answer of X if and only if QA (X, Y) and ENT (V, Y). U is an under-answer of X if and only if QA (X, Y) and ENT (Y, U). Our basic form can now be extended to:

$$(463) \quad ASK_1 \ (X) \ \text{if (i)} \ \dagger \dots \dagger \ \begin{Bmatrix} ANS_2 \ (Y) \ \text{if (i)} \\ \text{-}ANS_2 \end{Bmatrix}$$

The rejection of the assumption (i) by P2 cannot be regarded as an answer to P1's question though it can be understood as an answer in a certain sense if we start from a wider use of 'answer'. Here we have introduced this possibility in an additional intermediate component because the possibilities ANS_2 or $\text{-}ANS_2$ would again be open to P2 after such an attack has been parried. Thus only some intermediate components would be added to (463) in such a communication, as is provided for by the three dots. Another general assumption for ASK (X) → UTT (Z) implied by (i) is that

(ii) There is an answer to X.

And a third one on P1's side:

(iii) P1 believes that P2 may know of an answer to X.

In addition to the general conditions (i), (ii), (iii), there are presuppositions depending on X and Y which require the propositions as specifications of other act-patterns as well. We need not introduce them by way of the answer,[109] because we do not define presuppositions only in terms of truth-or-falsity. E.g. if P1 asks whether (442'), so that ASK_1 (whether (442')) → UTT (442), he presupposes at the same time that

(464)   Such theories can make sense.

Therefore asking a question means accepting the responsibility for its presuppositions. And so it is also possible to give information by questions. If P2 answers a question he presupposes the same things as P1 did when he asked the question. This is well known from certain dangerous questions in court or in interviews with interrogative sentences like

(465)   Why did you do that?
(466)   Why did you not stop HX-ing?

For if P2 answers these questions he acknowledges that (467') and that (468') because he presupposes that

(467)   I did that.
(468)   I HX-ed.

The presuppositions of P1 should be dealt with like assertions and he should be made responsible for them. In this context the question of an advisable use of ANS is at issue, a question we do not want to decide. Following our previous use of ANS, we could assume that the rejection of P1's presupposition by P2 is no answer. But there are often answers in our communications which concern a part of a presupposition of P1, especially in case of an "under-answer". E.g. if P1 asks with

(469)   Who constructed the theory?

and P2 answers with

(470)   It was a man.

this could be regarded as an under-answer in a certain sense, since P1 asks P2 to provide him with the possibility of identifying, by his answer, exactly the person who made the theory. If a direct answer to this question fulfilled this criterion and if we strengthened (iii) so that P1 believes that P2 knows a direct

answer then the utterance of (470) might be regarded as a partial rejection
of this assumption, which is open to P2 since it is usually obvious by
intonation, etc. that P1 asked a question. The extreme case would be where
P2 answers:

(471)   Somebody.

and thus completely rejects P1's assumption and only confirms a presupposition made by P1, namely that somebody made the theory. Another extreme
would be where P2 utters:

(472)   Nobody.

rejecting the assumption as well as the presupposition that somebody made
the theory. This shows that a strict separation between the rejection of assumptions or presuppositions, on the one hand, and the answer, on the other hand,
could turn out to be implausible.

Since ASK and ANS are instances of ILLOC they only admit as specifications propositional expressions or expressions with which one can refer to propositions. As for ASK, the specifications are restricted according to their syntactic form to 'whether S' and CS introduced by interrogative words, so-called indirect interrogative sentences; for ANS only 'that S' and CS introduced
by a zero-connective are possible.

A distinction is common between two kinds of question according to the
possibilities of answering them: yes-no questions and wh-questions. Yes-no
questions are such that the following holds for the answer:

$$(473) \qquad ANS_2 \rightarrow \left\{ \begin{array}{l} UTT_2 \ (yes) \\ UTT_2 \ (no) \\ \qquad . \\ \qquad . \\ \qquad . \end{array} \right\}$$

Correspondingly, the syntactic form of the specifications in ASK is always
'whether S'. With the yes-utterance P2 answers that S and with the no-utter-
ance that not S. The proposition in question must be gathered from the context. It is obvious that the communicative function of so-called minor sentences like 'yes' and 'no' is described in the communicative context, and also
that they perform in the same way as other sentences, for P2 could just as
well answer with the repetition of S or the utterance of 'not S'. Hence the
partition in (473) could be incomplete. Moreover it is questionable whether

it should be completed with answers which generate UTT (*maybe*), UTT (*possibly*) and the like. This again would affect the use of ANS, since one can assume that these utterances concern P1's assumptions and thus are relatives of the cases dealt with in (470), (471), (472). These possible alternatives are suggestive of a scale the outermost ends of which are 'yes' and 'no'. The decision as to which use of ANS is more convenient could only be provided by an extensive description which would have to describe these possibilities; in any case we shall retain the narrow use of ANS and extend our basic form for yes-no questions as follows:

$$(474) \quad (ASK_1 \text{ (whether S)} \rightarrow UTT_1 \text{ (Q.S)) if (i)} \dagger \ldots \dagger$$

$$\dagger \cdots \dagger \left\{ \begin{array}{l} (ANS_2 \text{ (that S)} \rightarrow \left\{ \begin{array}{l} UTT_2 \text{ (}yes\text{)} \\ UTT_2 \text{ (S)} \end{array} \right\}) \text{ if (i)} \\ (ANS_2 \text{ (that not S)} \rightarrow \left\{ \begin{array}{l} UTT_2 \text{ (}no\text{)} \\ UTT_2 \text{ (S1)} \end{array} \right\}) \text{ if } \underline{\text{(i)}} \\ -ANS_2 \end{array} \right\}$$

Q in UTT_1 (Q.S) represents the question operator mentioned in 3.3.1, the function of which should be determined more closely. For the newly introduced S1, the restriction has to be made that there is a special semantic relation between the corresponding propositions, namely INC (CS1, CS), as is intended in the specification of the generating ANS_2 by the insertion of 'not'. But 'not S', where 'not' must be understood as a sentence-negation, is only one case of the specifications of UTT within the partition. ANS_2 (that not S) can also generate UTT specified by other sentences, if only incompatibility holds. Therefore the uttering of (475) would be a generation for this member of (474):

(475)   No such theories make sense.

General violations of the incompatibility condition occur in sentences where one 'not' is already included which, obviously, is sometimes not used as a negation. The utterance of 'no' as a reaction to ASK_1 (whether (476')) by uttering

(476)   Isn't Bruno here?

can be understood as 'yes', thus as an act of ANS_2 (that (476')). In addition to the kind of yes-no questions in (470) where P2 has only two possible answers, there is another form where S in ASK_1 (whether S) stands for a sentence composed of *or*-coordinations of several sentences or *or*-coordinations of other syntactic positions:

(477)   Is he singing or screaming or crying?
(478)   Is that Bruno or Reinhard or Anna?

Such questions cannot be answered with 'yes' or 'no' and require an extension of our definition of yes-no questions. Therefore we assume as a new definiens that there is a yes-no question if and only if the specification in ASK_1 has the syntactic form 'whether S'.

In case of such yes-no questions with more than two alternatives the possible specifications of ANS_2 and UTT_2 change in such a way that one alternative is chosen from 'S1 or S2 or S3. . . . But in order to answer that S2 one need not always utter 'S2'. Maybe a minor sentence which we shall introduce when discussing *wh*-questions is sufficient.

Now *wh*-questions cannot be answered by uttering 'yes' or 'no'. The relation of the complement clauses represented by X and Y is somehow more complicated. The complement clause specifying ASK has the syntactic form of a CS with an interrogative word in one syntactic position: CS [CT + S], which again is a part of S. The main feature of these CS's is that one syntactic position is referentially left open. It is filled with an interrogative word which causes certain restrictions on the insertions in the answer but on the whole it is a kind of indicator for the fact that P1 wants P2 to insert a different syntagm in this syntactic position yielding a sentence uttered with assertoric force, i.e. with a truth claim. For this reason such interrogative words are introduced as pro-forms in generative theory. The corresponding complement clauses cause certain problems because they do not express complete propositions. For a CS like 'who sings' has to be completed first in order to be usable for the expression of a complete proposition, which comes out also in the fact that those CS's cannot be combined with 'is true'. Our analysis of illocutionary patterns demonstrated that there is good reason to assume that propositions are in play here as well. Only, stress is laid upon another component here, namely the referential component, whereas in most cases like ASS and yes-no questions stress is laid upon the truth component.[110]

The relations between CS1 and CS2, which are to be inserted for X and Y, can be described in terms of syntax as the relation between the corresponding sentence-parts S1 and S2. This relation here restricts the scope and the range of the QA-relation. The following holds:

(479) ASK_1 (CS1 [CT † S1 [. . .[K[q]. . .]]) † ANS_2 (CS2 [CT [that] + S2 [. . .[K [a]. . .]. . .]]),

174

where K stands for the syntactic position[111] of the interrogative q in question the syntactic category of which is the same for the answer syntagm a. But K is not to be understood as a variable for any syntactic position: There are positions where one cannot ask. This will not be discussed further. Nor shall we discuss an important *wh*-question with which one asks for a predicate:

(480)   What is he doing?

Since sentences like

(481)   He is grinning.,

which introduce parts of predicates or parts of predicates with complements, would be possible as answers to (480) they would not be covered by the general rule (479) either. Further restrictions are necessary since not every given a of the syntactic category K can be accepted in the answer sentence. E.g., (483) would not be possible as an answer to (482):

(482)   Who knows that?
(483)   Somebody knows that.

We have assumed that this is not sufficient because one already must assume that (483') if one asks (482') so that P2 would not give any information with such an answer. In addition certain changes of pronouns in S1 and S2 have to be taken care of for the case that a sentence contains a pronoun of the first or second person;[112] in answer sentences with a third person, subject-number congruence of the predicate must be secured.

As answer sentences to *wh*-questions certain elliptic expressions — or better, minor sentences — are possible, namely sentences which only consist of the answer syntagm a. Accordingly the partition of ANS_2 (CS2) is:

(484) ANS_2 (CS2 [CT + S2 [...[K[a]...]...]]) →
$$\left\{ \begin{array}{l} UTT_2\,(a) \\ UTT_2\,(S2\,[...[K[a]...]...]) \end{array} \right\}$$

This shows that the alternative generations are not completely equivalent. For with UTT_2 (a) one can only give the generating answer. But with the second utterance every given question of the same syntactic form can be answered, no matter which position K is or even whether a yes-no question has been asked. A more detailed syntactic description would dissolve this many-one relation because stress usually falls on a in the answer sentence.

When discussing yes-no questions, we already indicated with several alternatives the possible form of the answer, namely that there is a relationship between yes-no questions and *wh*-questions. This relationship gave rise to attempts to reduce one of the two kinds of question to the other. Katz-Postal[113] aim at the reduction of yes-no questions to *wh*-questions. For this purpose they introduce the 'or' in the more explicit basic form

(485)   S or not S?

as belonging to the syntactic category of sentence adverbs such as 'probably', 'possibly', so, too, for each expression in UTT (Z), e.g. 'yes', 'no', and complete answer sentences as well, for only then would the answer expression remain in the same syntactic category, as is required by (479). In this form the attempt is completely *ad hoc* and would have untenable consequences, e.g., all answer sentences would have to belong to at least two syntactic categories. But perhaps this reduction is possible in a different form. The yes-no questions mentioned above which cannot be answered with 'yes' or 'no' can be regarded as a special case of *wh*-questions where the alternative insertions for S2 would already be given. Therefore they do not include pure pro-forms. This can be made clear by changing the formulation:

(486)   Who is it: Bruno or Reinhard or Anna?

where we have a *wh*-prefix followed by three alternatives restricting the possible answers. In case of yes-no questions, which have to be represented in a form like

(487)   Will he or will he not come?

one had to assume a special prefix (say: 'Which is true?') which will not be discussed in detail here. But it is obvious that neither (486) nor (487) can be answered by uttering 'yes' or 'no' but only by the repetition of one of the alternatives.

I do not think, however, that this attempt is attractive either, because the syntactic and semantic form of (486) and (487) is not explained sufficiently. E.g. it might be assumed that (486) is to be reduced to a form like

(488)   Is it Bruno or is it Reinhard or is it Anna?

Like (486) yet unlike a yes-no question, this usually admits the choice of
'Bruno' and 'Anna', i.e. of two alternatives jointly, as an answer. But if each
of the possible answers always excludes the other possible answers, a question
can be understood as several succeeding yes-no questions and their answers:

(489)   Is it Bruno? No, it isn't.
        Is it Reinhard? No, it isn't.
        Is it Anna? Yes, it is.

Here we arrive at another attempt to reduce *wh*-questions to yes-no questions
– which would help us to get rid of the problem raised by there being a way
of asking which cannot be specified by complete propositions. This attempt
is made by Harrah[114] and seems to be plausible for the example (478).
Harrah proceeds as follows: He introduces all *whether*-questions as disjunctive questions of the form (487) or (488) among which there are special cases
that can be answered by 'yes' or 'no'. The *wh*-questions are only distinguished
from these disjunctive questions by the fact that they offer a great, maybe an
infinite, number of alternatives.

I do not want to recapitulate Harrah's technical devices. But the following
is important: In cases where the catalogue of alternatives is finite or known,
a *wh*-question could really be regarded as an abbreviation for a chain of yes-
no questions, but with this difference: using the abbreviation has considerable
consequences in communication and therefore cannot be considered as com-
municatively equivalent. A good example is the question game dealt with in
4.3.1, which could be mastered in two moves with *wh*-questions, but which
also shows that sequences of yes-no questions offer certain possibilities of
checking the answers which *wh*-questions do not offer.

In this context that case seems to me to be more important where the set
of alternatives is infinite, open, or not known, or where P1 does not know at
all according to which criteria such alternatives can be formulated. Here certain consequences result from the logic of lists[115] for the restriction of the
act-pattern ASK. For it is obvious that in this case a formulation of the corresponding sequence of yes-no questions is impossible, at least within a finite
communication which we have to assume. But the restriction to a finite number of alternatives does not seem to describe asking and our communication
in an adequate way at all. For it would require a determinate world and almost
omniscient agents. But one who asks a *wh*-question need not know the possible alternative answers, he need not even assume a definite scope for the answers. For he can accept an answer that does not fit the scope of answers he
had hitherto thought possible. This is one of the most important accomplish-
ments of asking for the agent's knowledge and for the extension of the world
of a social group.

3.5.2 *A restricted* why-*communication*

Why-questions and *because*-answers are of importance in various spheres of our life, e.g., in scientific explanation, in everyday arguments or when questioning norms. Even in creative intelligence tests the ability to answer *why*-questions is introduced as one dimension. The close relation of 'why' and 'because' to 'explain', 'cause', 'justify', 'causality', etc. is not that the use or the meaning of *because*-answers can be explained by words like 'cause' as some philosophers of science and semanticists have wanted to make us believe. Rather, words like 'why' and 'because' really are elementary, so that it is description of their use which is the basis for the description of 'explain', 'causality', etc.[116]

Our restricted *why*-communication is not likely to be found in such a simple form but embedded in a larger communicative context. Nevertheless it covers some essential problems occurring in normal communication. We assume n partners as participants in the communication. One of them, let us call him P1, opens the communication by asserting something. Thereupon the next one can react in two ways: he may ask 'why' or he may say 'that's wrong'. In the first case P1 has to justify his assertion, in the second case he can reply 'that's right'.[117] After this move of P1 it is P3's turn. He has the same alternatives as P2. The game goes on, such that P1 and the next in the sequence P2,. . ., Pn act alternatingly. We assume that the communication is finished if P1 gives up or if the branch with the alternating 'that's wrong': 'that's right' comes to Pn.

The formal description will be made in several steps. We begin with a simple representation of the first and of the second level in (490):

$$(490) \qquad ASS_1 \, (CS1)$$

$$UTT_2 \; (\textit{that's wrong}) \qquad\qquad UTT_2 \; (\textit{why})$$

This description is inadequate. For the possible utterances of P2 are generated by other patterns. If P2 utters 'that's wrong' he may negate what P1 has asserted, i.e. he asserts the contrary. Since $NEG_i \, (CS) = ASS_i \, (not \, CS)$, P2 asserts that CS1 is not the case by uttering 'that's wrong'. The right-hand alternative of P2 is also generated, since P2 asks with his utterance why it is the case that S1, which is only possible if he presupposes that S1. If we introduce these generations into our provisional tree, it has the following form:

$$(491) \qquad\qquad ASS_1 \ (CS1) \to UTT_1 \ (S1)$$

$$ASS_2 \ (not \ CS1) \to UTT_2 \ (\textit{that's wrong}) \quad \left. \begin{array}{l} ASK_2 \ (why \ S1) \\ \\ PRES_2 \ (CS1) \end{array} \right] \to UTT_2 \ (\textit{why})$$

As syntactic relation between CS1 and S1 we assume CS1 [CT + S1], more generally CSk [CT + Sk], where CT is the category of words like 'that', 'whether', etc. So we omit other parts of the partition of ASS (CS1). This is justified by the general restrictions of our communication as a result of which the partners cannot discuss the relation of CSk to Sk because they can only utter 'why' and 'that's wrong'. Concentrating upon the propositional expression CS1 also obviates the need to substitute personal pronouns. Nevertheless, the description (491) is not complete either, for by uttering 'that's wrong' one can not only assert the contrary of CS1 but also deny the presuppositions which P1 made when uttering S1.[118]

Let us take the sentence (492):

(492)   The present king of France is bald.

As is known, one of its presuppositions is:

(493)   There is a king of France at present.

I think the utterance of 'that's wrong' in reaction to the utterance of (492) can also be understood as a denial of the presupposition (493), but of course only if this is made clear by an addition, say: 'that's wrong because there is no king of France'. An addition is normally necessary for P1 to be able to decide (i) whether P2 had denied CS1 or attacked the presupposition; (ii) which of the presuppositions is under attack.

However, this differentiation has no effect here, since P1 in our communication would have to repel such an attack in the same way as the assertion of not-CS1. There are two possible ways we could introduce this into our description. We can start from the generation:

$$(494) \quad \left. \begin{array}{l} ASS_2 \ (not \ CS1) \\ ASS_2 \ (not \ CS) \end{array} \right\} \to \ UTT_2 \ (\textit{that's wrong})$$

and introduce CS as well as a variable for the presuppositions in the first speech act. But in this case ASS_2 (not CS) would be a blind alley since P1 cannot react to it in an adequate manner.

The second possibility would be not to differentiate at all between the act-patterns generating UTT (*that's wrong*). This is no solution because the utterance of 'that's wrong' will also occur in other branches of the tree where the twofold generation might be relevant. Thus we extend (491) in the following way:

(495)

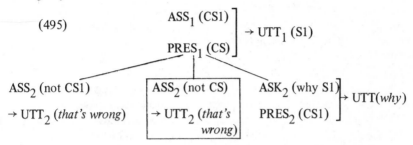

We frame the central node in order to indicate that this branch is blind. I don't try to remedy another weakness of description (495), the fact that UTT (*why*) is not always generated by ASK (why S1). It depends on the form of S1 whether this holds or not. In the case of performative sentences and coordinated sentences as well as subordinated sentences, P2 can ask why Sp, where Sp is a part of S1.

The case where you ask why someone did what he did, by uttering 'why', e.g. why he asked what he asked, is excluded, since it does not occur with ASS.

At the next level, in the left branch, P1 has to continue by repeating his assertion. Then P3 has the alternatives P2 had before. If he chooses the left branch, P1 has to answer anew and the game goes on to P4 and, in general, to $P(i + 1)$. If P3 chooses the right branch, the communication goes on just as it would have had P2 already done so. This can be introduced into our tree by a running index j for the agent and $j \neq 1$.

(496)

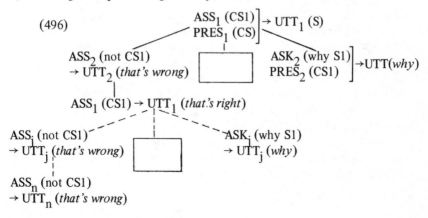

For simplicity the generated UTT_i could be omitted because of our restriction that there are no alternatives in the generated patterns. The alternatives generated by ASK_j (why S) in normal English communications could of course easily be introduced.

In (496) we have already reached one end of the communication, namely the end with $n = j$ in the left branch.

If P2 chooses the right alternative at level two, P1 has again only one possibility; he has to give a justification by uttering a sentence of the form 'because S2', more explicitly: ASS_1 (CS1 because S2) → UTT_1 (*because* S2). The expression 'CS1 because S2' might be syntactically misleading because it does not represent the fact that 'because S2' is a part of CS1, namely a subordinate sentence in S1. This does no harm, however, and we can use the less precise representation. But we need a more precise analysis of ASS_i (CS1 because S2) which tells us something about whether and in which way the pattern ASS_i can be distributed over CS1 and S2. The answer seems to be easy for CS1: we had a similar case on level two. There we assumed that an assertion of a sentence of the form S [. . .[A2]] , A2 standing for the syntactic position of a causal adverbial, is only possible under the condition that the sentence without the adverbial is presupposed. Thus it holds that ASS_i (CS1 because S2) must occur with $PRES_i$ (CS1). If P3 then reacts by uttering 'that's wrong' the case would be similar to that in the left branch: he might question both a presupposition and the assertion of CS1 made by P1 and P2. Since here the same holds as before, we omit this blind branch.

But how about S2? One might try to get details about whether CS2 is presupposed or asserted by considering further communications. E.g. what can P3 do by saying 'that's wrong'? Can he only question whether CS2 can be regarded as a reason for CS1, thereby assuming that both CS1 and CS2 are true? This possibility, (i), is rarely taken up (at least for the original German 'stimmt nicht'). We shall find a possible reason for this later when describing this case. Yet a further possibility is that (ii) P2 just questions CS2 with his utterance. But it is doubtful whether we can arrive at a conclusion in the case of the question whether CS2 has been asserted or presupposed by P1. We would be forced to assume that CS2 is asserted if 'that's wrong' were only used to negate an assertion and not in order to question a presupposition. It is true that we cannot advance arguments for the one or the other from our example, but it seems reasonable to assume that UTT_i (*that's wrong*) can be used in order to reject an assertion as well as a presuppositon, here as well as in the left branch.

Thus we have two possible ways of deciding for one of the alternatives (i) and (ii): we can go on analysing the use of 'that's wrong' or we can consider differnt uses of 'CS1 because S2'. I opt for the latter possibility because something still remains to be said about the case where P2 chooses the right branch. How can we understand P2's utterance of 'why', i.e. how does the communication go on? First of all, it is questionable whether UTT_i (why) is generated by ASK_i (why S2) or by ASK_i (why (S1 because S2)). Is what is in question the truth of the justifying sentence or the truth of the relation between the two sentences? Both seem to be possible here. However, the normal case is ASK_i (why S2) $\rightarrow UTT_i$ (why). The reason for this could be the increasing complication if acts were performed according to sequences of why-questions. For the following recursivity arises: ASS_1 (CS1 because S2) † ASK_2 (why (S1 because S2)) † ASS_1 ((CS1 because S2) because S3) † ASK_3 (why ((S1 because S2) because S3)) and so on. This seems to be difficult for speakers[119], and in consequence we have found a frequent restriction of our competence, namely the competence of questioning justifications, justifications of justifications, etc. It can easily be shown that the alternative (i) leads to the same recursivity which is reason enough for not using it very often.

Does not the case of ASK_i (why S2) $\rightarrow UTT_i$ (why) indicate that CS2 is also asserted in ASS_i (CS1 because S2)?[120] Otherwise P2's question would be about P1's presupposing. But this, too, is possible, and we cannot draw conclusions from this description for our starting question either, though it is useful as a part of our description of the whole communication.

In order to come to a decision about our question we can proceed in three ways: (a) We can consider reactions other than 'that's wrong' and in this way try to find a difference between reactions with which an assertion can be questioned and reactions with which a presupposition can be questioned. A typical indication for the fact that a presupposition is questioned is the utterance of a sentence of the form 'but surely not S2'. (b) We can examine the properties of 'CS1 because S2' as a specification of other illocutionary patterns and draw analogous conclusions for ASS. (c) We can examine 'because' in contrast to other subordinate sentence connectives such as 'if', 'although', etc.

Attempt (a) is not likely to be of much help because, in fictitious examples, the possibilities of questioning or rejecting an assertion are very much like those for presuppositions. In the case of presuppositions the sentence only needs to be completed by the addition mentioned above because a sentence expressing the presupposed proposition is not uttered and therefore cannot be referred to by P2. But even such sentences with additions can in fact be used in a reaction to the corresponding assertion. Perhaps differences may be brought to light by empirical inquiries. Here we shall not discuss attempt (a), for such additions are not admitted in our communication anyway.

Attempt (c) does not promise quick results either, because the connections of sentences behave differently depending on the distribution of the illocutionary patterns they specify. Consider the case of 'if' where the question whether CS2 in 'CS1 if CS2' is presupposed or asserted does not occur at all: it is neither presupposed nor asserted.

So let us turn to (b), which promises success because the question whether CS2 is presupposed or asserted is related to the question of ASS distribution in ASS (CS1 because S2), but is hard to decide here because of the close relation between ASS and PRES. If we assume that such an analogy is conclusive it would have to be decided whether for selected instances of illocutionary patterns (497) or (498) is valid:

(497) ILLOC (CS2) ⊏ ILLOC (CS1 because S2).
(498) PRES (CS2) ⊏ ILLOC (CS1 because S2).

Let us first take ASK and the specification (499):

(499) Is he coming because he is hungry?

which shows that ASK cannot be distributed to CS2, for with (499) one surely cannot ask whether he is hungry. This is rather presupposed, which can be shown by the possible answer (500) with the characteristic 'not. . . at all':

(500)   But he is not hungry at all.

We obtain the same result with ORD and (501):

(501)   Come, because I need you!

But this is somewhat more complicated, for only under certain conditions can (501) be uttered without deviation. E.g. if 'come!' had been uttered before and (501) is uttered as a justification in the face of a query. Obviously the ordering is what is justified and not what is ordered, which is more explicit in (502):

(502)   I order you to come, because I need you.

That's why we usually prefer the formulation:

(503)   Come! I need you.

Although we will not analyze these specifications of ORD precisely — a task which certainly involves difficulties — we may infer from this example that this instance of ILLOC cannot be distributed to CS2 either,[121] and we may transfer this to ASS. Now we shall continue our tree in the right branch (see figure (504)):

In the tree we have already passed this node and described how P3 continues. For 'that's wrong' as well as for 'why' we started from the use that includes the application to presuppositions. Yet we get only a four-way branching because the presupposition CS1 cannot be included. For, since P2,. . .Pn form a coalition, it can be assumed that P3 will not attack the presupposition CS1 made by P1 for being made by P2, too.

Certainly, P1 cannot know what P3 actually wants to do, for he has criteria neither for the choice among the left pair of nodes nor for the choice among the right pair of nodes. For this reason certain alterations of this communication would have to be introduced which indicate differences for the alternative generations of UTT (*that's wrong*) and for those of UTT (*why*). Obviously a feasible concept of polysemy might be introduced by the exact description of communications. But in the communication described here P1 would have a free choice between the two left nodes and between the two right nodes. Empirically it can be shown that usually, or almost exclusively, the inner alternatives are chosen, probably because of the recursion in the outer branches of this level, mentioned above.

Of course the ways in which P1 might react are now exactly the same as on the third level, except for the index of P2,. . ., Pn which will now be $k + 1$ and the indexes of the specification, where S2 occurs in the position of S1. In order to introduce this continuation into the tree we shall use circular dotted edges with inscriptions for the changes of indexes, and give as a description of the whole communication the following (see figure (505)):

NOTES

1. Cf. Austin (1971).
2. 'Reasonably short' means: can be used in communication in a similar way. A rather long explanation, for instance, cannot be used as a predicate, but 'Schlaf haben' can.
3. Quine (1963: 32).
4. Carnap (1955).
5. White (1952).
6. Cf. Geach's fallacy, Geach (1968: 61).
7. In other variations people talk of markers or features, which is still more misleading insofar as one loses hold of the fact that they are signs of a language.
8. I base my representation on the version developed by Heger (1964).
9. Cf. Bierwisch (1970).
10. Cf. the criticism Weinreich (1966) makes of Katz-Fodor (1963).
11. Cf. Heringer (1973: 118-22).

184

(504)

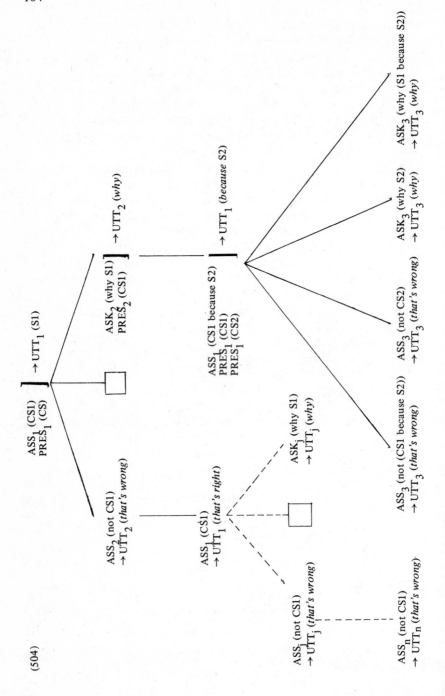

185

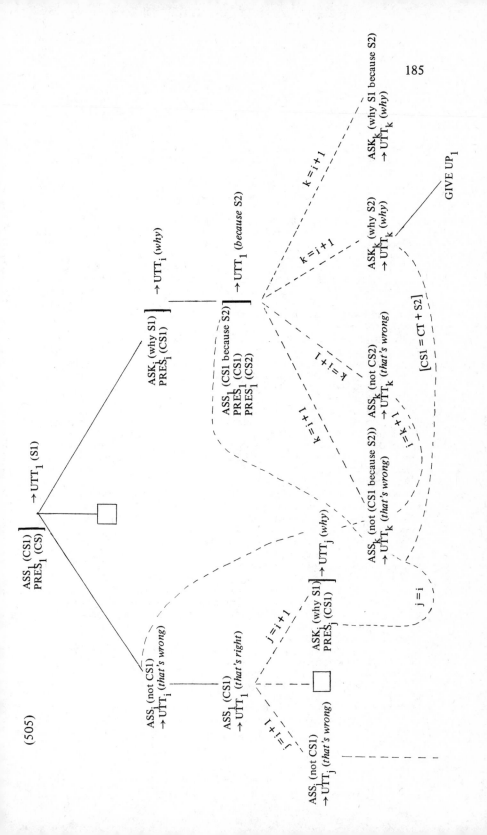

(505)

12. Chomsky (1971: 196).

13. Sometimes interpretation of the ultimate constituents or features is thought of on the lines of a model-theoretical interpretation.

14. Quine (1970).

15. The syntax is a simplification of one presented in Heringer (1972).

16. A more exact syntax would have to distinguish between sentences and sentence forms so that the same node does not occur three times.

17. Carnap (1964: 56): "Let us consider, as an example, the expressions '2+5' and 'II sum V' in a language S containing numerical expressions and arithmetical functors. Let us suppose that we see from the semantical rules of S that both '+' and 'sum' are functors for the function Sum and hence are L-equivalent; and, further, that the numerical signs occurring have their ordinary meanings and hence '2' and 'II' are L-equivalent to one another, and likewise '5' and 'V'. Then we shall say that the two expressions are *intensionally isomorphic. . ."*

18. Cf. the definition given in Mates (1950: 202): "A body of discourse A is a translation of another body of discourse B if and only if there is a correspondence between the meaningful parts of A and those of B such that corresponding parts are synonymous."

19. Cf. Austin (1971: 132). Obviously one has such cases in mind when one ends communications with utterances like "our difference is only verbal" and ignores the possibility that it is just not a question of words.

20. Many psychological theories and much of their technical vocabulary can be classed in this group, as well as certain semantic theories which want to explain the meaning of 'because' by means of 'causal'. As if our problems were of the sort where we did not understand 'because' but did understand 'causal'.

21. Cf. Wittgenstein's remarks on the task of philosophy, Wittgenstein (1953 : § 122-5).

22. Therefore the term 'context' is used here in a wider sense than usual. I hope that my hints will enable the reader to understand the wider use.

23. Perhaps we should pay attention to the fact that similar exotic considerations play a part in our everyday misunderstandings and that therefore this example is not far-fetched, thus the strange use of 'if' on which (254) is based is not rare, just as little as other cases where certain norms of others remain completely unintelligible to us.

24. Festinger (1957: 13).

25. Festinger (1957: 267).

26. Wittgenstein (1953 : § 124) assumes that his way of doing philosophy leaves everything as it is. But on the other hand he makes it clear that description in this sense is already normative as far as it deals with truth (cf. Wittgenstein [1970]). Moreover Wittgenstein's aim is to eliminate certain sentences.

27. An exception to this are so-called *wh*-questions: ASK (whom I wish).

28. Those admitted roughly correspond to ES art 1 in Heringer (1973).

29. Frege (1960: 62; 1967). Propositions in this sense are cognate to Meinong's objectives, Brentano's content of judgement, Bolzano's *Satz an sich* and recently to the propositions of Searle, who emphasizes the relation to Frege. These similarities are only to indicate a tradition, there are differences enough. E.g. Meinong assumes that p and q in 'if p then q' would be objectives. With Frege they would not express complete thoughts, cf. Frege (1960: 72).

30. Frege (1967: 21; 1960: 126).

31. In the following, '*that*-clause' will often be used for the part of the complement clause which syntactically corresponds to a complete sentence. Unlike this part the complement clause is no sentence at all, but a clause. In order to avoid confusions one would have to introduce a syntactic theory.

32. Frege (1967: 21; 1892: 38).

33. This does not affect the important connection of ASS with truth which Frege stressed. Although, this, too, should appear in a theory possessing the scope of Practical Semantics.

34. Cf. Prior (1971: Chapter 2).

35. Obviously this is thinking along the lines of the conceptual theories of meaning: propositions as sentence-meanings is a sequel to the myth of ideas as word-meanings.

36. Frege (1967: 37): "The thought, for example, that the tree there is covered with green leaves, will surely be false in six months time. No, for it is not the same thought at all. The words 'this tree is covered with green leaves' are not sufficient by themselves for the utterance, the time of utterance is involved as well. Without the time-indication this gives we have no complete thought, i.e. no thought at all. Only a sentence supplemented by a time-indication and complete in every respect expresses a thought. But this, if it is true, is true not only today or tomorrow but timelessly."

37. Quine (1970: 13).

38. Identification among all objects is presupposed in most accounts of definite descriptions (cf. Searle (1969: 79)) although there might be a more adequate theory of reference based on Kripke's rigid designators and emphasizing the historical and actional character of referring within everyday communication.

39. Cf. Lewis (1970: 24-25).

40. Cf. Ryle (1964: 15-35).

41. This has often been done. For an explication of 'symbol' as it is used here cf. Alston (1964: 50-61).

42. Cf. Kenny (1963: 91-2).

43. Cf. Grice (1968); Schiffer (1972).

44. Schiffer (1972: 1).

45. Grice and Schiffer give as one alternative of Meaning 'Meaning something by uttering y', Grice (1968: 226); Schiffer (1972: 63).

46. Cf. Stampe (1968: 140).

47. Kenny (1963: 172-6).

48. Since Meaning goes with symbolic acts and communication this is not to say I Mean something without a partner.

49. In greater detail: Linsky (1967: chapter 8).

50. Linsky (1967: 18).

51. Examples for such analyses are Grice's and Schiffer's although it is not really clear how 'intend' is used in the explanation of 'Mean' because the analogy is not represented in the linguistic form of the analysis. But I think that 'S meant something by (or in) uttering x if S uttered x intending. . .' could be paraphrased by 'S meant something by (or in) uttering x if S intended. . . by (or in) uttering x'. Cf. Schiffer (1972: 63).

52. Therefore, to the asymmetry of the arrow-relation there corresponds an asymmetry of 'y' and 'x' in (316).

53. They are mixed up in Schiffer (1972: 63): ". . . intending thereby to realize. . ."; ". . . with the primary intention that. . ."; "intended to be such that...".

54. This is not so with 'Mean that'. The greatest difficulties in clearing up the use of 'Mean' come from the great variety of complement constructions of the verb. Since to me the form (316) seems to be basic I concentrate on it although I cannot show the interrelation with other forms.

55. In the analysis of Grice (and Schiffer) it is assumed that the speaker intends that y have a certain feature, e.g. counting as x or being a symbol of a language, etc. But I do not think that a reasonable speaker can intend this. Perhaps Grice's wish to describe all conditions in an analogous way as intentions of the speaker leads him to this assumption.

56. The idea is due to R. Keller who uses it in his doctoral thesis for the definition of common knowledge avoiding the problems arising out of this in the definitions of Lewis' common knowledge and Schiffer's mutual knowledge*. It is obvious that the analysis of 'honestly' ends in 'believe' and is, in principle, no way out. But as 'honestly' covers at least both 'know' and 'believe', with respect to what it commits us to, it does better than either of them.

57. INTERPRET is related to 'understand' in the second use insofar as understanding is the result of INTERPRET.

58. Linguists who try to transfer methods developed by logicians in the construction of artificial languages start from the picture of naive communication and they adhere in a certain (the unhistorical) sense to the postulate of constancy of meaning, cf. 3.3.1

59. These difficulties in verifying (363) do not prove the weakness of our analysis. They only show that the same verification problems arise with communication.

60. Conditions for lying and irony are partly parallel but irony is no deception at all, not even in the case of communication between three partners where P3 does not understand irony, since then P1 does not communicate ironically with P3.

61. I hope it will be clear that I do not want to hold that Meaning is logically (or even historically) prior to meaning. That this would be nonsense is shown by the observation that in Meaning you are not free.

62. Notice that it is odd to say I understand P1 better than he does. The criterion for this being the agreement of P1 psychotherapy has to be based on the slogan 'understand P1 better than he d i d! '.

63. Cf. Lewis (1969: 36-41).

64. Labov (1972).

65. That we do not use 'is true' in a metalinguistic way is shown by the fact that we also translate the CS when we translate sentences of the form (370). Besides there is no metalanguage in public use beyond the use of natural language. In opposition to mathematics where there is one, explanation of natural language in terms of a metalanguage simply amounts to explaining the metalanguage by the natural language under analysis. Cf. also 3.1.

66. Frege (1967).

67. Ayer (1936: 88).

68. Danto (1973: 5).

69. Cf. Prior (1971: 4-13).

70. Cf. also Frege (1967); Strawson (1971: 194).

71. Cf. Winch (1972).

72. The differences between the dispositional and the activated character of 'believe' may also be comprehended in analogy to the distinction made by Ryle between dispositions and occurrences; Ryle (1949: 116-25).

73. I do not want to discuss the generation concerned here. Cf. generally Austin (1962); Furberg (1971: 197-98).

74. Yet adding a negation like 'not' need not have the consequence that the utterance of the sentence is generated by another pattern. With the utterance of 'I do not assert CS' one really can assert but not CS.

75. Austin (1962: 6).

76. I think it obvious from 3.3.1 why I do not consider that the sentence (397) can be true or false.

77. Furberg (1971: 195).

78. The definitions and attempts at definitions in Austin (1962), Alston (1964: 34-36) and Searle (1969: 25, 44, 46) differ from one another and do not convince me, above all because I do not regard a definition of PERLOC as possible which starts from the reaction or the result. This applies also to ILLOC. This does not mean that I do not think it important whether the success of an act is independent of a partner or not. Nor does it mean that the consequences of an act are not important. But illocutionary acts have consequences as well as perlocutionary ones. One has only to think of our Italian story.

79. It may as well have something to do with the fact that generations like ILLOC (CS) → UTT (*S) are deviant, and perhaps those with contradictory S as well.

80. Searle (1969: 25).

81. Austin (1962: 118); Searle (1969: 25) have WARN as an illocutionary pattern.

82. This is a suggestion of V. Beeh.
83. Strawson (1963: 175-76).
84. Nerlich (1965: 34). Frege tends rather towards the second alternative: Frege (1892); Black (1962: 50).
85. On this version it would still have to be decided whether the condition if X concerns UTT (Y), ASS (CS) or the whole generation. Certainly it will not concern UTT (Y) because this did not play a part at all in our previous considerations and if X does not hold, one certainly can utter the sentence corresponding to CS without deviating if one does not want to assert something by uttering it. Since the condition does not vary throughout the whole partition of ASS (CS), it seems to be advisable to restrict it to ASS (CS).
86. Strawson (1971: 13). Explanations of the form: with wrong presuppositions "the question does not arise" (Strawson [1963: 173-4]) can also be introduced into the theory through ASK since asking the question involves making the same presuppositions.
87. Cf. Geach (1965: 454).
88. The term 'entrenchment' as it is defined here should not be mixed up with other uses of the term.
89. Cf. for similar distinctions Beeh (1973: chapter 5).
90. This problem has been fully discussed in logic in connection with implication and entailment, cf. e.g. Benett (1954), whence one can follow up the discussion. Cf. also Strawson (1948: especially 186-87).
91. Notice that the condition of an illocutionary pattern is not entrenched. It is quite possible that I assert that S when I don't believe it. But it does not make sense for me to assert that S and that I don't believe it (Moore's paradox).
92. I am thinking of works like Beeh (1973).
93. In analogy to Carnap (1964: 10) one could say that necessary entrenchments are those which "can be established on the basis of the semantical rules" alone. This may work for formal systems where meaning is defined or laid down by meaning-postulates. But description of natural language is neither a matter of definition nor of postulating. Therefore such a principle would only beg the question: we are engaged in finding out the semantical rules and cannot presuppose them for any distinction.
94. The related objection that one could not calculate under operators such as 'normally' or 'probably' is exaggerated. Rules of inference under such operators have been given; rules that correspond more closely to what happens in natural languages; cf. Polya (1968). A conclusion of this kind is for instance one in court: P1: "Were you in a hurry? " P2: "Yes, I was." P1: "It is more probable that you caused the accident." We content ourselves with this hint because we do not want to go into details of the logic of the semantic relations and will leave open most of the problems in this area, especially the connections with ordinary logical relations. But I think we must be on our guard against using the looseness of semantic relations as a free ticket to forget the lessons that logic teaches us.
95. It is a slightly modified excerpt from Laffal-Ameen (1959: 267).
96. The example is too complicated to give an exhaustive description here. E.g. if P2 understood (c) as 'You do not mean that you know' he could react to this by (d) saying: I do not know this, the complement of 'know' not being the answer to the question asked by (a).
97. E.g. Strawson (1963: chapter 1).
98. Lyons (1968: 458).
99. Cf. Ziff (1960: 41).
100. Certainly this only holds for sentences with propositional content, not for 'hello' and the like.
101. Cf. Wittgenstein (1953: 23). The reduction to so-called assertoric linguistic act-patterns is important. This does not have to be ASS but might as well be ASCERTAIN or DESCRIBE and the like.
102. Moreover one could give a kind of answer with (443). E.g., if P1 has a bad temper

and P2 asks him what's the matter, (443) might be given as an answer but (442) is unlikely. This shows that the restriction to these sentences without consideration of the act-patterns does not make sense at all.

103. Frey (1965: 369); Katz-Postal (1964: 85) assume a relation with imperatives as well, but give as an equivalent an indicative sentence: 'I request that you answer. . .' and thus beg the question since the word 'answer' makes sense only in relation to 'ask' or 'question'.

104. As discussed in 3.3.1 it is important to secure continuity of reference in our propositional expressions. For this reason (447') 's pronouns in (453) must be changed correspondingly.

105. Another criticism of such attempts is made by Llewelyn (1964). They are often made without taking into account the act-patterns, e.g. Harrah's account in Harrah (1963), where a question is introduced as a disjunction of its answers, criticized by Hamblin (1963). Presumably such things won't be tried anymore in a description within action theory.

106. For this reason it seems that Harrah (1963: 28-29) does not correctly understand Wittgenstein, who dealt with ASK.

107. The specifications of UTT are not questions in the sense introduced, but at best interrogative sentences which have to be distinguished from questions, whereas the specifications of ASK have much in common with questions because we use 'question' in analogy to 'assertion' etc. for what is asked, that is, a proposition.

108. Cf. Belnap (1969: 27).

109. This definition by way of the answer is given in Belnap (1969: 32): a question X presupposes S if and only if S is a necessary condition for Y, one of the direct answers to X, being true or false.

110. In logical discussions of the question a sentence function with a question operator has been used: For which x (I see x). The incompleteness has been expressed by the variable which just keeps the place for an insertion and thus can be compared to an interrogative word. But this is nothing but another representation of incompleteness, not an explanation.

111. The cases where several positions filled by such interrogative words occur within one sentence are not considered here.

112. Cf. Katz-Postal (1964: 115).

113. Katz-Postal (1964: 95-102). Such attempts have long been available in logical discussion, cf. Prior-Prior (1955).

114. Harrah (1963: 32-34).

115. For open lists in a different context cf. Geach (1968: 184-91).

116. Cf. e.g. Bromberger (1966: 90-91).

117. For reasons of simplicity we ignore problems concerning the repetition of 'that' and 'it'.

118. Originally the description was made for German 'stimmt' : 'stimmt nicht'. So I am not sure to what extent the same holds for English.

119. Probably not because of embedding in the sense of Chomsky (1965: chapter 2).

120. This is assumed by Baker (1956: especially p. 375), presumably because he does not contrast ASS with other instances of illocutionary patterns. As for ASS the question of distribution has already been discussed in Frege (1892), where he explains the differences between clauses.

121. It seems to me that there are no commands expressed in clauses just as there are no questions expressed in clauses. This general principle seems to be, by analogy, a strong argument for the thesis that the proposition expressed in a clause could not be asserted but only presupposed.

4 COMMUNICATION GAMES

4.1 INTERACTIONS AS GAMES

In theoretical considerations human action is often compared with games. Probably this is often done because both are constituted by rules and the constitutive rules of games are simpler and clearer than those of serious action. On the other hand, both are considered to be so closely related that arguments about properties of games are carried over into the methods used to understand the structure of our action. In this case the playfulness of the game is left out of consideration, as for instance in Wittgenstein's language game or in de Saussure's comparison between language and chess.

The relation between games and serious action is usually put in the terms of mathematical game theory which, starting from the theory of parlor games, has gradually been generalized to such an extent that it may be applied to all human actions. 'Game' within game theory is used in such a general way that it no longer means unserious or playful action but can be used where it is a matter of life and death.

From a certain point of view social action can probably always be considered as interaction, for instance action against nature where people cooperate or at least depend upon what they have learnt when interacting with others. Since the courses of interactions are not determinate, the agents must have alternatives between which they can choose according to their aim. If the objectives of the partners are the same or partly the same they certainly can cooperate, otherwise interaction becomes competition.

The agents choose not only the act-patterns which they want to obey in order to reach their aims, but they can also choose their aims. It is said that so-called rational agents determine their aims in a way that secures the greatest utility for them. Certainly this is in some way a tautological assumption because the amount of the subjective utility of others is inferred from the choice of the aim. What counts as the greatest utility for an altruist or a masochist will not coincide with the estimation of many other people. Yet we assume that he reaches the greatest subjective utility given the aims he has chosen. We even conclude from these aims that someone must be an altruist or a masochist.

It is evident that a communicative problem exists here and that we are not allowed to assume that the criteria of preference are the same for different agents in this respect. This is the reason why the fairness of a game is not absolute. E.g., one might maintain that lotto is an unfair game, since only half the takings are paid out. But people do play it and from this one can conclude that lotto-players do not consider it to be unfair. The reason will probably be that they have a different preference function, namely that there is a fair chance of gaining so much money. How great this chance is is secondary.

There are similar problems in evaluating aims and about utility in scientific and political action. For example, one of the essential problems of the organizers of politically leftish parties in their attempt to join the workers is that their aims, which they want to reach for the benefit of the workers, are differently valued by the workers themselves. This shows that a real attempt to reach solidarity must not stand still on the assumption that the aims one assumes for others are somehow objective, but that it is important to influence the aims of others and to begin with one's partner's judgements and what he understands. Of course that does not mean that one would have to accept the preferences of others nor that these are inherent in the game. For that would not allow historical changes of or in the game, at best it would allow an alternative game the introduction of which would involve the same problems.

For the discussion of interactions with game-theoretical methods, the following properties are especially important: (i) the changes caused by interaction are neither accidental nor natural but caused by human action. (ii) For their action the agents have alternatives at their disposal, because action is not strictly determinate. (iii) In interactions each partner wants to reach certain aims. He evaluates the results of the interactions according to their utility with reference to these aims.

Since our formal description of interactions up to now has been conceived of in order to allow for an integration of game theory and since the theory of action can be considered to be a foundation for game theory in some respects, a description of interactions in terms of game theory and under the aspects of strategy and utility does not raise further difficulties. But since the formal description of interaction is not yet complete, the first task would be to produce such descriptions. In consequence the application of game theoretical procedures to these interactions remains very elementary, especially because an empirical theory of communication-utility is still pending. However, we want to give simple examples of communication games in relation to our theory of action which may show the way for further treatment, after having given a short introduction to the principal concepts of game theory.

4.2 BASIC CONCEPTS OF GAME THEORY

A game is a strictly alternating interaction between two or more partners. Thus we can represent a game as a tree, the so-called game tree where each branch represents one move of a partner in strict alternation:

(506)

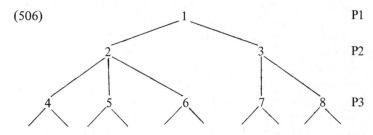

The branchings describe alternatives which are at the disposal of the player in question. Certainly, these alternatives are always determined by the preceding moves. For example: P3 can choose alternative 7 only if P2 chose 3 before. In this way each partner eliminates with his choice whole parts of the game tree which cannot be reached any more. A path through the game tree is called a play, that is, a sequence of act-patterns.

Accordingly plays, too, consist of patterns. Of course one always has to choose one of the alternatives if one acts according to such an interaction pattern, so that one realizes exactly one play if one acts according to a game. In this terminology the same play can be performed several times.

Within a finite game the number of vertices of the game tree is finite and so is the number of the edges. So, such a game consists of a finite number of moves. The end of every possible play of a game is determined by the final points of the game tree which represent the last play act of a partner. To each of those final points an outcome is attached by means of a function.

Each outcome consists of an n-tuple, the coordinates of which are attached to the players according to their numbers, such that each coordinate indicates the profit or loss of the player concerned. In the case $n = 2$ the pair $\langle 1, -1 \rangle$ might be attached to a final point thus indicating that P1 won 1 and P2 lost 1. Outcomes need not be money payments but increase in or loss of status, prestige, influence, punishment, etc. E.g., a game might end with the death of one player or with imprisonment. For in every game a set of outcomes and a function for the assignment of these outcomes to the final points must be given. If one additionally assumes a function for each player in order to indicate his utility for each outcome and if one sums up both functions, one obtains a so-called payoff function. As long as there is no empirical utility theory for the interactions and communications in question we content ourselves, for reasons of simplicity, with the outcomes and assume that the values given there are identical with the utility for the players. But it is consideration of the utility function which alone can lend interest to detailed strategic considerations.

If a player arrives in advance at a choice of certain alternatives we call the prescription he gives himself a strategy. E.g., a player could play by choosing the left branch at each branching. If one enumerates in a game with m moves the alternatives for P1 on each line from the left to the right with 1, 2,..., then one strategy of P1 can be described by an m-tuple of natural numbers such that each of its components represents the alternative chosen. In our example this strategy would be $\delta_1 = <1, 1,..., 1>$. In this way, shifting around nodes can be used to describe favored strategies in such simple ways as, for instance: Pi always chooses the left branch. The selection of a strategy by each player defines a play.

Certainly every player will choose a strategy with which he reaches profitable outcomes. However, he should also know the strategy chosen by his partner. Only then can he reach the highest possible profit. But as a player usually does not know his partner's strategy, the most interesting and most important applications of game theory come in here, namely to provide for the possibility of calculating optimal and winning strategies, strategies with which a player is bound to win.

Within the representation of a game, alternatives of different kinds may play a part. P1 can have three alternatives for one move at one place whereupon P2 can always continue differently as in (506). On the other hand, P1 may also have alternatives if he can carry out an act of HX at one vertex in different ways, that is, if HX generates alternative patterns:

(507)

$$HX_1 \rightarrow \begin{Bmatrix} HY_1 \\ HZ_1 \end{Bmatrix}$$

This representation does not seem to be favorable if the choice of an alternative influences the further course of a game. Perhaps it might be better in this case to omit HX and to begin with a tree like

(508)

HY_1 HZ_1

Hence we assume as a condition that every alternative relevant in this sense should be represented by a branching in the game tree. In this sense the generating pattern HX is not relevant for this game.

Now what about the case where the choice of HY or HZ does not influence the directly succeeding move of P2 but only a later one? E.g., if the results RY of HY and RZ of HZ with $RY \neq RZ$ later occur as conditions for acts of P1 or P2. In this case the choice would be relevant for the further course of the game. A representation like (508) would not be very economical if identical courses of the game follow after HY and HZ for a considerable length of time. In such cases one should choose the following form:

(509)

$$HX_1 \rightarrow \begin{Bmatrix} HY_1 \rightarrow RY \\ HZ_1 \rightarrow RZ \end{Bmatrix}$$

$$HA_i \rightarrow \begin{Bmatrix} HB_i \text{ if } RY \\ HC_i \text{ if } RZ \end{Bmatrix}$$

If the game continues all the same, the following representation would be possible also:

(510) HA_i

HB$_i$ if RY   HC$_i$ if RZ

Since we confine ourselves to two-person games, we can take for granted that there are two sets of act-patterns H^1 and H^2 where H^1 contains all act-patterns on which P1 can act, and H^2 all act-patterns on which P2 can act. Then a finite two-person game is a system which consists of

(i)   a finite game tree with a root; the tree arranges the patterns according to the criteria discussed.

(ii) a set of outcomes and a function which assigns to each final point of the game tree an outcome of this set.

(iii)   a rule that labels each act-pattern at a node with the number of the
        player who acts according to the pattern.
(iv)   a probability distribution for the alternatives of each move.
(v)   a partition of the set of vertices of the game tree into so-called inform-
        ation sets.
And among other things
(vi)   a utility function which gives the payoff for each player and each out-
        come.

We simplified (iii) by confining ourselves to two players and by stating that
the moves are strictly alternating, so that the assignment of act-patterns to
players is defined by the lines. In addition we shall sometimes use agent indexes, as we have done hitherto. The probability distribution in (iv) plays an
important part in connection with chance moves which are usually not due to
a partner and which therefore are introduced apart from H^1 and H^2, say by
H^0. Naturally there is such a probability distribution over the moves of P1
and P2 as well and in our normal action we make hypotheses about and on
the basis of this. For this reason the probability distribution should be empirically approached and related to the partners' judgements about the state of
the world and to their competence. Since we are not in a position to do this,
we start from the assumption that all alternatives of a move have the same
probability of being chosen. This simplification is related to another simplification made here, namely that we do not give well-founded utility functions
for each partner and thus leave aside a great deal of game-theoretical possibilities. Utility functions would demand extensive empirical investigations
which would have to be done after descriptions of certain interactions have
been made.

    For this reason it is convenient to content oneself with so-called zero-sum
games which are defined by the sum of profit and loss of both players where
this is O. We choose the three possible outcomes $<-1,1>$, $<1, -1>$ and $<0,0>$
and in this way give up the possibility of describing cooperative games which
would be especially desirable for ideal interactions.

    Furthermore, we deal mainly with games with two partners P1 and P2.
This restriction is related to our previous considerations. It will probably not
lead to any fundamental loss of generality, since extensions to $n > 2$ are
possible. But on one point one should exceed these restrictions, if one wants
to deal with the possibility of coalitions, which is only present where $n > 2$.

    Finally, one more restriction: we shall only treat games with perfect in-
formation, that is, games where each partner at any stage of the game knows
all alternatives chosen by both partners: he always knows where he is on the
game tree. That does not involve inadequacies for the communications chosen

by us, because it is assumed that both partners carry them out completely.

But for normal communications this assumption is not adequate because other, prior communications influence the choice of the alternatives of both partners.

For the calculation of optimal strategies two-person zero-sum games may be represented in the form of a matrix. For example, if P1 has at his disposal the strategies $\sigma_1, \sigma_2, \ldots, \sigma_n$ and P2 the strategies $\tau_1, \tau_2, \ldots, \tau_m$, then a_{ij}, the payoff for P1 for the strategies σ_i and τ_j, results from the game tree. If we are only interested in the payoffs for P1 for all possible strategies[1] we can represent all these payoffs within the following matrix:

(511)

	P2		
P1	τ_1	$\tau_2 \ldots \tau_m$	
σ_1	a_{11}	$a_{12} \cdots a_{1m}$	
σ_2	$a_{21} \cdots \cdots a_{2m}$		
.			
.			
.			
σ_n	$a_{n1} \cdots \cdots \cdot a_{nm}$		

Within this so-called normal form, the payoff for every possible play may be picked off. Therefore the matrix offers the players a basis for the choice of their strategy.

Let us take the following matrix as an example:

(512)
$$\begin{pmatrix} 5 & 1 & 3 \\ 3 & 2 & 4 \\ -3 & 0 & 1 \end{pmatrix}$$

P1 can expect the highest payoff for his strategy σ_1, namely 5. But if P2 then chooses the strategy τ_2 the payoff for P1 will only be 1, so it would be less than if he chose σ_2. In general P2 had better choose τ_2, because his average loss is smallest here. He would only have a chance to win if he chooses τ_1 and if P1 chooses σ_3 which is not favorable for him in any case. For these reasons P1 will choose σ_2 and P2 τ_2. It is also said that the game (512) has an equilibrium pair of strategies, namely the pair σ_2 and τ_2. Not all games in normal form have equilibrium pairs.

4.3 COMMUNICATION GAMES

4.3.1 *Question game*

Within this game a question communication will be described which, indeed, is not likely to occur in such a pure form but which becomes important because it plays a part in one form or other in many question communications and cases of problem-solving. The game works as follows: one partner P1 is supposed to find out from a set of objects $G_0 = [g_1, g_2, \ldots, g_m]$ a certain object x where $x \in G_0$ by asking P2 who has chosen this $x \in G_0$ previously. P2 may only answer P1's questions by uttering 'yes' or 'no'. P1 may only ask questions; because of the restriction on P2's possibilities of answering, P1 has to ask *whether*-questions. Accordingly the acts of P1 are of the pattern ASK_1 (whether S). The whole communication $GASK_{12}$ can be roughly described by

$$(513) \quad GASK_{12} = (ASK_1 \text{ (whether S)} \rightarrow UTT_1 \text{ (Y)} \dagger$$
$$ANS_2 \rightarrow \left\{ \begin{array}{l} UTT_2 \text{ (}yes\text{)} \\ UTT_2 \text{ (}no\text{)} \end{array} \right\})^n$$

Since P1's aim is to find out which g_i is the wanted x, the result of the communication is that P1 knows which $g_i = x$. Moreover, P2's possible answers can be further explained and related to each question of P1. We can assume that P2 affirms (AFF) the question put by P1 by uttering 'yes' and that he denies (DEN) the question by uttering 'no'. Since the repetition of the stereotype ANS_2 is redundant for the description of the communication and since the generation of AFF and DEN is constant, we might represent the communication $GASK_{12}$ as follows:

$$(514) \quad GASK_{12} = (ASK_1 \text{ (whether S)} \rightarrow UTT_1 \text{ (Y)} \dagger \left\{ \begin{array}{l} AFF_2 \text{ (that S)} \\ DEN_2 \text{ (that S)} \end{array} \right\})^n$$

$$\succ\!\!-\!\!-\!\!-\!\!- \text{ P1 knows, which } g_i = x.$$

Of course one cannot foretell how large n can be with such a loose description. We can assume that n becomes very large without additional restrictions, e.g. because P1 can repeat the same question though it has been answered with 'no' before. Besides, P1 could ask every possible *whether*-question according to our present description. For instance he might ask:

(515)   Do you have belly-ache?

without approaching his aim. Hence it makes good sense for P1 to adopt a criterion for the choice of his questions: if possible he should ask questions the answer to which (i) may well be that $x = g_i$ or (ii) help him to approach such a sentence. Both might apply to (515), for example if P1 wants to find out what is wrong with P2, what ails him or the like. But uttering (515) would not help to find out which brick P2 has chosen from a box of wooden bricks.

If we consider these two conditions, the limit of n still depends upon m: the highest value that n can reach in this case is $n = m - 1$. We shall demonstrate later how this equation comes about.

As concerns the instances for S one has to remember that P1 can indeed ask many different sorts of questions, but that he can ask two kinds of questions which we want to deal with separately. The relation between S and Y must be considered here, for P1 can ask the same question by uttering different instances of Y. The identity of questions is determined by the function of each question in communication. E.g., he might utter the following sentences:

(516)   Is the house the object wanted?
(517)   Is it the house?
(518)   This one?
(519)   Is it the third object from the left?
(520)   Is it the fact that you are hungry?

(516) - (519) would have the same effect in communication. P1 can refer with each of the questions to a certain g_i and ask whether this is the x wanted. It seems to make sense to regard all of them as sentences, since one can perform complete speech acts with them within such a communication. Since this completeness seems to be a condition for the acts of P1 and P2, only sentences which may be constituted out of a single word according to this sentence definition are justifiably admitted as instances of Y. As (516) - (519) in $GASK_{12}$ have the same effect, it is useful to take standardized expressions as specifications of ASK_1 which reflect the uniformity of (516) - (519). For this purpose we have already used a standardized form, namely $g_i = x$. So, if g_i is the object which is referred to when uttering (516), (517), (518), (519), then we could describe these phases of $GASK_{12}$, in a standardized way but certainly not extensively as concerns the generated patterns, as follows:

$$(521) \quad \text{ASK}_1 \text{ (whether } g_i = x) \quad \rightarrow \quad \left\{ \begin{array}{l} \text{UTT}_1 \text{ (516)} \\ \text{UTT}_1 \text{ (517)} \\ \text{UTT}_1 \text{ (518)} \\ \text{UTT}_1 \text{ (519)} \end{array} \right\}$$

It would be an important task to examine the form of those sentences with the utterance of which one can ask a question of the form '$g_i = x$'? Yet we shall confine ourselves in the following representation to the left part of the partition (521). Now we can describe GASK_{12} through the following tree where the results are marked at every final point. The communication of course ends there because P1 also knows this result (see page 201).

Now we recognize why the game is finished not later than after m-1 acts of both partners. After the m-1th move of P2, either the result of P2 in the left branch is reached or P1 can infer from P2's 'no' that it must be g_m, because it is the only object that remains.

P1's procedure consists here in asking about every single object from G_o, one after the other, choosing an ordering here represented by the ordering of g_i by means of indication. The order of P1's questions is not important; it is imperative only that he does not repeat himself. That is achieved in our description by keeping the names of the objects variable and by securing only the non-identity of g_i and g_j.

The indication allows the description, even in a relatively short tree, of the communication for every given m since the directly succeeding move of P1 always differs from the preceding one by the index i of g_i raised by 1.

In order to be able to interpret the communication of GASK_{12} as a game we have to give the outcomes in our tree. Since we restrict ourselves to zero-sum games and since we do not want to make further evaluations we simply determine that certain outcomes are valued as $<1, -1>$. We can do so by assuming that P1 has won if he reached his aim after $\frac{1}{3}m$ moves, so that all final points with $i \leqslant \frac{1}{3}m$ would have the payoff $<1, -1>$ and the rest $<-1, 1>$. Under this assumption we could calculate the utility for P1 and that for P2. The utility for both is plainly fixed, because neither of them has the possibility of influencing the course of the game, except by the chance moves before the game, where for example P1 determines the order of his questions and P2 singles out one of the objects according to the principle of chance. Since the probability is the same for each result, i.e. for each outcome, and since the probability of the whole is 1, the probability W_i for the outcome R_i is:

(522)

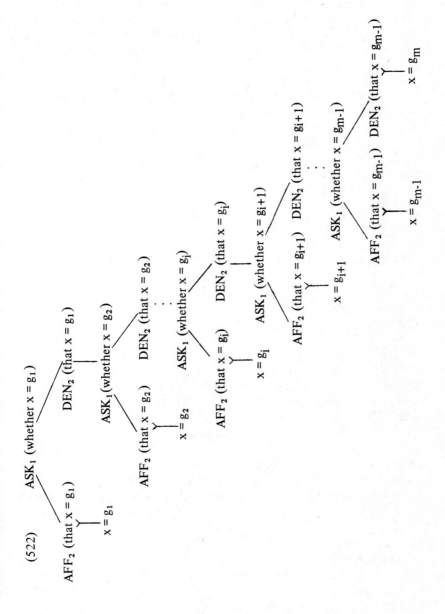

$$(523) \quad W_1 + W_2 + \ldots + W_m = 1$$
$$W_1 = W_2 = \ldots = W_m$$

$$W_i = W = \frac{1}{m}$$

Let U_1^i be the utility of the player P1 for the 1th outcome R_i, that is the first component of the corresponding two-dimensional vector, in our case 1 or -1. Then, the utility of the whole game U_1 for P1 is:

$$(524) \quad U_1 = \sum_{i=1}^{i=m} W \cdot U_1^i = \underbrace{\frac{1}{m} \cdot 1 + \frac{1}{m} \cdot 1 + \ldots}_{\frac{1}{3}m \text{ - times}} + \underbrace{\frac{1}{m}(-1) + \frac{1}{m}(-1) + \ldots}_{\frac{2}{3}m \text{ -times}}$$

$$= \frac{1}{3}m \cdot \frac{1}{m} - \frac{2}{3}m \cdot \frac{1}{m} = -\frac{1}{3}$$

Because of

$$(525) \quad U_1 + U_2 = 0$$

we get

$$(526) \quad U_2 = \frac{1}{3} ..$$

Because of $U_2 > U_1$, this game is unfair, it is in favor of P2. Indeed it is still more unfair in another sense, because P2 could cheat. E.g. if he did not have to lay down before the start just which g_i he had chosen and in such a way that P1 could check up on this, he could always say 'no' up to the m-1th move and would not even have to have any object in mind. In this way he could bring about the final points m or m-1, which secure him a payoff of 1. The utility of P1 would be $U_1 = -1$. It seems as if we are in a similar situation when we normally respond to a partner P1 with falsehoods. For it is hard to prove that P2 is lying if he does not make a mistake. In GASK$_{12}$ P1 could try to fool P2. If the latter does not act carefully and only counts the moves, P1 might repeat as the $(m-1)^{th}$ move one already made. If P2 says 'yes' he would have contradicted himself and he would have told a lie at least once. If he says 'no' P1 could make the mth move a test by repeating one that has already been made. If P2 said 'yes', and he would now be forced to, he would have contradicted himself, too. Cheating is not too easy.

We already mentioned that P1 can ask two sorts of questions by which he can obtain the answer 'yes' or 'no'. Up to now we have dealt only with the form $g_i = x$ for S and thus we have not taken full advantage of the alternative answer AFF (that S) and DEN (that S). P1 could ask questions of the other kind by uttering sentences like:

(527) Is the object wanted in the left half?
(528) Is it alive?
(529) Is it a tool?
(530) Is the cause a feeling?
(531) Is it an illness?

We want to represent the difference between these questions and those of the other kind within an analysis of S. It consists in the fact that here it is asked whether the wanted x is an element of certain subsets of G_0. As a standardized form for this way of asking, we introduce into ASK (whether S) the formulation '$x \in G_i$' where $G_i \subset G_0$. Here it would also be important to describe the relation between certain $x \in G_i$ and questions of the form (527) - (531). We shall see that it depends upon an appropriate set-theoretical partition of G_0 and that questions of the form (527) - (531) achieve just the same if they include, so to speak, expressions designating the same subsets, such that the structure of the partition may be represented in the questions. Besides, both of the possible kinds of answer of P2 to questions of this type have a function different from those in (522); namely, they are equally informative for P1, since he can infer that if x is not within the set G_i it must be in the remaining set G_{i-1} - G_i.

Now we want to draw the communication tree for this sort of question (see page 204).

The succession of the questions asked by P1 is based upon a set-theoretical partition of $P(G_0)$ which has the following form: (see page 205)

Here a set G^j is partitioned on the next level into two subsets such that it can be related one-to-one to both of P2's possible answers; if G_i^j were partitioned into A and B, P1 can infer as follows: '$x \notin$ A' $\Rightarrow$ '$x \in$ B' and vice versa '$x \notin$ B' $\Rightarrow$ '$x \in$ A'. Generally the partition is carried out in such a way that, if G_i^j is partitioned into G_{i+1}^{2j} and G_{i+1}^{2j-1}, (534) and (535) are valid:

(534) $G_{i+1}^{2j} = G_i^j - G_{i+1}^{2j-1}$

(535) $G_{i+1}^{2j-1} = G_i^j - G_{i+1}^{2j}$

Since the tree should if possible be symmetrical in order to keep n small, it is

204

(532)

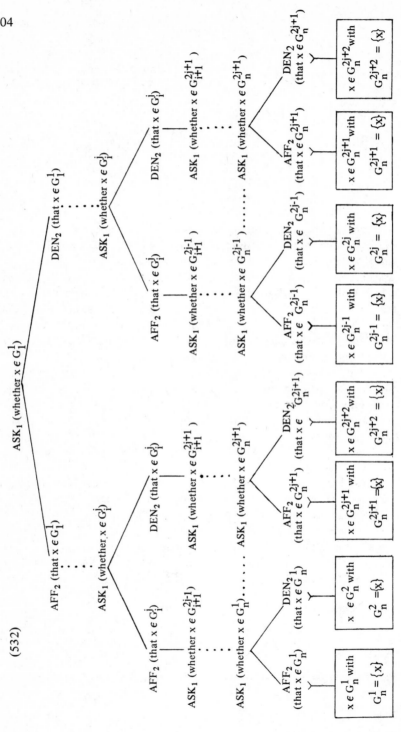

(533)

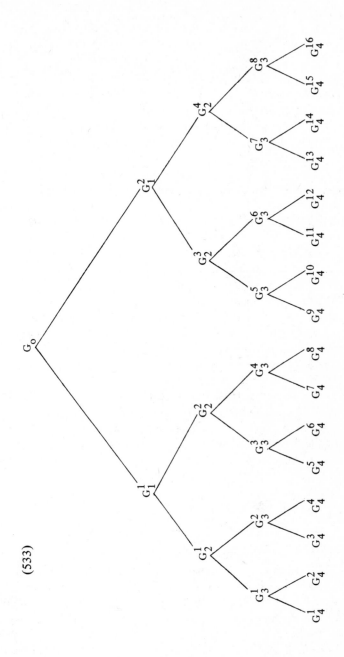

advantageous to partition G_i^j into equal halves, thus:

$$(536) \qquad |G_{i+1}^{2j}| = \frac{1}{2} |G_i^j|.$$

In (532), unlike (522), all final points are reached after an equal number of moves. Here, n also depends upon m. An outcome is reached if a set with only one element is reached with the partition:

$$(537) \qquad |G_i^j| = 1 \Rightarrow i = n.$$

It can be calculated from m after how many moves $|G_i^j| = 1$ is reached:

$$(538) \qquad |G_n| = \frac{1}{2^n} |G_o| \qquad \text{with } |G_n| = 1 \text{ and } |G_o| = m$$

$$2^n = m$$

$$n = {}^2\!\log m$$

If m is not a power of 2, a symmetrical partition certainly cannot be made. In the case that m is odd one has to take the next higher integer for n.

Certainly, the questions at the ends of (532) could be replaced by questions of the first kind, by asking for an element of the set G_n with only two elements. However, in general, mixing up both kinds of question is not to be recommended.

Our previous representation gave the impression that (522) and (532) were communications without interrelations. This impression is wrong.

Indeed we would have to represent the two trees in a single one, since P1 has the alternative of asking in this or that way at the beginning (and actually at every other place). This possibility would have to be represented, so that P1's first move would look like

$$(539) \qquad \left\{ \begin{array}{l} \text{ASK}_1 \text{ (whether } x = g_1) \\ \text{ASK}_1 \text{ (whether } x \in G_1) \end{array} \right\}$$

Now P1 ought to continue, depending on the kind of strategy chosen, just as in (522) or (532). P1 has, then, two kinds of strategy at his disposal in our restricted representation. No possibilities of choosing between different strategies are open to P2, since he chooses and determines all his alternatives before the beginning of the game; these influence the course of play only by chance.

We have seen that the game is unfair in favor of P2, under the assumption that all outcomes with $n \leqslant \frac{1}{3}m$ would have the payoff $\langle 1,-1 \rangle$ and the rest $\langle -1,1 \rangle$, because P2's utility is $U_2 = \frac{1}{3}$. In order to judge the two strategies σ_1 and σ_2, a calculation parallel to that described would have to be carried out for (532). We have already found out that the length of (532) in all branches is $n = {}^2\log m$. Since ${}^2\log m$ is smaller than $\frac{1}{3}m$ for all values of $m > 15$, σ_2 is a safe strategy for P1 in these cases. The utility of the game amounts for him to $U_1 = 1$ and thus $U_2 = -1$. Because of the utility principle

$$(540) \quad \sigma_i \geqslant \sigma_j \Leftrightarrow U(\sigma_i) \geqslant U(\sigma_j)$$

σ_2 should be preferred in these cases.

Now the cases $m < 16$ will be briefly considered. For $m = 1$, $n = 0$ holds for both strategies. Here the game is completely pointless because P1 knows everything from the beginning. For $m = 2$ one needs one move with both strategies and thus $n > \frac{1}{3}m$, so that P2 always wins. For $m = 3$ one needs 2 moves with both strategies. So here too $U_2 > U_1$. Besides, for all cases with $m > 2$ the general rule, $U_1 = \frac{1}{3}$, is valid. The utility of σ_2 only varies if m exceeds powers of 2. In this domain a mixture of σ_1 and σ_2 may even be advantageous.

The domination of σ_2 over σ_1 changes with the assumed limit where the payoff function changes. E.g., if the payoff were based upon some sort of lottery, which would give to every outcome the probability $\frac{1}{m}$, and if one payed proportionally to the probability of an outcome, one would probably approach our normal communication. Here the safe result with σ_2 for $m = 16$ after 4 moves would still reach a payoff 1, and would thus be four times better than the lottery.

4.3.2 *Assertion game*

The value of the description of communication games only becomes clear when one deals with a stretch of games instead of isolated games. A part of the structure of GASK, for example, can occur in other interactions as well. By a sequence of orders obeyed by P1 one after the other, P2 might get P1 to do something which P1 cannot do by obeying one single order or for which P2 does not know a single order. In this case the sequence of orders and acts might be based upon our partition (533). P2 could effect the same thing by orders that P1 achieves by questions in GASK.

In GASK we realized that not only can P1 choose to order his questions in a particular way but also that P2 is constrained in his answers by certain conditions. Since his answers are closely related to assertions, P2 has to maintain consistency, as the case of lying shows. In the same way, the rules of asserting form a part of the communication in 3.5.2. Because of this and the key role of the semantic relation INC, which was outlined in the formulation of the general aims of practical semantics, I shall now present a communication game which is based largely upon ASS and the relation of INC holding between specifications of ASS.

The game GASS is played by n players P1,..., Pn with m cards on each of which one indicative sentence is written, so that m sentences can be used. Each player is given $\frac{m}{n}$ cards which he turns up in front of himself, so that all players can look at all cards. For the sake of distribution it is desirable to choose a multiple of n for m. P1 opens the game, asserting a sentence by putting one card in the middle. Then P2 asserts a sentence from his set of sentences by putting one card to the right of the first card. Then P3 asserts a sentence from his set of sentences by putting one card to the right of the second card, and so on. After Pn it is P1's turn again. Conditions for putting down a card are: (i) that the references are possible and clear, (ii) that no contradiction arises. If a player cannot play a card under these conditions he passes. This can be standardized and introduced into the game: a player has to pass if the majority (or only one) of the fellow-players says 'that's wrong', 'that's a contradiction', or 'that's impossible' or the like. The game finishes when all players have to pass or when one of them has played all his cards. The number of points a player wins is determined by subtracting the number of cards remaining in his possession from the number his fellow-players are left with.

In a more formal representation GASS would have the following components:

(i) the set of players P1,...,Pn.
(ii) a set of sentences $\Sigma = \{S1, \ldots, Sm\}$.
(iii) a partition of Σ into n subsets $\Pi_1, \Pi_2, \ldots, \Pi_n$, all of the same cardinal number.
(iv) a set of outcomes and the n-place pay-off function which indicates the profit for each outcome and for each player.
(v) game trees for every possible partition of Σ.

It can be assumed that each partition of Σ defines one partial game. Since this partition precedes each partial game, it can be integrated as a move of a fictitious player, chance. Thus one obtains the whole game GASS.

In the game the players put their cards down one after the other and thus built up a maximal consistent chain of S's which we call M. The concept of a maximal consistent chain is related to that of a maximal consistent set in Hughes-Cresswell. Their definition goes:[2]

(i)   Let φ be a well-formed formula. A set of formulae is called consistent if and only if it does not include φ and $-\varphi$ at the same time (or φ and $-\varphi$ are both true formulae).

(ii)   A set of formulae is called a maximal consistent set if and only if it would become inconsistent by adding any formula which is not yet an element of the set.

For our purpose formulae must not be equated with the Si's, i.e. the elements of Σ. So we cannot simply define consistency by using the negation of Si. We have to go back to the semantic relation INC and hence to propositions. This is necessary because there are some elements of Σ with which different assertions can be made, as is shown by the description of a possible move in a game

$$(541) \quad \left\{ \begin{array}{l} \text{ASS}_i\,(X) \\ \text{ASS}_i\,(Y) \\ \cdot \\ \cdot \\ \cdot \end{array} \right\} \quad \to \quad \text{UTT}_i\,(S) \; \to \; \text{PUT}_i\,(x)$$

The alternative members generating UTT (S) are due to the fact that Pi can refer to different things with the same NP in different contexts. E.g., he can make different assertions with 'he boozes' depending on the object he is referring to with 'he'. Accordingly {*he boozes, he does not booze*} would not be inconsistent if the different occurrences of 'he' were used to refer to different persons. This shows why we should not talk of consistency in the case of such sets of sentences because the same set might just as well be consistent as inconsistent. The sequence of the acts of assertion and utterance becomes relevant here, the possibilities of reference usually being determined by the sentences uttered previously. This is the reason why we must not apply the conditions of consistency to sets but to chains of Si's. Furthermore, it must be noted that the condition of consistency is not restricted to elements of the chain but that, by the definition of INC, M is also inconsistent if S1, S2 ϵ M and CS1 entrenches not-CS2.[3]

A single round of GASS might be described as follows:[4]

$$(542) \quad \left\{ \begin{array}{l} \text{ASS}_1\,(X) \to \text{PUT}_1\,(x_1) \\ \text{PASS}_1 \end{array} \right\} \quad \dagger \quad \left\{ \begin{array}{l} \text{ASS}_2\,(Y) \to \text{PUT}_2\,(y_1) \\ \text{PASS}_2 \end{array} \right\} \dagger \dots \dagger$$

$$\left\{ \begin{array}{l} \text{ASS}_n\,(Z) \to \text{PUT}_n\,(z_1) \\ \text{PASS}_n \end{array} \right\} \qquad \text{where } x_1 \,\epsilon\, \Pi_1, \; y_1 \,\epsilon\, \Pi_2, z_1 \,\epsilon\, \Pi_n.$$

Of course, the Π_i's change in each round if Pi is not to pass.

The aim of each player Pi is to have put down more cards than his fellow-players and to make the gap as big as possible, that is, to render Π_i as small as possible and all Π_j with $j \neq i$ as great as possible because the n-place payoff function for each end point operates on the number of cards remaining to each player. If we write Π_i^e for the rest of Pi's set at the end point e the utility U_i, i.e. the ith component of the utility vector, can be calculated by means of

$$(543) \quad U_i = (|\Pi_1^e| - |\Pi_i^e|) + \ldots + (|\Pi_n^e| - |\Pi_i^e|)$$

We assume here that GASS is a zero-sum game, that is, if Pi plays the strategy δ_i, the following holds:

$$(544) \quad \sum_{i=1}^{n} U_i(\delta_1, \delta_2, \ldots, \delta_n) = 0$$

A partial game of GASS is defined by (i) the structure of Σ; (ii) the partition of Σ into $\Pi_1, \Pi_2, \ldots$. If the structure of Σ is left out of consideration m! different chains could be formed and thus m! different plays could be played, counting all possible combinations. But the possibilities are restricted by the conditions of reference and consistency. Reference above all is decisive because it excludes deviant chains according to the rules of English before the consistency condition operates. Non-deviating reference is a condition for ascertaining consistency. The consistency condition then excludes further chains.

Each partition involves a further restriction of the number of m! combinations because each player Pi at any given position in the chain can only put down a sentence from Π_i and not from Σ. For this reason there are not m but only $\frac{m}{n}$ alternatives at the first position and correspondingly fewer at the following ones.

In spite of all these restrictions I cannot describe the possibilities of GASS for every given n and m or how they depend on the structure of Σ. I shall rather confine myself to one example in order to demonstrate some essential strategic principles. The complexity of the example provides a justification for this procedure and for omitting the structure of Σ and thus essential strategic connections and rules. So it will be left to the players and to the reader to decide upon the possible contexts of Si according to their own competence, for the objective of the game is not to give an exhaustive semantic description of the sentences and their use in communication but to provoke the players, with a kind of model, into an insight into communication problems. The point of this will be quickly noticed by everyone who plays the game himself.

For example I choose n = 3 and m = 12. If any greater m and n were chosen the game tree would be very extensive, hard to draw and unsurveyable. But even the discussion of strategic questions with smaller trees allows a degree of penetration most unlikely to be obtained without the game-theoretical description. Let Σ be given by:

1   Jodok is not at home.
2   The telephone is ringing.
3   It is a boy.
4   It is a girl.
5   Grandfather plays with him all day long.
6   He has black hair.
7   Both are red-haired.
8   He loves his wife with all his heart.
9   He has no wife.
10   They had a child last Christmas.
11   He was murdered.
12   Thank heavens he is not yet dead.

The numbers in front of each sentence are a convenient abbreviation. We only use them for the description of this example.

The number of the possible chains for all partial games will not reach 12! because of the limiting conditions of consistency and reference and the rules of English. Probably only chains with 1 or 2 at the beginning are admitted. This seems to me a consequence of a rule that the whole story must begin by introducing referents and fixing some references. Ther are, however, counter-examples to this in poetry which show that the non-deviant chains cannot be plainly determined, for a fixed set of rules for English — as we have seen — does not exist. Thus a standard decision about which alternative can be chosen by a player in a certain context cannot be made. E.g. it can be argued about whether

(545)   ...5 8 9...

is to be admitted as a part of a chain or not. Some speakers will think the references difficult, expecially the jump in reference where 'he' occurs in 9 with which one must refer to the grandfather if the reference of the 'he' in 8 corresponds to 'him' in 5 and vice-versa. In other cases one can argue about whether there is a contradiction or not. In the following representation of the game I proceed by and large very restrictively by only admitting anaphoric references to directly preceding sentences and no multiple references. But this is only to be understood as a restriction for the convenience of description;

if GASS is played the decision about which chains are admitted as non-deviating and consistent will be made by the players themselves. For I do not assume that the meaning of a sentence is primary and that meaning-relations are derived from it, but rather that they are both interdependent. The possibilities of reference and compatibility or incompatibility are parts of the rule of use. And fellow-players will find out the meaning a sentence has for one partner by learning about the relational structure it is embedded in for him. This should be one effect of playing the game. However, from this point of view, it is a defect that the questions of reference and incompatibility are left hidden in the constitutive rules of the game. Any discussion of these problems remains outside the game and effort should be made to extend the game so that the rules of those discussions are introduced into the constitutive rules, or at least to exclude, by way of the strategic possibilities, the situation where players just settle on a solution or are even irresolute. Now these modifications should have the effect of institutionalizing certain liberties of the players, since given current standards, fellow-players tend rather to make strong restrictions, even stronger than those assumed here.

I shall now give the game tree for the following distribution of the cards: Π_1 = 7, 9, 10, 11 , Π_2 = 2, 3, 6, 8 , Π_3 = 1, 4, 5, 12 (see page 213).

The length of this game is at most 30 moves. For after 9 moves each player can still have exactly one card, so that the game would end with the next card player. But it is possible that it has been passed twice before so that the number of possible moves amounts to 27, up to this point. So if all players have to pass the game is finished after 30 moves at most, generally after 3(m-n) + n moves. Of course our game will end before then, because of the conditions and because no player will make the other players pass permanently. The longest play of our partial game is defined by the chain 2 1 9 6 12 5 8 7 10 3. Its length is 17. But by frequent passing the chain formed in this play has only 10 members, which is reached in 2 1 9 6 5 11 8 12 10 3 by a play of length 11. And this is the shortest play for the three longest chains.

The game tree shows P3 in a favorable position. He can decide the game for himself in his first move: by putting 4 he runs into a branch where he never can lose. He can even avoid his lowest possible profit, 1, by putting 12 and not 5 after the 7 of P1. The highest profit 5 for P3, however, can be avoided by P1 if he does not put down 9 in the 7th move. Since with the other alternatives he always loses 2, it does not matter for him whether he chooses 7 or 11. The important thing is that if P1 prefers P3 to win more than P2, then he has to choose 11, after which P3 wins 4.

But if P3 does not put down 4 but 1 by mistake or because he does not see the consequences, then P1 can decide the game for himself: by putting down 11 and later on 7 instead of 10 he will win 2. If P1 chooses 9 instead of

213

(546)

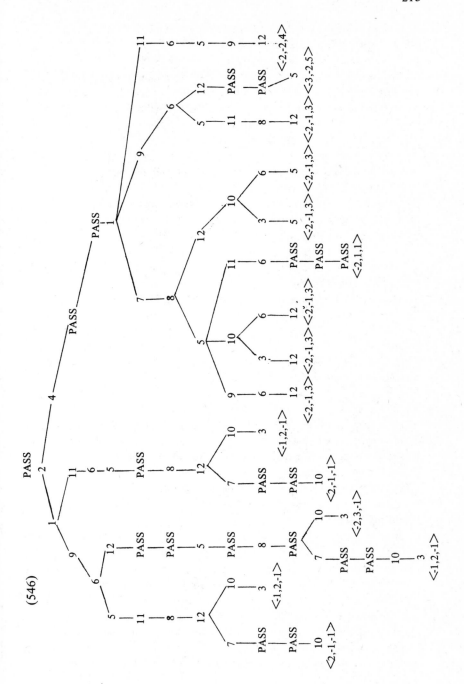

11 then P2 will have his chance since he can reach a profit of 3 after 12 and 10 or a profit of 2 after 12 and 7.

GASS is so extensive that we can neither draw the trees for all distributions nor for the distribution in our example. For this reason the game cannot be trivialized by giving strategies for all distributions and chances to win for all players. But as in the case of chess which is not trivialized either we can state some principles we learn by playing GASS and some strategic principles we read in the tree.

The most interesting principles we learn in playing the game concern the understanding of sentences in context. Thus, playing the game may be of heuristic help for the linguist who deals with rules of text formation as it may be for speakers of English who want to get insight into communicative methods to improve understanding. The following three principles seem to be important for communication in general:

(i) The possible interpretations of two sentences seem to correlate to the order of their utterances in historical contexts. Some interpretations easy to grasp in one order may become difficult or less probable in the reverse order. An example for this could be the chain 5 11 on the condition that we refer with the two 'he's' to the same person. Then we tend to assume an inconsistency because we tend to assume that one cannot play with a corpse. But, of course, one can, and we grasp this possible interpretation much more easily when the sentences are uttered in the sequence 11 5.

(ii) A known historical context seems to bind someone to certain interpretations, so that a creative act is necessary to get at alternatives which are open in the *langue*. An example for this is that because of the great number of occurrences of 'he' in our Σ it very often happens that one refers with 'he' to Jodok and by this makes him male. It is then, later, when playing other plays, not easy to see that Jodok might be female as well. The reason is that we cannot easily sever a historical context and the knowledge we have acquired in this historical context.

(iii) There is another principle which seems to contradict the one stated in (ii): The historical context opens up the way for possible interpretations. It often happens that after going through one path of the tree and there refraining from some partial chain one arrives, in the different context of another path, at a new interpretation of this chain and then one sees that under this interpretation it is also possible in the former path, so that one has to correct it. This corresponds to the familiar old truth that experience increases understanding.

Two more principles can be derived from our game tree:

(iv) We assumed above that the reference condition precedes the consistency condition. This does not mean that the latter could not influence the former. Usually, in communication, as in our game, referring with pronouns (and indeed with other NP's as well and even names) is by no means something which is uniquely determined. The rules for referring are so loose that one could refer with a pronoun to different objects or persons. Normally we refer with pronouns (except for special pronouns such as 'this one', 'that one' etc.) to the last mentioned object, if the pronoun can be used to refer to such a kind of object. But there are some conditions under which this is not so. One of them is the consistency condition, for if referring by 'he' to the last-mentioned person (or object) leads us to an inconsistency we go further back in the chain and search for another person (or object) in order to get a consistent interpretation. Now this is a rule followed blindly and not one involving reflection. Thus, in normal communication we follow the slogan "understanding before contradiction", which, however, is often not followed in scholarly communication. The slogan corresponds to a more general principle of communication, that whenever one finds that a partner has performed an inconsistent illocutionary act one has to improve one's own understanding, because no one really performs inconsistent illocutionary acts. This does not mean that it is impossible that someone interprets it as inconsistent nor does it exclude the case where the agent does not see the consequences because he does not know the whole implicit context or because he has another implicit context.

(v) In our game tree the most important card for P3 is 1. If he does not retain it he may lose the game. But if he holds it back he is bound to win. This seems to be a consequence of the fact that with 1 a new referent is introduced which allows the partners to assert new things about it and not to contradict themselves by asserting new things. So, in this game, it is risky to introduce new referents. And this is certainly a special quality of the game. For in normal communication, on the contrary, that someone enlarges the world is something which is very welcome. In our game this acts only to the detriment of the introducer because the game is strictly competitive. In a cooperative game it would be a social act to introduce new referents and fix references in order to allow the partner to give and to get more information about them.

Because of its strictly competitive character the important question of cooperation and especially coalition cannot be treated within the discussion of this game. As mentioned above P1 could, e.g., augment P3's profit at the cost of P2 by choosing the right alternative. But why should he do so? He would only be interested in doing this if he could hope for something for himself from P3 in another game, i.e., another partial game of GASS with a different distribution. We cannot study the problems of coalition more closely here but only remark that cooperation and coalition are of the highest importance in communication. In order to treat them in GASS it is not enough to consider only other distributions of Σ because we have not provided for the possibility of negotiation within the game which is essential for forming coalitions. In this form of GASS, coalitions would have to be based on silent understanding, e.g. P3 would have to understand that P1 was acting for his benefit. He must know that P1 has not merely made a mistake and cannot assume that he did not see the consequences of what he was doing.

NOTES

1. From which one can calculate the pay-off for P2.
2. Hughes-Cresswell (1972: 19; 151-154). I give a slightly modified formulation which can be better understood in this context.
3. This is included in the definition of Hughes-Cresswell by the recursive formation of the formulae.
4. Later we shall take into account the fact, provided for in (541), that a player can make different assertions within one move by playing the same card, viz. by uttering the same sentence.

BIBLIOGRAPHY

Alston, W. P.
    1964 *Philosophy of language* (Englewood Cliffs, N. J.: Prentice Hall).
Austin, J. L.
    1962 *How to do things with words* (Oxford: Oxford University Press).
    1971 *Philosophical papers* (Oxford: Oxford University Press).
Ayer, A. J.
    1936 *Language, Truth, and Logic* (London: Gollancz).
Baker, A. J.
    1956 "Presupposition and types of clause", *Mind* 65, 368-78.
Beeh, V.
    1973 *Ansätze zu einer wahrheitswertfunktionalen Semantik*. Dargestellt am
          Deutschen (München: Hueber).
Belnap, N. D.
    1969 "Questions: their presuppositions, and how they can fail to arise", in: K.
          Lambert (ed.), *The logical way of doing things* (New Haven-London, Yale
          University Press), 23-37.
Benett, B.
    1965 "Action, reason, and purpose", *The Journal of Philosophy* 62, 85-96.
Benett, J.
    1954 "Meaning and implication", *Mind* 63, 451-463.
Bierwisch, M.
    1970 "On classifying semantic features", in: M. Bierwisch and K.E. Heidolph (eds.),
          Progress in linguistics (The Hague-Paris: Mouton), 27-50.
Black, M.
    1949 "The semiotics of Charles Morris", in: M. Black, *Language and Philosophy*
          (Ithaca, N. Y. [5]1966: Cornell University Press), 167-185.
    1962 "Presupposition and implication", in: M. Black, *Models and metaphors*
          (Ithaca, N. Y. : Cornell University Press), 48-63.
Bloomfield, L.
    1933 *Language* (New York: Holt Rinehart and Winston).
Brand, M. (ed.)
    1970 *The nature of human action* (Glenview, Ill.: Scott Foresman & Company).
Bromberger, S.
    1966 "Why-questions", in: R. D. Colodny (ed.), *Mind and cosmos* (Pittsburgh:
          University of Pittsburgh Press).
Carnap, R.
    1955 "Meaning and synonymy in natural languages", *Philosophical Studies* 7, 33-47.
    1964 *Meaning and necessity* (Chicago, Ill.: University of Chicago Press).

218

Castañeda, H. N.
   1965 "The logic of change, action, and norms", *The Journal of Philosophy* 62, 333-344.
Chisholm, R. M.
   1964 "The descriptive element in the concept of 'action' ", *The Journal of Philosophy* 61, 613-624.
Chomsky, N.
   1965 *Aspects of the theory of syntax* (Cambridge, Mass.: MIT Press).
   1971 "Deep structure, surface structure, and semantic interpretation", in: D. Steinberg and Jakobovits (eds.), *Semantics* (Cambridge: Cambridge University Press), 183-216.
Danto, A. C.
   1963 "What we can do", *The Journal of Philosophy* 60, 435-445.
   1965 "Basic actions", *American Philosophical Quarterly* 2, 141-148, also in: A. R. White (ed.), 1968, *The philosophy of action* (Oxford: Oxford University Press), 43-58.
   1973 *Analytical philosophy of action* (Cambridge: Cambridge University Press).
Davidson, D.
   1963 "Actions, reasons, and causes", *The Journal of Philosophy* 60, 685-700.
   1967 "Truth and meaning", *Synthese* 17, 304-323.
Festinger, L.
   1957 *A theory of cognitive dissonance* (Evanston, Ill.: Row. Peterson).
Frege, G.
   1891 *Funktion und Begriff* (Jena). Cited from Frege 1960.
   1892 "Über Sinn und Bedeutung", *Zeitschrift für Philosophie und philosophische Kritik*, N. F. 100, 25-50. Cited from Frege 1960.
   1960 *Translation from the philosophical writings of Gottlob Frege* (P. T. Geach and M. Black, eds.) (Oxford: Blackwell).
   1967 *The thought.* Cited from P. F. Strawson (ed.), *Philosophical logic* (Oxford: Oxford University Press), 17-38.
Frey, G.
   1965 "Imperativkalküle", in: K. Ajdukiewicz (ed.), *The foundation of statements and decisions; Proceedings, International colloquium on methodology of sciences, Warsaw* 1961. (Warszawa: PWN-Scientific Publishers).
Furberg, M.
   1971 *Saying and meaning* (Oxford: Blackwell).
Ganz, J. S.
   1971 *Rules. A systematic study.* (The Hague-Paris: Mouton).
Geach, P. T.
   1965 "Assertion", *Philosophical Review* 74, 449-465.
   1968² *Reference and generality* (Ithaca, N. Y.: Cornell University Press).

219

1970 *A theory of human action* (Englewood Cliffs, N. J.: Prentice Hall).
Grice, H. P.
1968 "Utterer's meaning, sentence-meaning, and word-meaning", *Foundations of Language* 4, 225-242.
Habermas, J.
1971 "Vorbereitende Bemerkungen zu einer Thorie der kommunikativen Kompetenz", in: J. Habermas und N. Luhmann, *Theorie der Gesellschaft oder Sozialtechnologie* (Frankfurt/M.: Suhrkamp), 101-141.
Hamblin, C. L.
1963 "Questions aren't statements", *Philosophy of Science* 30, 62-63.
Harrah, D.
1963 *Communication: a logical model* (Cambridge, Mass.: MIT Press).
Heger, K.
1964 "Die begrifflichen Voraussetzungen von Semasiologie und Onomasiologie", *Zeitschrift für Romanische Philologie* 81, 486-512.
Heringer, H. J.
1972^2 *Deutsche Syntax* (Berlin: de Gruyter).
1973^2 *Theorie der deutschen Syntax* (München: Hueber).
Hughes, G. E. and M. J. Cresswell
1972 *An introduction to modal logic* (London: Methuen).
Katz, J. J. and J. A. Fodor
1963 "The structure of a semantic theory", *Language* 39, 170-210, also in: *The structure of Language* (J.A. Fodor and J. J. Katz, eds.) (Englewood Cliffs, N. J. 1964: Prentice Hall), 479-518.
Katz, J. J. and P. M. Postal.
1964 *An integrated theory of linguistic descriptions* (Cambridge, Mass.: MIT Press).
Kenny, A.
1963 *Action, emotion, and will* (London: Routledge & Kegan, Paul).
Kripke, S.
1972 "Naming and necessity", in: G. Harman and D. Davidson (eds.), *Semantics of natural language* (Dordrecht: Reidel), 253-355.
Labov, W.
1972 "Rules for ritual insults", in: D. Sudnow (ed.), *Studies in social interaction* (London: Collier-MacMillan), 120-169.
Laffal, J. and L. Ameen
1959 "Hypotheses of opposite speech", *The Journal of Abnormal and Social Psychology* 58, 267-269.
Lewis, D.
1969 *Convention* (Cambridge, Mass.: Harvard University Press).
1970 "General semantics", *Synthese* 22, 18-67
Linsky, L.
1967 *Referring* (London: Routledge & Kegan, Paul).

Llewelyn, J. E.
   1964 "What is a question", *Australasian Journal of Philosophy* 42, 69-85.
Lorenz, K.
   1970 *Elemente der Sprachkritik* (Frankfurt/M: Suhrkamp).
Louch, A. R.
   1967 *Explanation and human action* (Oxford: Blackwell).
Luce, R. D. and H. Raiffa
   1957 *Games and decisions* (New York-London-Sydney: Wiley).
Lyons, J.
   1968 *Introduction to theoretical linguistics* (Cambridge: Cambridge University Press).
Mates, B.
   1950 "Synonymity", *University of California Publications in Philosophy* 25, 201-226.
McKinsey, J.C.C.
   1952 *Introduction to the theory of games* (New York-Toronto-London: McGraw Hill).
Melden, A.I.
   1956 "Action", *The Philosophical Review* 65, 529-541, also in: Brand 1970, 91-99.
   1961 *Free action* (London: Routledge & Kegan, Paul).
Nerlich, G.
   1965 "Presupposition and entailment", *American Philosophical Quarterly* 2, 33-42.
Polya, G.
   1968 *Patterns of plausible inference,* Vol. 2 (Princeton, N. J.: Princeton University Press).
Prior, A.N.
   1971 *Objects of thought* (Oxford: Oxford University Press).
Prior, M. and A.N. Prior
   1955 "Erotetic logic", *The Philosophical Review* 64, 43-59.
Quine, W.V.O.
   1963 *From a logical point of view* (New York: Harper Torchbook).
   1970 *Philosophy of logic* (Englewood Cliffs, N.J.: Prentice Hall).
Ryle, G.
   1949 *The concept of mind* (London: Hutchinson).
   1964 *Dilemmas* (Cambridge: Cambridge University Press).
Schiffer, S.
   1972 *Meaning* (Oxford: Oxford University Press).
Scriven, M.
   1959 "The logic of criteria", *The Journal of Philosophy* 56, 857-868.
Searle, J.R.
   1969 *Speech acts* (Cambridge: Cambridge University Press).
Stampe, D. W.
   1968 "Toward a Grammar of Meaning", *Philosophical Review* 77, 137-174.

221

Strawson, P. F.
1948 "Necessary propositions and entailment-statements", *Mind* 57, 184-200.
1963 *Introduction to logical theory* (London: Methuen).
1971 *Logico-linguistic papers* (London: Methuen).
Weinreich, U.
1966 "Explorations in semantic theory", in: *Current Trends in linguistics III*
(The Hague: Mouton), 395-477.
White, M. G.
1952 "The analytic and the synthetic: an untenable dualism", in: L. Linsky (ed.),
Semantics and the philosophy of language (Urbana, Ill.: University of
Illinois Press), 272-286.
Winch, P.
1958 *The idea of a social science and its relation to philosophy* (London: Routledge
& Kegan, Paul).
1972 Understanding a primitive society, in: P. Winch, *Ethics and action* (London:
Routledge & Kegan, Paul), 8-49.
Wittgenstein, L.
1953 *Philosophical investigations* (Oxford: Blackwell).
1970 *Über Gewissheit* (Frankfurt/M: Suhrkamp).
von Wright, G. H.
1963 *Norm and action* (London: Routledge & Kegan, Paul). In part in: Brand
1970, 302-330.
Ziff, P.
1960 *Semantic analysis* (Ithaca, N. Y.: Cornell University Press).

INDEX

ability 60
act 21, 24, 110
–, basic 30, 40
–, negative 50f.
–, symbolic 113f.
action
–, common 132
–, inner 61
–, outer 61
–, social 53
–, solitary 63
action competence 30, 55, 58ff.,
    64f., 68
act-pattern 24ff., 58, 94, 140
–, illocutionary 144
–, simple 66
alternative 31
analysis of meaning 127, 130ff.
analytical 151ff.
analyticity 74
answer 162
arbitrariness 2
arrow of generation 29
arrow-relation 30, 52, 61, 68
assertion game 207
assumptions 126, 137f.
axiom of order 68
axiomatization 65

basic pattern 65f., 68
because-answer 177
bench 35
branch 64f.

can 59f.
category of conditions 33
codification 54
coherence 157
command 18, 19
commitment 167
common knowledge 124f., 137, 139,
    149
communication 64, 85ff., 96ff., 112
–, asymmetrical 168
–, conditions of 112ff.
–, ironic 126

–, naive 124
–, sceptical 124
communication game 96
communication pattern 162
competence 61ff.
competition 55, 62
component 44, 46, 54
componential analysis 77ff.
concept 5
condition 32f., 52, 55, 60, 95
conditional 151
consistency 208f., 215
consonance 93
content 1
context 88, 120
–, historical 88, 127, 214
context explicit 88f.
context implicit 88f., 149
contradiction 90
contradictory 158
conventionality 1, 14, 31, 50
cooperation 54f., 62
cross-operation 44ff.

deep structure 80, 110
deviation 14, 23, 51, 53, 98, 100
description 26
description of acts 22f., 95
description of events 23
description of rules 17
direct answer 169
disambiguation 120ff.
disposition 9
dissonance 92f.
distribution of acts 101
distribution rule 101

entrenchment 150ff., 158f.
equivalence 74
essential 154
eternal sentences 106f.
event 22
explanation 79
expression 1
extensionality 27

relation 67
relation between acts 24
response 7
role 52, 55
rule 11, 13, 18, 33, 51, 54, 62, 122,
    131, 191
rule and law 18
–, being master of a . . . 13
–, constitutive 19
–, expression of the . . . 17
–, following a . . . 15, 23, 122
–, strategic 19
rule-formulation 16, 19
rule of inference 41, 43
rule of use 104

segmentation 161
semantic description 1, 71, 76
semantic relation 5, 40, 81, 149, 157
sense 4
sentence
–, analytical 74, 146, 151
–, eternal 105, 108
–, performative 141, 143
sentence definition 98
sentence-meaning 71, 104, 120
sequence 45, 101, 193
sequence, direct 45
sequence of questions 203
sequence-pattern 45, 57, 101
specification 37ff., 63, 97
specification of speech acts 100ff.
speech act 11
speech and action 140ff.
stimulus 7
strategy 192, 194, 197, 200, 206f.
strategy tree 57
subjective utility 191
subpattern 37ff., 44, 149
surface structure 110
surplus 32, 41
synonymy 72, 74, 80, 86, 103
syntagmatic relation 161
syntax 161f.
syntax of the noeme-language 78

thought 102, 146
to act symbolically 112
to answer 198
to ask 198ff.

to assert 146ff., 160, 167, 182, 207
to communicate 64
to count as 122
to denote 117
to describe the use 12
to deviate 14
to intend 118f.
to know 59, 153
tolerance 94
to mean 114ff., 119, 123
to mean as 113f.
to refer 117
to think 61
to understand 123
transformation 109
translation 83
tree 57
tree C^*_i 61
trough 36
truth 87, 128, 134
–, absolute 135, 138
–, condition 111, 129
–, eternal 136
–, tacit 132
truth value 105, 108, 145f.
types of acts 21

under-answer 169
understanding 13, 86f., 91, 93, 123,
    125, 127, 137ff.
unfair 192
use 11, 87
utility 191
utility function 194
utterance 96f.
utterances of the sentence 104

vagueness 152f.
verb, performative 142
verification 134
Verstehen 23f.
vertex 58

wh-question 146, 171, 177

yes-no-question 171ff.

zero-sum game 196

†-relation 25